LEADING AND MANAGING EDUCATION:
INTERNATIONAL DIMENSIONS

Educational Management: Research and Practice

Series Editor: Tony Bush

Managing People in Education (1997)
Edited by Tony Bush and David Middlewood

Strategic Management in Schools and Colleges (1998)
Edited by David Middlewood and Jacky Lumby

Managing External Relations in Schools and Colleges (1999)
Edited by Jacky Lumby and Nick Foskett

Practitioner Research in Education: Making a Difference (1999)
David Middlewood, Marianne Coleman and Jacky Lumby

Managing Finance and Resources in Education (2000)
Edited by Marianne Coleman and Lesley Anderson

Managing Further Education: Learning Enterprise (2001)
Jacky Lumby

Managing the Curriculum (2001)
Edited by David Middlewood and Neil Burton

Research Methods in Educational Management and Leadership (2002)
Edited by Marianne Coleman and Ann Briggs

The Principles and Practice of Educational Management (2002)
Edited by Tony Bush and Les Bell

Leading and Managing Education: International Dimensions (2003)
Nick Foskett and Jacky Lumby

This series supports the MBA in Educational Management offered by the CELM, (previously EMDU), University of Leicester.

The modules in this course are:
Leadership and Strategic Management in Education
Managing Finance and External Relations
Human Resource Management in Schools and Colleges
Managing the Curriculum
Research Methods in Educational Management

For further information about the MBA in Educational Management, please contact CELM@le.ac.uk. For further information about the books associated with the course, contact Paul Chapman Publishing at www.paulchapmanpublishing.co.uk.

LEADING AND MANAGING EDUCATION:

INTERNATIONAL DIMENSIONS

Nick Foskett and Jacky Lumby

P·C·P
Paul Chapman
Publishing

First published 2003

 Paul Chapman Publishing
A SAGE Publications Company
6 Bonhill Street
London EC2A 4PU

SAGE Publications Inc
2455 Teller Road
Thousand Oaks, California 91320

SAGE Publications India Pvt Ltd
32, M-Block Market
Greater Kailash - I
New Delhi 110 048

Library of Congress Control Number: 2002107131

A catalogue record for this book is available from the
British Library

ISBN 0 7619 7202 1
ISBN 0 7619 7203 x (pbk)

Typeset by Anneset, Weston-super-Mare, Somerset
Printed in Great Britain by Athenaeum Press, Gateshead

CONTENTS

SERIES EDITOR'S FOREWORD

The world is becoming a smaller place. Developments in information and communications technology, and faster and more frequent air travel, mean that the perspective of governments, businesses and many individuals is increasingly global rather than national or local. Globalisation has at least five major dimensions:

- political
- economic
- cultural
- environmental
- managerial.

Political globalisation means the proliferation of political bodies above and beyond the nation state (Bottery, 1999). In Europe, for example, nations have ceded many powers to the European Union (EU) and the relationship between the EU and its constituent states is a topic of continuing debate. According to Jones (1998, p. 149), sovereignty and the notion of statehood are 'eroding and very quickly'.

Economic globalisation refers to the organisation and integration of economic activity at levels that transcend national borders and jurisdictions. Multinational companies pay little regard to national issues and are increasingly beyond the control of nation states. The world is dominated by international brands, most of them American, including Microsoft, Boeing, Ford, McDonald's and Coca-Cola. McDonald's success is based on a standard formula that means that a 'Big Mac' is the same all over the world.

Education is valued all over the world for its ability to develop human potential and contribute to economic growth. It is no accident that countries with highly developed education systems are also those with successful economies and high standards of living. As economies become more dependent on high-technology industries and on the service sector, the desire for a well-educated and highly trained work-force becomes an imperative.

Popular culture has become dominated increasingly by the West, through its control of the mass media and its huge purchasing power. Satellite television and the Internet ensure that western lifestyles are promoted and often emulated. Film and television are available almost everywhere throughout the world. Popular culture has a particular impact on children and young people and this, in turn, affects the nature of the educational process.

The threat to the environment from the practices of governments, businesses and individuals is well beyond the control of nation states. Global warming and the 'greenhouse effect' impact on everyone and state action, although welcome where it occurs, can do little unless the response, like the problem, is global.

Management theory and practice, both within and outside educa-tion, are becoming increasingly global. This includes notions of lead-ership, marketing, human resource management and total quality man-agement. These international concepts make it possible to compare management practices but raise fundamental questions about the importance of context and culture in the organisation and management of schools.

It is within this increasingly global context that Nick Foskett and Jacky Lumby have chosen to publish this important new book on inter-national aspects of leadership and management in education. While they rightly warn of the dangers of glibly claiming an international perspective, the book is timely in seeking to locate the widespread interest in educational leadership and management within a global framework. The dominance of the English language means that most of the academic literature on education is produced in the English-speaking world, notably the USA, the UK and Australia. Perhaps inevitably, the dominant perspectives of this substantial body of writ-ing are those directly relevant to policy, theory, research and practice in these three countries. Because of the paucity of literature in many other countries, academics and practitioners tend to rely on these 'international' texts, leading to a false premise of a global perspective.

It is now widely accepted that managers in education require spe-cific preparation if they are to be successful in leading schools and colleges. The development of effective leaders and managers requires a range of strategies, including high-quality courses and tuition, mentoring by experienced and successful principals, opportunities to practice management at appropriate stages in professional careers and an appreciation of research methods. It also needs the support of literature that presents the major issues in clear, intelligible language while drawing on the best of theory and research. The aim of this series is to develop a body of literature with the following characteristics:

- Directly relevant to school and college management.
- Prepared by authors with national and international reputations.
- An analytical approach based on empirical evidence but couched in intelligible language.
- Integrating the best of theory, research and practice.

Leading and Managing Education: International Dimensions is the tenth volume in the series and it aims to provide a new perspective on educational leadership and management, going beyond the dominant western culture whose authority 'verges on the absolute'. The authors draw on a wide range of approaches from different parts of the world, including developing as well as developed countries and the great traditions of the Islamic world, Africa and Asia. They hope that this diverse and eclectic stance will help readers to challenge the 'accepted' norms in educational leadership and management. This book provides valuable insights for all those interested in seeking out the educational and managerial implications of globalisation.

Tony Bush
University of Reading
March 2002

PREFACE

Those of us who lead or manage in education are encouraged to think of ourselves in an international context, to look to what is happening elsewhere in the world and to learn from each other. Adjectives such as worldwide, global and international, slip readily into so many aspects of our working lives that they are in danger of losing meaning, passing by unnoticed, a token gesture to how the world is changing. In this book we have tried to move beyond such glib rhetoric, to consider afresh what an international perspective might mean. The exploration is a vehicle to create a connection to all those who have a role to play in education – teachers and lecturers, classroom assistants, regional and national administrators and policy-makers in all parts of the world. Whether formally studying educational leadership and management or simply reflecting as professionals, we hope that this volume will offer stimulation to consider the aims and practice of education beyond the limitations of national and cultural parameters.

Thinking outside of lifelong patterns established by culture and practice is a demanding discipline. Just as in an optical illusion, great concentration is needed to see something other than the first immediate image, so becoming aware of and side-stepping the cultural assumptions which colour our view of education demands constant vigilance. The familiar, the habitual, the unconscious bedrock of the values and beliefs laid down by a lifetime's pattern of thinking regain a hold with consummate ease. The authority of culture verges on the absolute. We have tried to challenge this authority and to show how things might be perceived differently. Specifically we have tried to balance the dominant perspectives drawn from research and writing which has its provenance in the West, particularly the UK and the USA, with those reflecting thinking in other parts of the world. This book is, therefore, not for those who wish to identify 'good practice' internationally, but for leaders and managers who wish to locate their thinking and practice within a range drawn from different parts of the world in order to develop, change or confirm their appropriateness.

Presenting things in a new light is by nature iconoclastic. Pointing out the weaknesses or problems associated with any suggested policy or practice is relatively easy. Finding solutions, which tend to be contingent on local conditions, is not. Consequently, prescriptions for the way forward risk re-creating the 'one set of assumptions for all' that this volume aims to question. This book problematises many of the current, dominant theories and practice in educational leadership and management, and demands from its readers a proactive response. In encouraging educators to step outside their habitual way of thinking, to view their beliefs and activity in a wider perspective, we hope they will become active collaborators in using the text, adding their own creativity and judgement in deciding on the implications for action.

Walking the line between the negative and the positive is a difficult balancing act. We can only hope we have got it right.

THE STRUCTURE OF THE BOOK

Beyond the introductory chapter (Section A) this international review of leadership and management in education is organised into a five-section structure which moves outwards concentrically from the key *raison d'être* of schools and colleges which is learning:

Section B examines those management issues relating to the learners (pupils and students) and to learning, with Chapter 2 providing an overview of the management of teaching and learning, and Chapters 3 and 4 focusing on learner outcomes and on quality

Section C considers the people and communities that work in schools/colleges and whom the school or college serves. Chapter 5 provides an overview of the cultural influences on the management of people in schools, while Chapter 6 considers issues of the performance of people. Chapters 7 and 8 focus on the external peoples of schools/colleges by considering external relations management and links with parents and communities.

Section D moves to the wider perspective that is incorporated in the management of strategy and resources. Chapter 9 examines strategic planning, while Chapters 10 and 11 look at the management of resources at whole system and school levels of analysis.

Section E looks at some of the wider issues of future development in education policies and systems, by considering the ideas of widening participation and the development of learning organisations to see how far they are concepts of global significance rather than simply the current priorities and preoccupations of western economies.

Section F concludes the review by focusing on the issue of leadership and seeking to identify what the international analysis tells us about leaders, leadership and management in schools and colleges.

Thanks are due to many people for the help they gave. Tony Bush was supportive as series editor. Marianne Coleman and Daniela Sommerfeldt gave detailed and insightful comments on drafts and were consistently encouraging. Ann Briggs provided useful comments and ideas on the title. The support of Leicester University in providing study leave to complete the book is also acknowledged. Thanks, finally, are due to our families for living with the long hours involved in producing a book of this nature alongside other responsibilities.

We learned a good deal in writing this book, about our own perspectives and about different ways of seeing. We hope we may pass on something of this learning to those who read the volume.

Nick Foskett and Jacky Lumby
University of Southampton and University of Lincoln
March 2002

Section A: Introduction

1

INTERNATIONAL PATTERNS IN EDUCATIONAL MANAGEMENT AND LEADERSHIP

WHY READ THIS BOOK?

Amongst the wide range of academic skills that we emphasise to our students on programmes in educational leadership and management is the need to be critically aware of the motivations and intentions of authors in the literature they consider. In our case, justifying and explaining a book which contributes to the as yet poorly developed literature on international facets of educational leadership and management is not difficult, for we have set out to try to address the growing expectation that practitioners and students will have an international perspective on their roles, responsibilities and tasks. This is not just a personal value statement or academic judgement. Governments promoting the development of educational management and leadership in many countries are expecting that an international perspective will be incorporated in training programmes. In setting up its National College for School Leadership, for example, the British government has stressed that 'in a world class education service our teachers and school leaders must keep pace with developments in other school systems' and that leadership development must incorporate 'the building of international networks of school leaders to debate and exchange practical experiences' (DfEE, 1999, p. 6). However, the book is not just a response to government exhortation, but the result of a personal commitment to respond to the growing pressures of globalisation and the increasing stress felt by educators worldwide by confirming the validity and celebrating the range and richness of practice. Within such a grand purpose, though, this book has a number of more precise and specific aims:

1) To map the international landscape of leadership and management in

education, to provide an overview of the range of approaches and practice in many different national settings, and to seek to identify any
global patterns and trends that may exist.
2) To challenge some of the 'accepted' norms and paradigms in educational leadership and management by providing a range of perspectives
on key themes, drawing on contrasting examples of practice from different national and cultural settings
3) To reduce isolation and build confidence in educational managers as
part of a global community of professional educators, and to support
informed choice about policy and practice amongst practitioners in a
wide range of settings from government to school.

Within this introductory chapter we shall explore these aims in more
detail, and examine some of the significant generic factors that underpin
an understanding of international patterns in educational management and
leadership.

MAPPING THE GLOBAL LANDSCAPE OF EDUCATION

Education is a global-scale enterprise. The provision of school-based education is a firmly established component of the social and political landscape of every state across the world, and towards the end of the twentieth
century primary and secondary schools were providing education for
approximately 1.5 billion children and employment for some 50 million
teachers, using some 4 per cent of the sum of global gross national product
(GNP).

Despite this clear commitment to education on such a vast scale, the
contrasts that may be seen in even a cursory examination of patterns of
provision and experience are huge. Three strong themes emerge from such
an overview. First, although education is global, participation by children
and young people is by no means universal. In the world's developed
countries enrolment rates are virtually 100 per cent for children of primary
and secondary school age, yet in the least developed countries enrolment
rates average only 71 per cent for primary age children and only 19 per
cent for secondary age children. The potential for and pressure towards
increasing the scope and extent of educational provision is still considerable, therefore. Secondly, beyond simplistic comparisons that identify
schooling as, in the main, a process involving teachers in 'classrooms'
working with children, there lies a multiplicity of aims, ideologies, practices and outcomes. The daily experience of children, teachers and principals in schools around the world differs fundamentally in the context
of extremely diverse expectations from government, community and
family. We cannot assume that the motivations for providing education in

any specific setting are similar to those elsewhere. Liberal-humanitarian views of the role of education as developing the whole child as an individual stand in stark contrast to utilitarian views of education as training young people to contribute to economic growth and development. Thirdly, the notion of 'school' is itself a diverse idea, for there is little in common between the rural school in Africa, with no buildings or physical resources, and the sophisticated technology colleges of the UK or the USA.

Contrasts in educational provision and participation are also characterised by sub-national contrasts. These may appear as 'simple' socio-economic patterns with a geographical expression – between urban rich and urban poor, between urban and rural or between core and peripheral economic regions. More frequently this pattern is related to a much wider range of factors, however, in that it reflects the values, histories and cultures of a range of communities and, very frequently, ethnic or religious groups. These factors frequently shape the patterns we can observe in the organisation and management of the education and training system, and either generate or require different responses from national and regional education authorities. Brace (2001) shows, for example, such contrasts within Australia in the patterns that can be seen between Aborigine and other ethnic groups. Demographic contrasts mean that a much higher proportion of Aborigines than other groups are in the under-15 age group and hence in the compulsory school-age phase, yet levels of educational achievement are much lower – only 13.6 per cent of Aborigines possess a post-school qualification (compared with 34 per cent of other groups), only 74 per cent of 15-year-olds remain in full time education (cf. 92 per cent) and only 12 per cent of 19 year olds are in full time education or training (cf. 33 per cent). Such contrasts in outcomes raise fundamental leadership and management challenges to national and state governments and to the political systems of Australian society, and emphasise how dangerous to real understanding generalised interpretations at the national scale can be.

Mapping the international landscape of policy and practice provides a significant challenge in that the precise shape and system of educational management is unique to every national, regional, local or individual school setting. Notwithstanding claims to uniqueness though, we have sought to identify some of the principal approaches that can be observed internationally. Our examples are drawn from every continent and seek to examine patterns from within the major global economic and cultural contrasts – from the Organisation for Economic Cooperation and Development (OECD) countries, the newly industrialising countries, the world's debtor states and the world's least developed countries, and from the major cultural traditions of the West, the Islamic world, Africa, and the great eastern cultures of China, Japan and southern Asia. Our 'mapping' seeks not to be comprehensive but to be indicative, and to represent the range of policy and practice in educational leadership and management.

So far we have sketched in the book's key purposes. We now consider the two central generic themes that emerge throughout the rest of the book, and which underpin a considerable part of our perspective on leadership and management in education – the nature and impact of the processes generically termed 'globalisation' and the centrality of culture in understanding management.

GLOBALISATION, EDUCATION AND MANAGEMENT

'Globalisation' is a term commonly used to describe a range of processes and effects that have emerged from the rapid growth of international interactions in trade, travel, communications and culture that has characterised the last three decades. Waters (1995) has identified three interwoven strands to globalisation. Political globalisation is the emergence of groupings and organisations that operate at a wider scale than the single nation state (for example, the EU, the OECD, or the United Nations Educational, Scientific and Cultural Organisation (UNESCO)), and which shape policy and practice within many individual countries. Economic globalisation is the growth of international trade and exchange, and the operation of markets and businesses at a scale above that of individual countries. Cultural globalisation involves the international exchange of values and beliefs. While rooted in part in economic processes, it is strongly driven by the communications revolution, dominated by western corporations, which makes access to the images and symbols of other cultures available to many through television, film and music. This process is multi-directional, but is regarded by some as cultural imperialism with the spread of western, particularly American, values and symbols across the globe, and the challenging of indigenous national cultures. This spread of western culture is, of course, not an unplanned side effect of economic and political globalisation, but a key and driving part of it. The success of western business in the global economy is dependent in part on the successful selling of the culture and values on which it is based, or what Beare, Caldwell and Millikan (1989) have described as the 'entrepreneurialism of culture'.

Globalisation is, of course, a misleading term, in that it implies that each of these forces is acting to reach and impact upon all parts of the globe. The processes outlined here are, in fact, rather uneven in their impact and penetration, but are characterised by operating at a scale which is larger than that under the authority of single nation states. The processes operate at an international rather than a national scale with a potential for impacting anywhere on the globe. Equally it is important to recognise that forces of globalisation generate negative responses or rejection at times and are certainly mediated at the national level in terms of how the forces impact. The effects are not homogeneous, though, since the nature of the interaction between external forces of 'globalisation' and the existing cultural characteristics, with their own inherent pressures of conservatism and/or change, means that a unique outcome is likely in every national setting. Rhoten (2000, p. 615) writing in the context of decentralisation in the education system of Argentina, for example, emphasises that 'supranational policy paradigms on which national policy agendas are based are neither universal nor inevitable in the processes and outcomes they produce'.

Indeed, writers such as Waters (1995), Parsons (1995), Naisbett and Aburdene (1988) and Brown and Lauder (1997) suggest that the 'direct threat to nation state legitimacy' (Bottery, 1999, p. 302) generates a reaction in governments to at least retain their own national values in the changes that arise from such global forces. In some cases governments may eschew those changes altogether and proclaim the retention of existing values and perspectives that may be in explicit contrast to the values underpinning globalisation. For most national governments, though, there will be the ongoing, and perhaps increasing, tensions between the pressures to respond to global economic and political forces in a way that optimises benefits at the national level, and the pressures for increasing participation, democracy and self-determination at regional, local and individual levels of operation. An important outcome of globalisation is the increased instability, contradiction and ambiguity in the environments within which governments, managers and individuals must operate.

Overall, globalisation is perceived as the spread of western values to the rest of the world. In the context of education we may see this in terms of the promotion of policies on educational outcomes and practices that have emerged in western political settings, and the adoption of western approaches to management. Bottery (1999) identifies the latter phenomenon as 'managerial globalization', and illustrates the concept well in the context of educational management. Specifically, Bottery suggests that the dominant themes in the literature of educational management in the developed world in the last two decades have been:

- a consideration of the public/private/voluntary sector divide, with an emphasis on adapting and adopting approaches from the business world to the world of educational management
- a consideration of educational management practice in other countries.

The consequence of the dominance of these themes lies in the convergence of the perspectives that they generate. The emergence in the literature of business management terminology and the rise in the emphasis on business-based forms of accountability 'infiltrate educational language and begin to spin their conceptual webs' (Bottery, 1999, p. 303). Similarly, as practitioners and governments seek to adopt the 'best' ideas from the international literature on education there begins to emerge a common perspective that may 'define what looks increasingly like a global picture of management practice' (Bottery, 1999, p. 303). We must be aware that the spread of 'good practice' internationally, through the educational management literature, through the actions of international organisations such as UNESCO and through the impact of professional development programmes, all of which are dominated by the perspectives of western educational management practitioners and academics, is in danger of presenting such a global picture of good practice.

The educational management literature with which this volume is particularly concerned may be characterised as promoting certain practice as 'good' to the extent that it not only appears normative but takes on a mythic nature. Turner (1990, pp. 3–4) defines myths as 'unquestioned assumptions' or 'a frame of thinking' which serve a variety of purposes. They reassure people that the way they think is the only way, thereby excluding the need for messy and stressful decisions and change. In confirming that the accepted way is the only way, myths may also stabilise and protect existing power structures. Both Schein (1997) and Argyris and Schön (1981) have written about the function of myths in organisations, and the sacrosanct nature of stories and beliefs which are clearly in contradiction to actual practice. Both emphasise the ability of myths to withstand change in the face of all but the most dramatic events. An organisation must be near the point of collapse before long-standing myths about the appropriate way of doing things will be dented. The reason for the degree of resilience of myths is rooted in the important needs they serve. Turner (1990, pp. 4–5) identifies four such purposes, categorised as follows:

1) Myths that create, maintain and legitimate past, present and future actions and consequences.
2) Myths that maintain and conceal political interests and value systems.
3) Myths that help explain and create cause and effect relationships under conditions of incomplete knowledge.
4) Myths that rationalise the complexity and turbulence of activities and events to allow for predictable action-taking.

All these purposes are served by myths within organisations, but equally can be applied to the body of literature in question. For example, the concept of leadership, and particularly leadership of the principal, is increasingly stressed by governments and governing boards of schools and colleges. The 'story' of the criticality of the principal's leadership to the success of learners is widespread. The extensive literature on educational leadership contributes to what may be a myth, which can be related to all four of the purposes of myths outlined above. The myth legitimises the increasing powers being devolved to principals and also serves to place the responsibility for failure at their door. The reasons for failure in educational institutions, which are complex, and to which the relationship with leadership is not clearly understood, can be simplified and reduced to explorations of the nature of leadership on the unquestioned assumption that it is of great importance, despite the fact that some evidence questions whether the role of the principal is indeed critical to improving the experience and achievement of learners. Of course, not all the literature on leadership promotes such ideas, but the work *as a body* has this effect. Our aim, and it is very challenging, is to make explicit some of the myths in the research, writing and thinking about educational leadership and management, and to contribute to some degree to stepping outside the existing largely western frame of thinking to question how far the norms and assumptions within the literature are justified. It is challenging for the writers because stepping outside existing frames of thinking is a hazardous enterprise which risks failure and, even if successful, may provoke resistance and criticism. It is hazardous too for the reader because 'myths enable people to feel better about what they do' (Turner, 1990, p. 5) and questioning them may be uncomfortable.

THE CENTRALITY OF CULTURE

A second generic theme is the importance of considering the role of culture within any meaningful analysis of educational leadership and management. O'Neill (1994) has illustrated how any organisation has three key but interdependent dimensions of structure, activities (processes) and culture which define the essence of that organisation. Culture is that set of values and beliefs, both explicit and implicit, which underpins the organisation and provides the basis for action and decision-making in the absence of direct instructions – it is 'the way we do things around here'. Beare, Caldwell and Millikan (1989) suggest that culture is expressed:

- conceptually, through the valuing of particular ideas, which will be expressed in any explicit aims that the organisation has
- verbally, through the adoption of specific discourses and usage of terminology
- behaviourally, through rituals, ceremonies and social interactions
- visually, through designs and styles adopted by the organisation, perhaps, for example, in dress or uniform.

Prosser (1998) shows how culture is expressed at a range of operational scales within an educational system – at the level of individual classrooms, at the level of teams within the school, at whole school level and at the level of the communities (local, regional and national) within which the school exists. 'Sub-cultures' (Goodson, 1988) and even 'counter cultures' (Beare , Caldwell and Millikan, 1989) may operate, therefore, within organisations and systems, although dominant values and beliefs will be strongly identified. Understanding culture, therefore, is important to interpreting schools and colleges as organisations, and we must recognise that:

> Education, as an essentially human activity, is culture bound. Policy makers and school leaders, therefore, need to be mindful of societal and organisational cultural characteristics when formulating, adopting and implementing policies. The prospect of successful implementation is enhanced when the policy makers and school administrators adopt policies consonant with the characteristics of the prevailing societal culture.
>
> (Dimmock, 1998, p. 366)

Furthermore, we must recognise that the implicit influence of culture will strongly shape the patterns that emerge and that while we must not impute a deterministic relationship between culture and organisational/operational outcomes, culture will provide strong boundaries and constraints to 'what will work'. This is at its most significant in examining patterns of change within national settings in the context of increasing international influence on policy and practice. Change results from the interaction of indigenous and exogenous forces promoting and restraining that change, and that interaction provides a battleground that is 'both the site and the stake' (Bowe, Ball and Gold, 1992) of change. For example, the so-called metatrend of decentralisation in education may confront government with the need to consider the adoption of some form of delegated system of school management. The change itself will be an issue for debate and decision-making, but may also provide a focus for debate on a wide range of matters relating to the nature and purpose of education in the social context of that country's own culture and heritage. The outcome will be a compromise between the extremes of 'no change' and the adoption wholesale of an externally generated initiative, which will itself reflect the impact of cultural values and beliefs on the decision.

At the national scale, plurality of culture is an increasing phenomenon in society as a result of processes of internationalisation and globalisation. However, the existence of specific characteristics in national cultures is clear and their impact on policy and practice in educational management is important to recognise, even though 'minimal research on cultural dimensions has taken place in educational administration' (Dimmock, 1998, p. 367). Much of the understanding of culture in the context of management is based on the ideas of Hofstede (1991), who identifies five dimensions of culture, each comprising a bipolar spectrum, against which a country may be profiled. Hofstede's five dimensions are:

1) Power–Distance (PD). The distribution of power and acceptance of that pattern varies significantly between societies. In many western societies inequalities of power and the acceptance of considerable distance between the least and most powerful members of society and

organisations are much less pronounced than, for example, in many Asian societies. Hence China may be seen as having a high Power–Distance Index (PDI) while the UK and the USA have a much lower PDI.

2) Individualism–Collectivism (IC). This reflects how far the society emphasises responsibility to the group (the state, family or community) rather than responsibility to the individual. Many African societies are strongly collectivist, in contrast to, for example, the USA and UK, which Hofstede identifies as having the strongest individualist cultures. Societies with low PDIs tend to be strongly individualist.

3) Masculinity–Femininity (MF). The MF dimension illustrates how far the organisation of society reflects the stereotypical male attributes of assertiveness or the female attributes of caring and modesty. Many Latin American or Islamic cultures, for example, are strongly masculine in their culture.

4) Uncertainty Avoidance (UA). Uncertainty avoidance reflects the culture's tolerance of risk, change and ambiguity. In those cultures where UA is high the emphasis may be on stability and security within existing systems and practices rather than on the adoption of new ideas and approaches, and limited tolerance of a range of ideas. Uncertainty avoidance is often low in plural societies and in those societies emphasising the individual and entrepreneurialism. Islamic nations frequently have high UA, whereas western and Asian cultures frequently have low UA.

5) Long-term–Short-Term (LS). This reflects how far the society is focused on long-term perspectives, with a tolerance or avoidance of short-term 'costs' in the interests of long-term gains. Dimmock (1998) shows how in many societies these factors are finely-balanced – for example, in Confucian Asian societies 'the values associated with long-term orientation, such as thrift (and) perseverance . . . are counterbalanced by values associated with short-term orientation such as respect for tradition, fulfilment of social obligations and protection of one's face'.

It is important to stress that these dimensions provide a broad, subjective, general analysis of national organisational cultures, within which sub-cultures and counter-cultures will be identifiable, and the ideas of cultural determinism proposed by Parsons (1966) must be strongly rejected. However, such analysis does provide a useful starting point for understanding the cultural setting within which specific patterns of policy and practice have emerged. For example, the importance of understanding the inherent cultural values that underpin the education system is emphasised by Chang (2000) in the context of Singapore and by Hallinger and Kantamara (2000) in the context of Thailand. Chang (2000) has examined 'state' values and individualism in the development of education in Singapore in contrast to those in North America or Western Europe. He asserts that:

> In North America and Western Europe the individual is given primacy in relation to society. It follows that access to education ... is perceived of as an uncompromising right of the individual ... [T]he guiding principle of the Singapore government's education policy is to give top priority to the overall interests of society.
>
> (Chang, 2000, pp. 28–9)

Chang describes this focus on the interests of society as 'communitarianism', and places it alongside five other core state values in Singapore in influencing education – pragmatism; neo-Darwinism; conservative liberalism; good government (government which is 'clean, honest, capable, efficient, forward-looking and firm' [Chang, 2000, p. 28]); and a commitment to the Confucian concept of zhongyang ('golden means oriented rationalism') which promotes the view that the best solution to any problem is located between two sets of alternatives, and so excludes both excessively radical or conservative perspectives.

Hallinger and Kantamara examine the introduction of the western concept of school-based management into Thailand, and conclude that 'the values and assumptions underlying these modern educational practices run counter to traditional cultural norms of Thai society' (Hallinger and Kantamara, 2000, p. 191). The government strategy to promote school-based management, therefore, has required significant attention to management within the cultural constraints and to the development of strategies to overcome traditional deference (*greng jai*) which runs counter to the cultural assumptions of devolved responsibility.

The processes of globalisation may be interpreted as leading to the spread of western culture and values to most countries and societies, where there is an inevitable interaction with the existing societal culture. Cultural change is inherent in all societies, although it progresses at differing speeds, but confrontation with western values may lead to more rapid change. Understanding the possible outcomes of that interaction necessitates a clear knowledge of both the inherent components of existing culture and the areas in which exposure to western culture will generate tensions and frictions.

INTERNATIONAL RESEARCH IN EDUCATIONAL LEADERSHIP AND MANAGEMENT

There are difficulties in using existing literature to support such a critical view of policy and practice taking account of the centrality of culture. Research in educational leadership and management, while extensive and productive in quantity, has considerable imbalances in its coverage. The literature from the western, developed, English-speaking world is substantial and wide-ranging. This literature contains research-based studies at a range of scales, and a wide literature representing analysis, reflection and experience-based perspectives is also readily available. Outside English language journals, however, the range of literature is extremely limited. The output from research and debate in other cultural settings often finds its only outlet in the English language literature, or is based on research undertaken by western scholars examining other cultural settings only as interested outsiders. We have been aware in selecting material, examples, ideas and critiques for this book, therefore, of the imbalances in what has been available to us, and the issues that this raises. We recognise, for example, the danger of implicitly promoting the western, Anglo-Saxon perspective implicit in the majority of the literature we have used, and as authors we recognise that we are ourselves the product of the paradigms and cultures that we inhabit. We have tried to provide breadth and balance in our coverage of geographical and cultural realms. However, this has provided a challenge to selection in relation to the developed world, and a major task of exploration and discovery in relation to other environments. We have tried to apply our typical standards of critical review to all the materials we have used, but recognise that reliance on single sources or official government publications in some spheres has made this very difficult.

Against such a picture of the evidence base it is inevitable that we would emphasise the need for more research into both comparative aspects of educational management and into the practice of management in a range of social, cultural, economic and political environments. However, it is also clear that our own commitment to research-based decision-making, policy-making and action, based on western academic standards, is neither practical nor necessarily valued universally. In many cultural settings the encouragement of critical or reflective practice is not welcome, for example, and may challenge fundamental social values. While our own commitment to the importance of research in informing understanding and practice is an unequivocal ideal, the opportunity to reflect, develop and improve practice globally cannot wait on the emergence of a comprehensive research base. Rather we would seek to promote reflective practice at all levels of management, leadership and policy-making, from government office to classroom, through the use, where appropriate, of informed dialogue, sharing of ideas and perspectives and appropriate professional development. Small-scale research projects in the traditions of action research may provide a useful adjunct to this. Overall we are stressing the importance of recognising what can and cannot be achieved in each individual reader's own professional setting, and the support of appropriate (sometimes primitive or intermediate) professional development technologies.

To summarise, despite the almost overwhelming pressures of globalisation which militate against celebrating difference, and despite the limitations of existing literature recognising the important centrality of culture, any perspective on educational leadership and management must emphasise the need to:

- not accept uncritically any concept or approach developed in different cultural, economic and political environments
- recognise that there is no single universal principle of educational management that is not shaped by contextual factors at a local, implementational level
- recognise that the values of education are frequently different from those of business, and that the emphasis on management as a term risks detracting from the wide range of social and cultural purposes of education
- recognise that educational management is about operating in a range of contexts from global to local, but where the local factors will always shape to some extent the precise nature of the educational process.

Such a perspective underpins the ideas presented elsewhere in this book.

BUILDING AN INTERCULTURAL COMMUNITY

The previous discussion has elaborated our first two aims of mapping the international landscape and challenging accepted norms. The third aim relates not solely to the knowledge that educators bring to their task, but also to how they feel about their work. Isolation is a constant reality for many in education, working as a sole adult with children or adults, confined to a single classroom for the majority of time. Educators struggle to find time and space to share their experience with others working in the same institution, let alone people working in schools and colleges elsewhere in their country or in other parts of the world. To address the third aim of reducing isolation and building confidence, this volume attempts to offer a bridge, to link all those contributing to the endeavour of educating children and adults wherever they may be. In reading and responding to ideas drawn from different parts of the world such isolation may be reduced as people can reflect on their engagement with the international community of educators. If such a sense of a global community is truly to be attempted, it is likely to be created not just at the technical level, by exchanging pedagogic or management practice, but also more fundamentally by some connection of values, of shared understandings while avoiding, even by implication, the promotion of selected values and philosophies as in some sense the norm. It is a very challenging intention to communicate with educators throughout the world and find a means of engaging them without recourse to justification or motivation that is culturally bounded. However demanding to identify, a common ground platform for communication is needed and must offer the chance for sharing and evaluating practice without assuming shared values.

Ironically, a concept that is one of the most widely contested, the concept of professionalism, may offer a possible framework for intercultural communication. The history of those who work in education is the history of the struggle for professionalisation. Teachers and principals have striven for their role to be recognised as having critical importance to individuals and to society, and to involve high-level skills and dedication (and commensurate rewards). Eraut (1994) reminds us that professionalism is a concept which can be understood in a number of ways, relating not only to the ideal type traits of high-status professions such as medicine and law, but also to class power struggles, with professionalism as a means of securing and protecting status. He also suggests that amongst the traits of professionalism in the lists compiled by various writers are some which are culturally dependent. It is not our intention to debate the wider aspects of definitions of professionalism, but to find in the concept a means of supporting our aim to communicate with educators throughout the world, by focusing on two selected defining characteristics that may be universal. First, professionalism rests on the acquisition of knowledge and expertise. Professionals spend time and effort learning how to fulfil their role. Consequently, we hope that by exploring policy and practice in different parts of the world we will contribute to the knowledge of educators, wherever they work and whatever their role. Secondly, professionalism depends on self-regulation (Bergen, 1988). Judgements must be made on how to act, based not solely on the compulsion of external authority, but on the intrinsic arbiters of values, knowledge and understanding.

We are well aware that choices may be made at different levels within any educational system, and that the degree of freedom to use judgement may be shaped by how the role of a teacher, principal, classroom helper, regional or national administrator/manager is viewed. Nevertheless, it is our belief that all those who work in education do make choices, and that a greater understanding of the range of practice throughout the world may usefully inform such choices. Knowledge is a key component of such professionalism. Within this notion, though, we must reiterate the 'health warning' stressed earlier in this chapter. Exploration of the international range of policy and practice may be founded on a spectrum of approaches from the normative to absolute relativism. Both extremes are equally unhelpful. The normative approach, suggesting one method is universally applicable or in some sense preferable to others in any environment, is to deny the richness of different contexts and desired outcomes of education throughout the world. However, the converse extreme, of accepting any current practice as somehow justified by accepted tradition and beliefs is equally unacceptable, inviting complacency and stasis rather than stability or improvement. The appropriate selection of practice will lie somewhere between the two ends of the spectrum and the choice is likely to be guided most fundamentally by values. It is our belief that the values of an individual or team are elastic. They can be stretched, but parameters will remain beyond which fundamental principles cannot move. Through this volume we hope to increase knowledge and understanding of leadership and management in education and to encourage the elasticity of values in thinking through or rethinking choices about developing practice in the individual context of the school/college or role, between the extremes of normativism and relativism. In this our central value as authors is a belief in the ability of every individual in education to make a contribution to improving education and the achievement of the desired outcomes.

Section B: Learners and learning

Teaching and learning are the core of education. Supporting learning is the purpose of all leadership and management activities, either directly or indirectly. It is fitting, therefore, that the first main section of this book focuses on this central purpose. The first chapter in the section explores what is expected of education, how this may be changing and how educators are responding. The following two chapters examine two of the most significant international trends that have resulted, a move to outcomes-based education and efforts to improve quality.

2

LEARNING AND TEACHING

FORCES FOR CHANGE

The changes in the global context for education outlined in the introductory chapter exert profound forces which translate most fundamentally into a pressure to change the way children and adults learn. The exhortation to rethink the nature of teaching and learning resonates in the words of researchers and writers on education (Bowring-Carr and West-Burnham, 1997; Stoll and Fink, 1996) and in those of many governments (Tan, 2001). At least in the rhetoric, there is a demand for thinking schools, learning schools and learning societies, reflecting changing expectations amongst many of the groups with an interest in education. In tension with the ubiquitous call for change is an assertion of school and college inertia, that there is 'a more or less universal classroom reality' and that this has not and is not changing (Beattie, 1990, p. 28). There is, of course, truth in the assertion. Similarities exist and reflect enduring practice. All over the world learners are grouped largely by age and taught in a classroom or workshop by a single teacher. The profile of subjects they are taught is similar and the activities, certainly of older children, generally teacher directed and conventional, are based on a transmission model of knowledge and culture (Roelofs and Terwel, 1999; Tan, 2001). A further common denominator is the poverty which haunts innumerable pupils not only in developing economies, but also in the developed world (De Voogd, 1998; Thaman, 1993) leading directly or indirectly to the physical and often emotional deprivation which underlies a capacity to learn. The power of poverty to shape an individual's encounter with learning dwarfs the impact of government or educators' intentions. Finally, throughout the world, the most coveted outcome of education is not the publicly articulated goal of fulfilling intellectual and emotional potential but 'the acquisition of credentials' (Olson, James and Lang, 1999, p. 75) as a route to a better income, status and security in the future. Whatever the mythology,

it is expanding credentialisation, examinations and their resulting qualifications, which are the currency of education.

Despite the inertia of existing practice, changing economic, societal and
technical factors are compelling change. The expansion of education with
a higher proportion of the population in compulsory and post-compulsory
sectors has challenged educators to provide quality education for much
larger numbers and a more diverse range of ability and attainment (Qui,
1988). New technologies have opened up different methods of learning.
Teaching and learning are escaping from their previous domain. Students
with access to such technology are no longer dependent on the school or
college teacher. The means for learning can be accessed independently.
Learning can also happen in a wider range of places. Increasingly, educators are seeking ways of supporting learning outside the classroom environment, in the home, on employers' premises, in drop-in centres, even
on the streets haunted by the homeless or disaffected. An emphasis on
lifelong learning has legitimised learning as a pervasive activity which
happens beyond educational institutions, defying the limited age span of
schooling and the direct control of professional educators.

In synthesis these pressures have led to differing expectations and
demands for a new kind of learning. This chapter will explore how far
the apparent calls for fundamental shifts in teaching and learning are
reflected in reality in modified policy and practice, and how far this results
in changes to how learning happens, where it happens and to what
purpose. This chapter questions what sort of learning is envisaged for the
first part of the twenty-first century, and what the practical implications
are for those who lead and manage in education. The key questions are:

- What are various stakeholders' expectations of education?
- Has this led to paradigm shifts in learning?
- How have national governments responded?
- How have schools and colleges responded to the challenge to manage
  this change?
- What are the resourcing implications?
- Has this led to changed roles for teachers, students and parents?

MEETING EXPECTATIONS

There are two dominant perspectives on the aims of education. On the
one hand, there are calls for education to fulfil the intellectual and emotional potential of the individual; the liberal approach. On the other,
meeting the social and economic needs of the family and the state drive
the design of educational systems; the instrumental stance. Whatever the
perspective, there is much dissatisfaction. Criticism that education is not
matching the needs of the twenty-first century has come from a number
of sources. Researchers accuse education of being stuck in methods appro-

priate to an earlier era. Stoll and Fink, (1996, p. 1) claim many of our schools are good schools 'if this were 1965'. Hargreaves (1994), Caldwell (1997) and Bowring-Carr and West-Burnham (1997) all argue that schools are outdated in their aims and methods. The common thread appears to be a belief that, comparing the three outcomes of education cited by Stoll and Fink, being (affective skills), doing (practical and cognitive skills) and knowing (memorisation of facts), it is the latter which has, inappropriately, by far the greatest emphasis. However, this critique tends to emanate most strongly from western perspectives. Some cultures approve the primacy of knowing and wish the curriculum to remain concerned largely with knowledge and therefore culture transmission. They do not seek fundamental change (Oman Ministry of Information, 2000).

Nevertheless the prevalence of reform implies that many governments share a critical view of education. Aedo-Richmond and Richmond (1999, p. 196) refer to the 'pervasiveness of curriculum change' across OECD member states. The introduction of the National Curriculum in England, Outcomes Based Education in South Africa and the Target Oriented Curriculum in Hong Kong are examples of wholesale national reform in three continents. Curriculum development may also be seen as a means of 'trying to meet the challenges of independence and decolonisation', for example in Pacific island countries (Thaman, 1993, p. 77).

However, the ubiquitous clamour for change may obscure differences in desired goals. Writers on education demand more emphasis on learning output rather than teaching input. Government reform may apparently aim at a similar shift, for example in the burgeoning of outcomes-based curricula, but the retention of assessment systems which focus on knowledge transmission essentially confirms the age-old goal of getting as many children as possible to pass examinations primarily through testing their memory. Resource levels which result in large class sizes, compelling whole-class teaching, have the same effect. Whatever the rhetorical intent, while qualifications are achieved by assessment systems which are founded on knowledge, class teaching will focus on knowledge transmission. Teacher input and examination results, not learning, will remain central. The publicly-expressed wish of states to move away from historic forms of education which use the transmission and testing of knowledge to rank citizens, thus circumscribing their life opportunities, to a greater emphasis on providing lifelong skills seems something of a myth. The retention of existing assessment systems effectively ensures that little will change.

As a consequence, teachers are trammelled by the system. Even where they may wish to change, the expectations of government and of parents deter. In some cases, for example in South Africa, teachers need children to pass the standard test, so they can move on to the next class (Pell, 1998). Internationally, league tables, formally published or informally compiled through discussion amongst parents, enforce concentration on examination results. Accountability to parents and to government is enacted through measurement of results, and memorisation of knowledge is amenable to measurement. Teachers want learners to succeed, but where the measurement of success focuses on knowing, rather than being or doing, it is knowing which will easily carry the day as the centre of teaching.

Parents are well aware of this and consequently the expectation of many is that schools and colleges teach learners how to pass examinations. In Japan even primary age children work additional hours after school in an effort to help them pass examinations which will give entry into a prestigious school and then a prestigious university (Sugimine, 1998). In Korea and Singapore, despite rhetoric from the government about encouraging creativity and whole-person development, schools' major aim is to achieve examination success (Le Metais and Tabberer, 1997; Stott and Walker, 1992). The key point is that, as confirmed by Metais and Tabberer in a survey of 16 countries in Europe, Asia, Australia and America, the nationally and institutionally stated values of education are not necessarily reflected in the assessment process.

Expectations of education also relate strongly to economic aims, at both family and national level. Governments stress a strong link between developing education and strengthening the economy (see Chapter 12). As argued above, parents may view education as the passport to a brighter economic future for their family. However, such expectations are not universal. The economic situation of both the family and the nation influences the expectations of schooling. For example, in rural India, in the absence of alternative employment possibilities, knowing that education has little relevance to their future work in agriculture, children drop out early or, when they complete compulsory schooling, cannot afford to proceed to further training or, if they do train, can find no work locally (Dyer, 2000). Expectations of education on the part of teachers, students and their families may not be high. Even in more developed economies, for example in Hong Kong, the multiplicity of social and economic problems on urban estates may lead to a sense that, realistically, the expectation of what education can achieve for individuals and for the community is limited (Cheung, 2000).

In the contested area of the aims and process of teaching and learning, children's views are not given much attention. In some cultures, it is considered appropriate that children should be subject to the decisions of adults. However, change is creeping in. Outcomes-based curricula emphasise working with individuals to set and achieve targets necessitating the involvement of the learner. The advent of quality processes, particularly total quality management, with its emphasis on the views of customers, has to a limited degree legitimised listening to the views of even child learners. Where such views are reported, learners generally indicate a wish to move away from expository styles of teaching, to enjoy a more equal relationship with teachers. They want not merely to know, but to understand, and admire staff who help them achieve deep learning (Chan and Watkins, 1994; Harrison, 1997).

THE PARADIGM OF LEARNING

The expectations of education are, therefore, ambivalent, on the one hand both created by and reflected in assessment systems and resulting teaching methods where a central aim is to rank children and, on the other, reflecting a desire to educate children and adults to equip them with life-long skills and confidence. In relation to the latter, there is growing dissatisfaction with current teaching and learning which is perceived as encouraging dependence and passivity in learners (Morris and Adamson, 1998). The process is described variously as, for example, 'arcane pedagogical rituals' (Olson, James and Lang, 1999, p. 70), or 'a passive atomistic and mechanical process' (Roelofs and Terwel, 1999, p. 221). The problems associated with current practice are a belief that it does not equip learners with the autonomy and confidence to manage their learning outside school/college and throughout their life, it does not connect with their experience outside the classroom, and it often results in overload both within the curriculum and in the amount of work learners, especially young children, are expected to undertake as homework. The perceived irrelevance or unconnectedness is contributing to disaffection amongst young people even in societies which traditionally could expect obedience and respect. Whether it is an American city, an industrial area in Hong Kong or a township in South Africa, students reacting to an educational ranking process which confirms their already bleak future prospects, may opt out of the system by passive lack of interest or aggressive revolt (Cheung, 2000; De Voogd, 1998; Jansen, 1998; Sernak, 1998).

The emerging alternative is based on a new paradigm, which emphasises a more holistic approach to teaching and learning, influenced by movements from psychology such as situated learning and constructivism (Gipps and MacGilchrist, 1999). Such perspectives maintain that learning is not a discrete package that can be delivered in the classroom by a teacher/lecturer, but is constructed by the learner through connecting new experience, facts and emotions to previous experience and knowledge. The new paradigm marks a shift to what Roelofs and Terwel (1999, p. 201) term 'authentic pedagogy', the most important characteristics of which are:

> The meaningfulness of the learning context; the connection between learning and behaviour; knowledge as a tool rather than as a goal in itself; the significance of the interactions among learners; the influence of cultural attitudes; the idea of the learner as an active researcher; less emphasis on the teaching of facts and greater emphasis on the personal aspects of knowledge; more attention to coherent

forms of knowledge as well as greater emphasis on the way in which the learner arrives at a solution; more focus on the complex problems that learners (re) structure for themselves; application of the 're-invention' principle ; and the acceptance of more than one solution to an existing problem.

(Roelofs and Terwel, 1999, p. 205)

They describe how secondary schools in the Netherlands attempted to reform the curriculum to achieve this metamorphosis in the nature of teaching and learning.

Morris and Lo model a similar shift in relation to the reform of the curriculum in Hong Kong, the introduction of the Target Oriented Curriculum (see Table 2.1). The shift indicated from subject-based, norm-referenced, didactic teaching to an interdisciplinary, criterion-referenced, learner-centred approach is a profound challenge not only to centuries of teaching practice but also to the underlying Confucian values of Chinese society. The technical reform of teaching practice is the surface expression of deep changes in power relations within society, implying a more equal relationship between teacher and pupil, and potentially more equity in life chances for all. The competence or outcomes-based movement has been used throughout the world to try to engineer a culture change, a transfer from a concern for input and traditional modes of assessment to a concern for output and less emphasis on ranking in the assessment process. The next chapter explores this phenomenon in more detail.

As Roelofs and Terwel (1999, p. 205) point out, 'it is not the case that education is authentic or not authentic; authenticity is always a matter of degree'. It is not suggested that whole-class teaching or memorisation are never appropriate. Rather the shift in paradigm suggests that though the current ranking assessment and teacher-centred system dominates, there is a growing intention to change this situation and to break free from learning which, rather than being constructed, is constricted.

DEVELOPING TEACHING AND LEARNING: GOVERNMENT RESPONSE

The discourse on developing teaching and learning has to some extent been dominated by two concepts, effectiveness and improvement. The former grew out of a wish to validate factors present in schools deemed effective. It was hoped the identification of such factors could be used to underpin particularly national reform. Since its inception in the 1960s, effectiveness research has grown in sophistication and devised ever more complex multi-level models of the variables which influence educational outcomes. Major criticisms have shadowed this work, including the contingent nature of many identified variables which therefore may not

Table 2.1 Reform of the curriculum in Hong Kong

	Old paradigm	New paradigm
PEDAGOGY	Whole-class teaching/teacher centred, textbook/syllabus-oriented, strong frame	Group-based pupil activity/interaction. Cater for pupil differences, resources/task-based learning, weak frame
ASSESSMENT	Summative, norm-referenced, focus on established knowledge	Identification of progressive targets, formative, continuous, criterion referenced, focus on knowledge as constructed
CURRICULUM AIMS/ CONCEPTIONS	Academic rationalist, strong boundaries between subjects, focus on subject-specific goals, product oriented	Social efficiency, weak boundaries between subjects, focus on broad generic skills (problem-solving, reasoning, enquiry, communication and conceptualising), process oriented

Source: adapted from Morris and Lo, 2000, p. 177.

transfer easily, and the lack of connectivity between factors of effectiveness and the process of becoming effective. Improvement research has attempted to rectify this fracture by focusing on the change process, though again the features of successful change may be highly contingent (Teddlie and Reynolds, 2000). The impact of effectiveness and improvement approaches are examined in more detail in the next chapter. The two approaches are conceptually and methodologically very different but do share a common feature in that both direct leaders to focus on the centrality of the instructional process, teaching and learning in the classroom and the department.

Governments have tried to find ways of metamorphosing teaching and learning. Often underpinning action for reform is a common belief that teachers will not change their practice themselves without considerable pressure or even demand to do so (MacGilchrist, Myers and Reed, 1997). Also, in many countries the formulation of policy is seen as a prestigious task, reserved for those with high status, contrasting with the much less prestigious task of implementation (Dyer, 2000). As Olson, James and Lang (1999) remind us, ideas for reform are likely to come from a number of sources, are melded and result in policy which is rarely fully formed and is infrequently trialled. While it is easy to heap criticism upon governments which impose change quickly and with insufficient development, it is the case that at national level there may be difficulties such as a paucity of resources and/or experience, or a long-standing historical domination by colonial culture which undermine the capacity to develop policy. Fergus (1993) cites the Caribbean and Malta as two such cases. The result often is that 'a range of poorly-planned initiatives are dumped' upon teachers (Jansen, 1998, p. 81). Havelock and Huberman's 1977 model (Figure 2.1) is still a compelling description of the frequent outcome.

This model suggests that the speed and scale of reform provoke resistance, and change, if it takes place at all, is rapidly submerged as previous practice reasserts itself. Ansoff and McDonnell's 'law' (1990, p. 416) that 'resistance to change is proportional to the size of the discontinuities introduced into culture and power, and inversely proportional to the speed of introduction' suggests that resistance is indeed predictable. Resistance and failure in the curriculum reform process can happen at a number of levels. Dyer describes how 'Operation Blackboard', an Indian reform to improve the physical facilities in elementary schooling:

> moved through no fewer than four tiers of government, from the capital in New Delhi through the State to the *Panchayati Raj* in the District to the *talukas* or Municipal Corporation. As it passed from level to level, it encountered and was shaped by a local agenda and the *modus operandi* of each administrative tier. In many places, administrative discretion was retained and used to dilute or defeat policy objectives even though everyone seemed to agree that the notion of improving physical facilities in schools was very important and long overdue.
>
> (Dyer, 2000, p. 156)

As has been argued elsewhere, outstanding merit in any reform does not guarantee success (Lumby, 1998). Change can be subverted by regional and local administration, but its most fundamental barrier is within schools and colleges themselves. Even where there is a determined attempt to involve representative teachers in shaping policy, and/or where teachers are in agreement with the proposed change, the ultimate touchstone of successful change, a different or improved experience for the learner, may not happen. Roelofs and Terwel (1999) conducted a three-year study of the process of implementing the national curriculum for Dutch secondary schools, which aimed to achieve 'authentic pedagogy' and found few changes in teachers' practice. The reasons for this lay with structural and timing issues, and the way that the school day and the division of labour were constructed. It is within schools and colleges themselves that the management of change can secure improvements in learning or block them.

Antecedents	Implementation	Immediate outcomes	Short-term outcomes	Longer-term outcomes
$\rightarrow$	$\rightarrow$	$\rightarrow$	$\rightarrow$	$\rightarrow$
Pressure for massive change	Decision to make major reforms	Overload of structure	Delays Unexpected events	Project reduced in scale
	Rapid planning and execution	Demand for rapid behavioural changes	Passive resistance or exhaustion	Traditional structures swallow up changes

Figure 2.1 Change outcomes
Source: Havelock and Huberman, 1977 (quoted in Dyer, 2000, p. 61).

DEVELOPING TEACHING AND LEARNING: SCHOOLS' AND COLLEGES' RESPONSE

Dimbleby and Cooke (2000, p. 79), writing of the development of teaching and learning in further education, quote an address to the USA's League for Innovation in the Community College, which berated educators for failure in innovation because they 'focus on everything but learning'. Managers are accused of focusing on, for example, structures, organisational charts, administrative processes, business partnerships and quality systems rather than learning. But the point is surely that educators cannot focus directly on learning. Learning is a process which happens within individuals. It is internal and can only be indirectly observed through *post facto* behaviour, hence the reliance on assessment systems as a proxy for learning. Inevitably then, to develop learning, educators have no option but to focus on learners and on factors which may influence learning rather than learning itself. The structures in place, the assessment systems and, most fundamentally of all, the practices of teachers are the features that can be reshaped to impact on learning.

Learners themselves recognise that the relationship with teachers and the activities with which teachers lead them to engage are the most critical element supporting their learning (Chan and Watkins, 1994; Harrison, 1997; Martinez and Munday, 1998). Changing teachers' practice in any radical way is a very challenging task. New teachers quickly develop what Olson, James and Lang (1999, p. 72) term 'craft and survival norms', a range of skills and routines which allow them first to survive and hopefully to achieve some success in the existing system. Survival is important, given that pupils may not always be easy to control, and that time to cover the crowded curriculum and other administrative demands is seen as inadequate. Drawing on a study of English, French and German teachers, Pepin (2000) reports that all felt they had insufficient time, and that innovations required of them were perceived as robbing them of time in the classroom with their pupils, the most important element of their job. Innovations to improve teaching and learning might therefore be seen as achieving exactly the opposite. Similarly, as reported in one study in Hong Kong, teachers would not welcome change or additions to the curriculum because they felt they already had insufficient time to accomplish what was required of them (Lee, 2000). They would only co-operate on the basis of some quid pro quo, that is the principal deleting another activity, for example assembly, in order to create time for the new activity. Even with such an arrangement, any development activity equates to more work in the teacher's perception. For those already overstretched, whatever the merit of suggested change, the proposed development may be dismissed as 'impractical' by teachers (Carless, 1997).

If, as Carless found, only change which is compatible with existing classroom practice is seen as being practical, then radical change is pre-empted. Teachers often have, in any case, a predilection towards current philosophy and practice, as they themselves have achieved success by means of the existing system. Where they are secure and confident in their knowledge of their subject or vocational area, moving out of this secure zone into new methods and relationships different to those that have led to their own success, and on which their practice is based, is asking a great deal. Their reaction may involve more than an innate conservatism, which implies a rather static refusal to change. Rather, a dynamic conservatism may lead teachers to fight hard to preserve the status quo. Where teachers' grip on their subject or teaching methods is insecure, due to inadequate initial training, they may view emotional support for children as a sufficient substitute for the development of pedagogy. In a study of rural teachers in South Africa and The Gambia, 'the rhetoric of "child-centred learning" was strong, but teachers generally failed to point to activities that might lead to improved pupil learning' (Jessop and Penny, 1998, p. 397). Instead, teachers proposed 'loving children' as their most important quality.

The underlying causes of change failure are likely to be complex. Teachers and lecturers will need much support to work together to develop appropriate confidence, skills, structures, materials and teaching methods to develop students' learning. Managers may also need to facilitate different structures to underpin new ways of working. For example, Roelofs and Terwel (1999) found a number of barriers to 'authentic pedagogy' which were structural. Teaching needed to be in long enough time blocks to allow multi-disciplinary and multi-tasked activity. Teachers needed the practical conditions to allow them to co-operate together, to break out of single subject boundaries. Olson, James and Lang (1999) confirm this finding, noting also the anxiety created by moving away from secure subject parameters. Appropriate resources help, including information and communications technology (ICT) and library facilities, or textbooks which allow room for individualisation of task and tempo. Assessment processes may need review, moving, as Roelofs and Terwel (1999) suggest, from norm-referenced examinations to criterion-referenced portfolios. Content of teaching materials may need development, to incorporate more problem-solving and use of elements perceived by the student as connected with their life outside the school or college. The latter is particularly challenging, as students' experience and perception of 'real life' may differ markedly from that of teaching staff. Above all, as Spratt (1999) suggests, teachers may need to build more time into lessons for evaluating activities, including careful listening to learners.

RESOURCE IMPLICATIONS

In developing teaching and learning the availability of resources is key (Aedo-Richmond and Richmond, 1999; Wu, Li and Anderson, 1999). Class size is a critical factor in allowing individualisation of learning. Where classes are typically 40 to 50 children or more, pedagogy is inevitably constrained. The use of double-shift schooling is one method to limit class size where resources are limited (Bray, 2000). However, even with large classes and virtually no teaching resources, imagination can open up new ways of teaching. Field notes from a visit to South Africa record that in one rural primary school, local mud, stones and sand had been used to allow children to model animals and to create a display area in the classroom of local wildlife. With nothing available but earth and stones, the teacher had introduced experiential learning, allowing children to model the shapes and relative sizes of animals and to address issues of ecology. In contrast, in a second school, teachers displayed to visitors the excellent transparencies provided by the regional administration to support the transition to the Outcomes Based Curriculum. The school unfortunately had no projector so the transparencies were useless. High technology solutions are not always the best support for learning. However, a small injection of technology has the potential to make an enormous difference. Jessop and Penny (1998, p. 396) note the delight and wonder of a South African teacher whose school had acquired a photocopier and was able to produce 'wonders' for the first time.

Teachers, however, are the main resource, and their cost takes up the vast majority of available funds. Although they may argue that they are underpaid, the cost still stretches economies in both developed and developing economies. Two issues emerge in the attempt to respond to this problem: the use made of existing teachers and the potential for supplementing or substituting their work through use of para-professionals.

In Chapter 5 the range of teachers' hours will be discussed in more detail. Where teachers are working 60 hours per week, as in Chile (Avalos,

1998), they are already working in excess of what could be reasonably expected. In other parts of the world, such as China, where the usual weekly teaching load for primary schools and vocational colleges is up to 15 hours and eight hours respectively, there may be more room for manoeuvre (Cortazzi, 1998; Lumby and Li, 1998). The action which is most often seen as a solution, employing considerably more teachers, is equally often seen as financially impractical, or where there may be funds, trained teachers are in short supply. One strategy is to employ those who are not trained teachers as an additional support for learners, or as in the case of some non-governmental organisation schools in Bangladesh, to substitute with local women who are qualified to secondary school level (James, 1998). Educators who rightly take pride in their knowledge, training and experience fear that such initiatives may result in a degradation of teaching. However, the current Platonic model, with an expert teacher relating to one class may not be sustainable, or even preferable, as participation in education expands and the new paradigm demands individualised support. The model to support teaching and learning for the future may be more appropriately a flexible range of staff within whom trained teachers are valued and central, but where para-professionals of different kinds, instructors, technicians, information access specialists and literacy helpers all contribute to the process of supporting learning.

CHANGING ROLES, CHANGING POWER

Fundamental changes in any system are likely to involve challenges to existing power structures. Many of the players in the arena of education may perceive proposed change as a threat to their power. However, power does not function in only one way. While it is true that an individual or group can seize power and use it to enforce their wishes, it is also true that, paradoxically, relinquishing power may result in strengthening it. For example, a government that increases the democratic rights of the people may thereby increase its own power. Empowerment of others does not necessarily result in the diminution of those who empower. Currently, fear of losing power and/or control is constraining change. National and regional policy-makers and administrators are often reluctant to lessen control, both for altruistic reasons, as they wish to retain the power to lead change for the benefit of learners or the country, and/or for personal reasons, as control is the means of making political capital. Parents and children may have some power through their ability to make choices of attending one institution or another, but once there, they may be locked out of any meaningful involvement in planning and developing teaching and learning. The role of parents as seen by teachers in European schools, reported by Pepin (2000), is to appreciate the work of teachers and to come into contact with them infrequently and in ways controlled by teachers. Morris and Adamson

(1998) writing of Hong Kong confirm this picture of parents having little influence on the curriculum.

Learners themselves, though most centrally involved in learning, are not usually involved in contributing to its development. Generally, they are expected to accept what educators believe to be an appropriate learning experience, and to be respectful of their expertise and authority (Cortazzi, 1998; Pell, 1998; Pepin, 2000). Teachers assume that they know what the preferences of learners are, though studies show that this is not necessarily the case (Chan and Watkins, 1994; Spratt, 1999). Teachers appear to overestimate how positively students feel about them (Roelofs and Terwel, 1999). In many parts of the world the absolute authority of teachers over learners is seen as entirely appropriate, but individual educators and governments are beginning to challenge the exclusion of learners from decisions as being in the best interests of learning: 'In my experience there are many and often limiting assumptions made about what the young child can and cannot do and about what the young child can and cannot understand. I find it challenging to explode what I refer to as the "they are only little children" myth' (White, 1997, p. 172). This principal believes that even infant children could make a contribution to planning and developing teaching and learning. Reforms to increase the involvement of both learners and parents in governance, for example in South Africa and New Zealand, have begun to challenge the limitation of children and parents' involvement.

The principal is often cited as key in achieving improvements in teaching and learning, though there is dissenting evidence which suggest that others such as deputies or heads of department may be alternative leaders of the process (Dimmock and Wildy, 1995). The power relations between staff and principal vary. Hofstede (1980) devised five spectra to measure culture, the first of which is power–distance (PD). The distribution of power and acceptance of that pattern varies significantly between societies. In many western societies inequalities of power and the acceptance of considerable distance between the least and most powerful members of society and organisations are much less pronounced than, for example, in many Asian societies. Hence China may be seen as having a high power–distance index (PDI) while the UK and the USA have a much lower PDI.

In Asian cultures the principal may often be viewed as having absolute authority, though of course even in such a case instructions can be subverted (Quong, Walker and Stott, 1998). In European cultures, the principal is viewed often as an honorary teacher, there to support but not 'to interfere with teaching' (Pepin, 2000, p. 25). The power–distance relationship will inevitably vary from culture to culture. Perhaps as a general point, large power difference differentials at any level, between learners and teachers, teacher and principal, school staff and parents and regional/national administration are unlikely to provide the collaborative effort required to secure development and sustained improvement. All these individuals and groups are able to constrain change. Some degree of support from all, or from a sufficiently powerful coalition of some, may be a prerequisite for the radical change which has been mooted in this chapter.

THE CHANGING ROLE OF TEACHERS

The literature on managing change in education has tended to emphasise the need to empower teachers and to give them ownership of change, as it is they who do the work. It is they who teach and have day-to-day contact with learners. However, the concept of giving ownership to teachers is problematic for the reasons discussed in this chapter. In undertaking innovation, teachers may have little experience of school-based innovation. For example, while the culture and history of Chile and China are very different, one resulting factor in their education systems is similar: teachers in the post-Pinochet and the Communist context have had little say in what is to be taught and how, and therefore have no legacy of involvement with curriculum development on which to draw. In many parts of the world, teachers may see radical change as impractical. They may veto change as involving them in more work or eroding their power. They may have an optimistic view of how learners view them. They may have inadequate training. The changes that are mooted are risky, asking them to collaborate with other teachers, to move outside their own discipline, to not provide a single authoritative answer to any problem but to encourage seeing alternatives. For all these reasons giving teachers ownership of change cannot be enough. The role of parents and learners to act as a conservative brake or to support change has perhaps been underplayed. It is not just a question of empowering teachers but empowering a range of groups. This does not mean less power for some. Rather, it is a change of role which increases power. Teachers as role models of lifelong learning, who can cope with uncertainty, who are willing to take risks, who can lead a flexible team of educators with different contributions to make is an enhanced role, and one which is far more credible for the twenty-first century.

MOVING ON

Despite calls for rapid change, it is more likely that the development of teaching and learning will happen piecemeal and over a lengthy timespan. Even during revolution, continuities remain. The current assessment systems and the ubiquitous public and government requirement for examination success constrain education. There are many profound difficulties to overcome. Teachers are busy surviving and may have little energy to engage with fundamental change. Principals may lack the training to tackle development. Parents and students may be deeply conservative, indifferent or hostile. Governments persist in imposing the latest scheme. Some teachers long for a previous era 'when students were still under the Confucian values in regard for study and to respect for elders' (Cheung, 2000, p. 227) or when teachers decided what was to be taught and how. If they ever existed, such times will not return.

As Harley and Wedekind (1999) suggest, major curriculum change will happen in response to major societal change. Global technological and local societal changes will continue to impel change in teaching and learning. There is much to build on. More learners are in schools and colleges and many of them value the efforts of the staff. Information and communication technology facilities are creeping or blasting their way in. In many countries, educational managers and teachers are experimenting with new structures, new resource arrangements and new teaching methods to support learning. Although the forces of inertia and resistance may be strong, change is seeping in as a result of the determined efforts to improve the experience of learners and to make learning relevant to their lives in this century. Critical questions emerge, though they may remain the questions that have always been central. What are the aims of education? Looking beyond the rhetoric of public pronouncements, what are governments, teachers, and families truly wanting from education? Is education a means of replicating or changing existing social structures and values? If change does not happen, it may be because there is no real desire for change, that governments, teachers, families and teachers want a continuation of their own experience of education. If change is a genuine aspiration, then there is much that we know about the process of learning that can support reform at every level. We shall examine some of these questions in Chapters 3 and 4, which consider two specific foci in the management and leadership of learning and learners – managing learner outcomes and managing 'quality'.

3

MANAGING LEARNER OUTCOMES

THE RISE AND RISE OF OUTCOMES-BASED EDUCATION

In Chapter 2 we examined the broad picture of the changing nature of learning and the views and attitudes that underpin this turbulent arena for school and college managers. Amongst the most significant of the changes that can be observed has been the emergence of a focus on learner outcomes, for it has required a fundamental reassessment of the epistemologies underpinning education and training, a restructuring of the management of learning, and a root and branch change in the day-to-day lives of teachers, pupils and school managers.

Outcomes-based education has its roots in a range of perspectives on the purpose and organisation of schooling. Specifically it is based on:

- a view that school should be focused on the learning needs of pupils, not the knowledge transmission wishes of teachers
- a view that assessment of pupil achievement should be based on 'objective' measurement of what pupils know, understand and can do against predetermined assessment criteria
- a view that we can identify in advance, determine and plan for the specific knowledge, understanding and skills which pupils should achieve from education or training.

This trend to outcomes-based education may be seen in part as a response to liberal ideologies that focus on the individual and their personal development, but its spread is more properly explained in a conservative perspective on education. Such a view not only sees the purpose of education as providing the skills and knowledge necessary for direct utility in the labour market, but also seeks ways of demonstrating the effectiveness of investment in education through measurable outcomes. Its impact within the management of educational institutions occurs at two levels, therefore. At the level of the classroom and the individual teacher it demands a changing approach to the management of learning, for 'the focus of attention has moved from the intentions of the lecturer, that is, teaching, to the experience of the student, that is, learning' (Lumby, 2001, p. 122). This is a cultural and operational challenge for teachers, making considerable demands on their skills. Thomas (1995, p. 1) identifies these demands as:

- an ability to see the learning process in context
- within that context, an ability to identify the learner's needs
- an ability and willingness to respond to the learner's capabilities, expectations and uncertainties
- skill in taking into account a number of learning variables, such as available technology, sources of expertise . . . in the design of a learning solution which meets the purpose.

At institutional level it places on schools and colleges an obligation not only to facilitate those classroom-level changes but also to be accountable for outcomes and 'performance' at the whole-school level. In all cultural settings schools have always been accountable to some degree for the progress of their learners. In the last two decades, though, from out of the advanced western economies has emerged a powerful and persuasive movement in which the active management of learner outcomes has moved to the centre of the educational stage. Its motivation is the raising of standards of achievement of pupils/students, prioritising (Joyce, 1991):

- the identification of specific, measurable student learning outcomes, which become the target for management action both by teachers and school leaders.
- the monitoring of those learning outcomes through a range of formal and, normally, quantitative methods, using the evidence both to inform the identification of new targets and plans and, as a basis of accountability, to measure the effectiveness of the school.

This focus on learner outcomes has established a high profile in educational policy in many developed countries. In schools, a wide range of initiatives and development projects promoting school improvement strategies based on the evidence of school effectiveness research have emerged in the last two decades. In post-compulsory education and training below university level the historical emphasis on 'training' and vocational skills has seen the emergence of 'competence-based' approaches to learning and assessment in many countries. Hargreaves et al. (1998) show evidence of its adoption across the countries of the OECD, with a particular political primacy in the UK, the Netherlands, Scandinavia, the USA and Canada, and Australia and New Zealand. Its diffusion into the countries of eastern Asia has been a characteristic of the latter part of the last decade, with Japan, Hong Kong, Malaysia, Singapore and Taiwan aspiring to adopt the pathways to raising learner achievements that outcomes-based approaches signpost (Watkins, 2000). In the less developed world its growth is less marked, although some governments, notably in South Africa (South Africa Department of Education, 1995) have moved in a substantial way towards a competence-based curriculum in both schools and training.

For education managers the development of outcomes-based education raises many technical, organisational and policy questions. Placing learning at the centre of the education and training process does not mean that students are given complete choice and total control over their learning, since this is implausible, but it does demand 'a balance of input into designing a learning programme from both learner and [teacher]' (Lumby, 2001, p. 123). Such an emphasis provides a fundamental cultural challenge to educational leaders, and confronts class teachers with a new responsibility for their own leadership backed by systems of accountability. A number of important questions emerge from such processes of change:

- What do we mean by learner outcomes?
- What impact does the emphasis on learner outcomes have on the organisation and management of schools and colleges?
- What impact do such developments have on the culture of schools and on the lives of teachers and pupils?

We shall explore these questions with particular reference to schools, where the growth of the school effectiveness and school improvement movements has been built largely on a presumption of the importance of outcomes at the level of individual pupils and whole institutions. In so doing we shall address a number of ideas about outcomes-based education which have acquired significant veracity but will be shown to be myths:

Myth 1 Outcomes-based education is a clearly understood and shared concept.
Myth 2 Outcomes-based approaches will inevitably improve learning.
Myth 3 Outcomes-based learning is driven by educational rather than political principles.

THE NATURE OF LEARNER OUTCOMES

What are learner (or learning) outcomes and what is their significance in school environments? At a simple level learning outcomes represent all of the changes that occur to learners as a direct result of the experiences they have in school or college, whether cognitive, affective or in the development of physical skills. These outcomes may express themselves in

terms of acquired knowledge and understanding, or in changes in attitudes, skills and behaviours. At the level of the individual learner the outcomes may be explicit and observable, or implicit and largely private.
Where observable they may be measurable, as in tests of knowledge and
understanding, or they may not, as in changes of attitude. They may be
short term in their impact, for example in gaining the qualifications for
higher education entry, or long term in raising the economic capability or
social capability of an individual over their lifetime. Levačić (2000)
emphasises that within the academic field of the economics of education
there is a distinction between educational outputs, which are the short
term and direct effects of a school, and educational outcomes, which are
the long-term benefits that the individual and society as a whole gain from
the educational system. However, it is more common to use the terms
'learning outcomes' or 'learner outcomes' to cover the broad range of gains
that individuals and society may accrue.

The growth of competence-based curriculum and assessment has been
important within the learner outcomes movement. Competences are skills-
based statements of what a pupil/student can do, and the notion of competence-based education and training has emerged from the arena of
vocational training. The value of competence-based approaches lies in
their close linkage to the demands of particular vocational fields and the
relative ease of recording whether an individual has or has not reached
the required level of competence. Armitage et al. (1999) identify some of
the concerns over such approaches though in relation to:

- their lack of distinction between levels of performance, where there is
  only a 'can do/can't do' distinction
- their emphasis on behavioural and performance elements of learning
  rather than cognitive dimensions
- the fact that the assessment of competences is frequently judgemental
- the fact that competency-based approaches make learning assessment
  led.

Outcomes-based models of the curriculum, whether competence-based or
not, inevitably require the measurement of pupil achievement in relation
to desired outcomes, and two challenges arise when we seek to undertake
such measurement. First, many of the outcomes are not readily measured,
particularly those which are implicit, linked to affective or attitudinal
aspects of development, or linked to long-term (lifetime!) benefits. The
desire to measure, though, is strong and leads to the prioritisation of those
elements of pupil learning which *can* be measured, and a resulting dis-
tortion in the emphasis that schools place in the application of their
efforts. Inevitably, if schools and teachers are to be measured (and hence
judged) in relation to pupil outcomes, resources will be prioritised on
those areas of the school's work that will have most positive impact on
the measurements. Secondly, schools and pupils are in large measure the

product of the socio-economic environment in which they operate. Pupils do not start school with equal skills, knowledge and achievements, nor do they have equal support as they progress through school. Hence measuring outputs alone may provide only a limited picture of the progression of the individual through school, and measures of value-added (for example, Fitz-Gibbon, 1994) may provide a more meaningful picture of the benefit the pupil gains from his or her school experience.

The development of information technology has been an important catalyst to the emergence of the emphasis on learner outcomes at institutional level. The quantities of data that potentially might be collected about pupil performance and progress are enormous, both at the level of the individual pupil and at a school system level. The emphasis on quantitative data that information technology (IT) requires, though, both prioritises a reductionist, numerical system of outcome measurement and implies a highly rationalistic, algorithmic, cause–effect model of the learning system and the way pupils learn. The importance of IT also acts as an economic constraint on the diffusion of such strongly quantitative output systems. In most countries of the world the possibility of large-scale measurement, data collection and analysis systems at institutional level is highly constrained, therefore, and the emphasis on outcomes-based learning may only progress at the classroom level through, for example, the development of portfolios.

LEARNER OUTCOMES AND INSTITUTIONAL DEVELOPMENT – THE SCHOOL EFFECTIVENESS AND SCHOOL IMPROVEMENT MOVEMENTS

We shall consider the prioritisation of learner outcomes in education through a review of the school effectiveness and school improvement (E + I) movements of recent decades. These international movements have drawn strongly on an epistemology of outcomes-based education, and their successes and failures illustrate well the challenges to managing in educational environments where learner outcomes are at the heart of ideology and practice.

The period since 1980 has seen the development of research, scholarship, debate and political rhetoric on the connection between the activities of schools and the outcomes achieved by their pupils. The roots of these movements are found in the large-scale studies undertaken in the UK by Rutter et al. (1979) (*Fifteen Thousand Hours*) and Mortimore et al. (1988) (*School Matters*). These challenged the view that either heredity or the socio-economic environment had a deterministic impact on pupil achievement by suggesting that 'schools can do much to foster good behaviour and attainments, and that even in a disadvantaged area, schools can be a force for good' (Rutter et al., 1979, p. 205).

The broad thesis, therefore, has been that it is schools, the way they are managed and operated, which make the difference to learner outcomes. The emphasis of researchers such as Edmonds (1979) in the USA, Sammons, Hillman and Mortimore (1995) in the UK, and Creemers (1992) in the Netherlands has been to identify the significant factors within the influence of schools that can be managed and manipulated to impact on the effectiveness of schools. More recently Barber (1996), Reynolds (1992) and Hargreaves and Hopkins (1991), working at the heart of the school improvement movement, have considered the application of key ideas on school effectiveness in a problem-solving approach, which suggests that school effectiveness research can identify strategies for action in schools that will lead to the raising of achievement and outcomes. School effectiveness research began with the identification through large-scale statistical analysis of the impact on outputs of a wide range of school processes.

From the early days of the lists of the characteristics of effective schools, the E + I movement has progressed, and headteachers in schools in many OECD countries have been 'directed' to follow. Hopkins and Reynolds (2001) have identified three phases in the implementation of E + I developments in schools and through government policy, all with an international profile. The first phase was founded in the OECD International School Improvement Project (ISIP), with its emphasis on the management of change at an institutional scale and on the identification of outcomes through processes of school self-evaluation. From the *School Matters* research of the 1980s Mortimore et al. (1988) had identified those factors that make for effective junior schools, and these became the mantra for those involved in school improvement, used to direct the strategies to be adopted by school management. The list is well known – effective schools are believed to have:

- shared, purposeful and participative leadership of the school by the head or principal
- shared vision and goals between managers and teachers
- an attractive and orderly environment in which pupils work
- concentration on learning and teaching and a focus on achievement within the school
- purposeful teaching that is well organised, appropriately paced and clearly structured
- high expectations and self-esteem among teachers and pupils
- a positive climate in the school, with an emphasis on rewards and praise rather tha sanction and punishment
- careful monitoring of pupil progress
- an emphasis on pupil rights and responsibilities that enable them to engage in the life of the school
- an emphasis on the school as a learning organisation for staff and pupils
- home–school partnerships that encourage and promote parental

support and engagement with the school.

Changes were not strongly concerned with enhancing student learning outcomes though and the impact on classroom practice was limited, despite a high profile in development planning and policy documentation in schools.

Phase 2 dates from the early 1990s, and saw the adoption of statistical methods that enabled the disaggregation of whole-school performance data down to the level of individual departments and pupils through the introduction of, *inter alia*, value-added methodologies. The prioritisation of learning outcomes within school development planning was facilitated by the statistical methods that emerged, and high-profile school improvement projects were adopted at a national scale by many OECD governments. However,

> (d)espite the dramatic increase in education reform efforts in most OECD countries, their impact upon levels of student achievement is widely seen as not having been as successful as anticipated. Although there may be pockets of success, such as the British National Literacy and Numeracy Strategies, and although there may be individual programmes which appear to be effective, such as 'Success for All' (in the USA), most persons in the school improvement community regard the improving of educational outcomes as a mountain still left to climb.
>
> (Hopkins and Reynolds, 2001, pp. 460–1)

The 'Third Age' represents the most recent period of school improvement that has emerged from those perceived underachievements, and is typified by the 'Improving the Quality of Education for All' (IQEA) Project in the UK, and the 'National School Improvement Project' in the Netherlands. Hopkins and Reynolds (2001, pp. 460–1) underline the new management and leadership focus within Third Age schemes:

1) An enhanced focus on pupil outcomes.
2) An increasing focus on the learning level (i.e. classrooms and learners rather than the whole school) and the actions of teachers.
3) A culture and staff development perspective that enables best practice and the findings of research to be implemented.
4) An emphasis on 'capacity building'.
5) An increasing recognition that qualitative data can provide valuable perspectives alongside highly quantitative methods.
6) An increasing recognition of the need to ensure reliability in the adoption of new approaches and methods.
7) A recognition that cultural change is essential in schools if school improvement is to be embedded.
8) An emphasis on training, coaching and development programmes for teachers.

Within this developing perspective, four particular priorities for leadership and management are identified by Hopkins and Reynolds (2001) as holding the key to future school improvement developments. The first three relate to leadership and management *within* schools.

First, each school must recognise that school improvement is highly context specific and that understanding the characteristics of the school, its pupils, its teachers and its processes is essential, and the strategies to be adopted will differ between and within schools. This underscores the view of Reynolds that 'the traditional belief that schools are effective or ineffective for all sub-groups of pupils within them is [not] . . . tenable in view of the evidence that there can be different school effects for children of different ethnic groups, ability ranges and socio-economic status within the same school' (Reynolds, 1992, p. 22). At the level of international analysis this is a critical notion, for the transferability of lists of school improvement factors between national settings is problematic. Two examples will illustrate this idea. In the transfer of E + I to Singapore, school improvement approaches were adopted early from practices in the UK. The government's report *Towards Effective Schools* (Singapore Department of Education, 1987) identified from UK evidence those characteristics of effective schools that would be most significant in the context of Singapore and used this to promote a 'pivotal focus on schools and a continuous effort . . . to encourage schools to excel and to forge their own identities' (Chang, 2000, p. 14). Chang's research suggests, however, that on the basis of ten years' experience of implementation there is now a clear recognition that while there is some overlap between factors in successful schools in the UK and Singapore, the lists are different, and differ between schools.

A second example is drawn from Hong Kong, where Morris and Lo (2000) provide a critique of the introduction of the 'Target Oriented Curriculum' (TOC) in primary schools in the mid-1990s. They perceive TOC as an explicit attempt by the Hong Kong Education Department and Education and Manpower Branch to adopt outcomes-based education in the light of global developments in curriculum reform. The difficulties of implementing the programme and achieving its ambitious goals are explained by Morris and Lo as the result of insufficient consideration of the cultural context of Hong Kong primary schools, which, in effect resulted in a cultural clash between western and Chinese educational values and approaches. This perspective is confirmed by Watkins (2000), who identifies important differences in learning and teaching styles between Chinese and western classrooms. Drawing on the work of Jin and Cortazzi (1998) he identifies the preference in Chinese classrooms for rote learning as a route to deep understanding, and a traditional teacher–pupil relationship that he equates to that of 'father and son'. Furthermore approaches to group work and questioning have different priorities and operational systems. Watkins concludes that 'Educators in Hong Kong (and Singapore and Japan) are currently trying to propose reforms that will encourage more independent, creative learning outcomes. Perhaps, before rushing to adopt western methods, they should look more seriously at the validity of these views . . . in their own cultural contexts' (Watkins, 2000, p. 171).

The second priority identified by Hopkins and Reynolds (2001) is to recognise that 'teacher and classroom variables account for more of the variance in pupil achievement than do school variables' (Creemers, 1992, p. 20). In other words, it is in the management of learning in the classroom by individual teachers that any impact on pupil performance is likely to be achieved. Stigler and Heibert (1999), for example, describe the positive impacts in Japanese schools of a focus on classroom-level developments, and report how schools have promoted active approaches to the review and studying of lessons by groups of teachers with a focus on problem-solving and enhancing pupil performance.

Thirdly, an emphasis on establishing systems to support capacity building is prioritised to embed school improvement practice and culture. Fullan (2000), for example, stresses the importance of in-school and inter-school teacher networks with a commitment to sharing practice and collaborative planning. Harris and Young (2000) identify the Manitoba School Improvement Project (MSIP) in Canada as amongst the most successful school improvement approaches in terms of its impact on enhancing learning outcomes. Since 1991 MSIP has funded projects in over 30 secondary schools, and its requirements emphasise the priority for networking in support of capacity building. Projects are required to focus on pupil learning, but to do this through teacher initiatives that are collaborative and participative. In particular, key success factors have been identified through evaluation as the devolution of leadership to middle management and class teachers, and the strong engagement of both internal and external agencies in the networks that are established.

The fourth priority emphasises the need for leaders to have more evidence for their attempts to improve practice. This suggests that continuing work, both by experienced academic researchers in the field and by classroom-based practitioners, must seek to refine the understanding of the relationships between the complex raft of factors in school improvement by seeking to develop better methods for collecting, utilising and applying data.

The E + I movement, with its emphasis on learner outcomes, has had considerable political and practical appeal, and has stimulated developed and newly industrialised nations to reflect on their existing curriculum to seek ways of raising standards. As Chitty (1997, p. 55) has indicated:

> [it] has had many wise and important things to say about the practical ways in which schools . . . could work to improve the quality of education for all their pupils. It provided an antidote to the pes-

simism and fatalism of the 1970s – and particularly to the view that schools situated in working class neighbourhoods were bound to be unsuccessful – just as much as it provided a jolt to schools that were failing to make efforts or make changes . . . It also provided a much needed warning to those who might be expecting far too little from those they taught – simply assuming they were likely to produce little.

CHALLENGING THE E + I AGENDA

The prominence of the work of the E + I movements has been considerable, and has changed the face of school leadership and management in many countries. Yet the basis of school effectiveness and improvement has been subject to considerable criticism, not least because the impact of applying school improvement measures is not always readily identifiable. The belief that E + I is the holy grail that provides the single routeway to success is open to serious challenge, for a number of reasons.

The first group of concerns relates to a view that schools and colleges are limited in the impact they can make because of external sociocultural factors. Principal amongst these concerns is that E + I simplifies the complex nature of school processes, that it prioritises only measurable outcomes, and that it largely ignores the wide range of contextual and school mix factors which influence pupil achievements and progress. In so doing it has often ignored those factors within the school 'equation' that are outside the school's control – for example, ethnicity and social class. However, once the most effective ways of manipulating the factors within the control of schools have been identified, the fact that their influence on the total output may be rather small is largely forgotten. Reynolds (1992), for example, suggests that controllable variables may account for only 8–15 per cent of performance differences between schools, with the rest accounted for by external environmental, social, economic and cultural factors that schools can do little to influence. Scheerens and Bosker (1997, p. 308) emphasise that 'our findings call for a modest view on the degree to which schooling in general is malleable'.

A second concern over the impact of E + I strategies lies with the view that the internal social and political processes of schools mean that the use of school improvement strategies may reinforce differences between schools and between particular groups of pupils in schools, enhancing polarisation and social differentials in achievement. Indeed, the research evidence suggests that even where improvement can be identified it is naive to see the enhancement as solely, or even principally, the outcome of the work of schools and their leaders. Evidence from New Zealand (Lauder and Hughes, 1999; Thrupp, 1999) and from the UK (Gorard and Fitz, 2000) suggests that 'school mix effects', which are the product of the socio-economic characteristics of the pupils, are more significant in shaping the school's performance than the application of school improvement strategies. Polarisation of schools according to socio-economic status results from three components of these school mix effects:

1) 'Reference group effects', which are the reinforcing of social and cultural values within the social group that makes up the majority of the school's pupils. This in turn impacts in a reinforcing way on two further effects:

2) 'Organisational and management effects'. This reflects the fact that most schools are acculturised to middle-class ethos and values, so that managing a school where pupils reflect this ethos is easier than where they do not. Hence middle-class schools can direct more of their management effort in to enhancing learning outcomes rather than pastoral or behaviour management.

3) 'Instructional effects'. This relates to the engagement of children with the curriculum, which in most schools is defined principally by middle-class values. Most E + I research assumes that the curriculum is neutral in promoting or impeding pupil performance. However, we must recognise that the curriculum is socially constructed and dynamic and reflects specific cultural, social and political influences, and may therefore advantage or disadvantage particular pupil groups within the system.

Thirdly, beyond the concern over the validity of the argument in relation to school improvement, there is concern about the impact upon teachers and schools of the race to school improvement. Two significant negative impacts on teachers can be identified – a reduction in teacher morale, often resulting in an increase in teacher stress, and the deprofessionalisation of teachers as a consequence of the top-down implementation of change in schools predicated on a mechanistic, learning and teaching technology view of schools. E + I, with its emphasis on continuous improvement and accountability in terms of performance indicators, promotes the 'politics of blame' within and between schools. After all, if we know what makes schools better, then failure to achieve sufficient improvement must be the teachers' fault. The promotion of value added measures, while seeking to level the playing field of comparative data, may compound this issue, since it removes from the equation those environmental factors that teachers cannot influence. Similarly, while at first sight recognising the importance of the work that teachers do in the classroom, the priority of improvement drives schools to limit experimentation and innovation outside the limits defined by imported notions of 'what works'. In a context which 'replaces political questions with technical ones' (Lingard, Ladwig and Luke, 1998, p. 24), the empowerment of teachers may, ironically, be the first casualty of the war on pupil performance.

CHALLENGING THE MYTHS

The rhetoric of the ability of schools to manage their operations in such a way as to enhance learner outcomes is clearly very strongly rooted, therefore. As we have identified earlier they have become imbued with a mythology that has been a key driver in their impetus. Outcomes-based approaches to education and training, though, do not provide either a straight or uncontested road to universal pupil improvement, for they are based on assumptions about the aims and purpose of education and about the ability of teachers (and managers) to meet the professional challenges that such approaches bring. Teachers and managers, of course, would emphasise that their work *can* change children's performance and achievement, but the approaches to management that work are much more context defined and less identifiable. There is a risk that 'effective school research . . . [is] a two-edged sword. It has raised the possibility that (teachers and schools) can make a difference to educational outcomes . . . [but] saddled them with responsibilities over which they would claim to have little control' (Lauder, Jamieson and Wikeley, 1997, p. 1). Indeed, Goldstein (2001, p. 440) is critical of the use of approaches emphasising measurable learner outcomes: 'there is a great deal of inappropriate use of performance data for judging schools and teachers. Despite much research data back to the 1980s, government has largely ignored its findings about the limitations of such data in terms of its practice, even while accepting the limitations in theory'.

With such concerns for the nature of the outcomes-based movements we might reasonably ask why they have become so strongly influential. The answer lies in their political appeal, for they provide a number of important opportunities for government. First, they provide a simple and straightforward formulaic approach to raising achievement in schools. Secondly, they provide an agenda for action for governments who in the timescales available between elections can demonstrate an active programme of reform and change in schools and colleges. Thirdly, they provide the opportunity for government to distance itself from direct responsibility. If schools make the difference, then it is schools, headteachers and teachers who are responsible for success where it occurs (using, of course, government promoted approaches!), but are also to blame when it does not work.

It is easy to see the potential for teachers to be the victims of the drive towards an emphasis on learner outcomes. Gilham (1995), for example, has identified some of the consequences of such developments for teachers as an increase in workload, a period of acute anxiety, feelings of confusion and disorientation, and the growth of disbelief and cynicism about innovation. However, what a focus on learner outcomes *can* provide is a stepping stone to enhanced professionalisation, by giving to teachers the opportunity to innovate and take the lead in curriculum reform – but this can only occur where the political system creates the right conditions. First, the growth of centralised curriculum control in some countries acts as a brake on the very innovation and responsiveness that school improvement promotes. Reduction in central intervention in the detail of the curriculum would seem to be an important step in facilitating educational improvement. Secondly, the significance of sociocultural factors in performance must be repeatedly underscored. It is entirely appropriate that schools and colleges should use the best of E + I evidence to influence the 10–15 per cent of performance that is within their direct influence, and the successful manipulation of this margin can have a substantial impact on learner, institutional, government and community confidence. However, government must recognise that the other 85 per cent of influence on learner outcomes is the product of fundamental characteristics of society and culture that educational leaders and teachers cannot take direct responsibility for. This responsibility lies, rather, with government to 'extend the boundaries of social reform' (Thrupp, 1999).

Outcomes-based education can provide valuable strategies for enhancing learner achievement and rewarding persistence and ability – but at the same time it can make pupils and teachers fall prey to the tyranny of accountability through outcomes and become subject to the politics of blame. It is perhaps ironic that an ideology that seeks to liberate and empower the learner and the teacher has been hijacked to meet the political needs of governments in a globalised and competitive world.

4

A PASSION FOR QUALITY

THE EMERGENCE OF 'QUALITY' IN EDUCATION

The previous chapter explored the 'war on pupil performance', linking it particularly to an emphasis on outcomes and to the research on effectiveness and improvement. The 'war' has also led to a largely independent further focus, the theory and practice of raising quality. The insistence on assuring quality in education is a relatively recent phenomenon. The latter half of the twentieth century reflected initially an anxiety not about the quality of education, but the numbers receiving it. Quantity, not quality was the overriding concern. This is, of course, still an issue in many countries, for example, in ensuring access to primary schooling for all children, or in more developed economies ensuring that young people stay in education for a longer number of years. However since the 1980s, as access to education has expanded, the focus on participation in education has been matched by a zeal for improving quality (Duraisamy et al., 1998). Chapman and Adams (1998) point out that virtually every country in Asia has placed improving the quality of education as a top national priority. Government agencies to assess quality have sprouted all over the world (Vroeijenstijn, 1999) often underpinned by commissions to set the quality improvement agenda (Yin, 1999). The by now unshakeable governmental conviction of a connection between national economic success and the quality of education has ratcheted up demands for the assessment of quality to enable the state not only to assess and demonstrate national improvement, but also to exhibit international equality or, preferably, superiority in the quality stakes (Crocombe and Tuainekore Crocombe, 1994).

In searching for the means to achieve improvement, governments and educators have looked to the quality techniques developed in business and industry to provide suitable tools. The effort to become more 'business-like' is certainly a metatrend discernible in government policies, and quality is a prime example of the transfer to the public sector of methods that were designed essentially to increase the profit of companies. The mantra of quality and its attendant techniques, quality assurance, total quality management, the business excellence model, and particularly the numeric measurement of processes and outcomes have all infiltrated the management and leadership of schools and colleges.

Thus, interest in quality is fuelled by increasingly frequent measurement of education and publication of such measurement. Chapman and Adams list eight countries, including China, Nepal, Pakistan and the Philippines where surveys have assessed educational quality and reported severe problems. International comparison is perceived as a necessary element not only to assess quality, but also to increase determination to improve it. International league tables, such as that compiled by the Third International Mathematics and Science Study (Plomp, 1998) involving a comparison of the achievement of students in 45 countries, fuel the gloom of many countries whose performance is not at the top of the league and fire the determination of all either to rise towards the top of the list or to stay there.

In the face of such a high profile given to quality issues it is easy to assume that all share this commitment. In fact it is not apparent that parents, students and teachers are equally vehement. Those who individually or whose families have benefited from the status quo may resist change which might threaten existing advantages. The connection between economic success and the quality of education may not be evident to parents who make a cool assessment of the relative advantage to the family finances of sending a child to school or to work (Verwimp, 1999). The pre-eminence of quality as an issue is predicated on a deficit model of education, which may not be shared by many of the stakeholders. While most governments and many parents, employers and learners may indeed be very concerned to increase the quality of education, this cannot be assumed to be universal. Equally, the commitment to improve quality may vary across different phases of the education system and be supported by differential resources. Consequently the determination to improve quality may be differentially implemented, with most effort going into the higher prestige or most valued parts of the system. The strongest driver is the underlying conviction that improved quality in education will strengthen the economy. This belief is contradicted by Morley and Rasool (2000) who assert that macro socio-economic factors override the contribution of education. They give the collapse of the Japanese economy as an example, the latter being due to global forces that could not be countered in any significant way by raising the achievement of pupils. Despite this weakness in the instrumental argument driving quality, the search for international means of assessing quality and for improving it continues apace. The questions that result are:

- How is 'quality' understood by individuals and groups with a stake in education?

- What means are being adopted at national level to assess and to improve quality?
- What means are being adopted at institutional level to assess and to improve quality?
- Are the activities to assure and to assess quality making a difference to teaching and learning?

The promotion of quality systems as key has gathered support to the degree that adherence has almost become an expected orthodoxy. In addressing the questions above, this chapter will explore how far the belief that quality systems improve quality is myth or reality.

DEFINING QUALITY

On one level it is easy to define quality. Verwimp (1999, p. 169) defines a good school as one which is able 'to enrol more children, to keep them in school, and let them perform well'. The basic elements of quality as attracting and retaining learners and helping them to achieve are common in many countries. However, this apparently simple formula begs a myriad of questions. For example, which individuals or groups decide what is adequate or better achievement? As long as the terms remain general, learners 'doing well' or 'achieving', agreement is possible. However a more detailed consideration of how the general terms can be defined or recognised leads to debate and a range of views on how quality can be understood and how it is to be achieved/improved. Over time, quality has come to be conceptualised in a number of ways, but all involve a process of comparison. Quality can be understood to be a match to different types of comparators:

- standards
- expectations
- a future improved state.

Standards

Chapman and Adams (1998) identify that standards can be set for:

- inputs, e.g. number of teachers, equipment, etc.
- processes, e.g. the way learners are taught or assessed
- outputs, e.g. qualifications achieved, value-added
- outcomes, e.g. the number entering employment or further education.

Chapman and Adams (1998) argue for the helpfulness of developing an international minimum set of standards which schools must match. There is some evidence that achievement of basic standards of inputs does influence teaching and learning outcomes. For example, Duraisamy et al. (1998), surveying schools in Tamil Nadu, discovered a correlation between pupil–teacher ratios and examination passes. Extrapolating, it would seem that ensuring a minimum standard of pupil–teacher ratio would maintain or increase the output of examination passes. Parents too may be reassured by standards of inputs. Verwimp (1999) suggests that the level of enrolment in Ethiopia, currently very low, would be increased by assurance of minimum input standards. Parents are more likely to send their children to school if there are, for example, adequate seats, textbooks and latrines.

However, while the literature may offer evidence of a link between assured standards of education and *attracting* learners, the evidence on a link between standards of inputs and the *achievement* of students is far less certain and consistent.

A second school argues that the pressure towards a universal set of standards is not desirable as standards are related to cultural and contextual variables. For example, Woodhead (1998) and Siraj-Blatchford and Wong (1999) both argue that what is considered an appropriate standard for early years education in one part of the world is not necessarily seen in the same light elsewhere. The small class sizes seen as crucial for quality in the UK and USA may not be seen as especially relevant in societies such as Japan where large groups are viewed as a norm. Equally, theories of childhood development and learning will underpin what is viewed as appropriate education and will vary considerably throughout the world. The growing frequency and detail of international comparisons encourages a trend towards universal standards which some countries do not have the resource to achieve and which may be culturally inappropriate. The pressure is towards cultural homogeneity. However, Woodhead (1998) argues that absolute relativism in relation to quality is as unhelpful as universal standards. He suggests that the danger of assuming that standards should be determined only in relation to local conditions is that this may encourage complacency. Lack of resources or the existence of particular traditions or practice may be taken as justification for allowing unsatisfactory conditions in schools, or retaining outdated teaching and learning methods. He suggests that governments and institutions may need to approach achieving quality in a way that is 'relative' but 'not arbitrary'. They need to negotiate standards in the light of competing views of what constitutes 'good' education, including local views, rather than adopting the latest 'international' set of quality techniques or indicators. Such a process is micropolitical and will reflect the relative power of players and how far a tradition of democracy or collegiality exists at national or institutional level. The use of quality standards, whether imposed nationally or negotiated locally, is often seen as a rational and objective process. It is in fact a micropolitical process of control or accommodation, with the choice of standards reflecting the views of those in ascendancy. For example, the use of competency standards for assuring the performance of principals reflects the choice of some governments (DfES, 2000). They have the power to impose such standards, providing them with convenient lists of criteria to be ticked, despite the many recognised weaknesses in judging holistic teaching performance by fragmented competencies. Principals have insufficient power to resist and insist on an alternative system.

Expectations

A second common approach to defining or recognising quality is to compare the expectations with the experience of students and/or other stakeholders: quality defined as matching or exceeding expectations. Li and Kaye (1999) argue that expectations are complex and dynamic, and may not only differ amongst students but may change over time and in relation to different aspects of the educational process and outcomes. Consequently the identification of quality as matching expectations is bounded by limitations. The upsurge in internal mechanisms to measure the perceptions of students in post-compulsory education, and the delineation of quality as, for example, achieving 90 per cent satisfaction scores from students, can be at best only a rather blunt instrument. Students' experience is too complex to be captured in this way. At worst, such an approach may mislead managers into an ill-founded sense of certainty of having achieved quality. It also sidesteps the fact that different stakeholders may have contradictory expectations and so satisfying all may be impossible.

Continuous improvement

The third way of defining quality is to match the current state with an imagined future improved state. In other words, individuals or groups do not necessarily take as their comparator an existing standard or expectation but, rather, work creatively to suggest ways in which a current aspec of education could be improved. This definition is pragmatically based in working from what exists to what could be achieved. It is universally applicable in theory in that ideas for improvement will take into account resources and political realities. However, the emphasis on continuous improvement is predicated on a degree of autonomy and power that may not exist in all institutions or cultures. If governments impose a structure or curriculum on schools/colleges, or if the internal management structure is hierarchical and controlling, then the freedom of staff, parents and students to suggest ways forward is clearly constrained.

SYNTHESISING THE THREADS

The standards movement is situated within a quality assurance approach. Schools and colleges attempt to define what is acceptable by means of a set of standards, for example in a quality assurance manual, and then ensure all comply with the stipulated standards. Benchmarks or targets are set and their achievement measured and publicised. Measurement and response to stakeholder satisfaction may be part of this scenario. Quantitative measurement of the achievement of targets or compliance with procedures provides managers with information on how far what has been planned has been achieved.

By contrast, the attempt to achieve continuous improvement is located within the total quality movement, with more emphasis on internally generated action. Student and stakeholder expectations are central, and matching or exceeding expectations is the measure of quality. Self-assessment processes which require staff to use customer feedback to identify and rectify weaknesses and build on strengths are founded on such an approach.

In practice different approaches may be used concurrently within an institution. The adoption of a particular approach or approaches is clearly a micropolitical process with contestation of views and power bases (Roberts, 2001). Governments or their agencies, and/or the principal and senior management team may impose quality systems. Morley and Rassool (2000) argue that internationally the quality movement, while apparently overtly about improving education, is actually a diversionary tactic to disguise the redistribution of power;

> The construction of the individual and the organisation as being in deficit and in need of continuous improvement is a powerful regulatory device. It forces a docility and compliance and shifts attention away from values and ideologies towards technologies and operational factors. Hence, vast amounts of energy are invested in enhancing effectiveness, quality and productivity rather than questioning whose interests are being served.
>
> (Morley and Rasool, 2000, p. 177)

In this view, the pursuit of quality can be viewed in micropolitical terms as a vehicle to regulate interests and power, rather than as designed primarily to improve the experience of learners. Government-imposed quality systems or initiatives to improve quality constrain the freedom of others, particularly teaching staff, to choose how to act in the best interests of the institution or the learner. Quality initiatives can therefore be a means by which governments control educators or by which senior managers in schools and colleges control their staff. Alternatively, the pursuit of quality may be seen as a genuine attempt to ensure learners have the best experience possible. In the latter case, the perceived existence or improvement of quality depends on its definition. The choice of comparator, for example international standards of achievement or student satisfaction levels, provides the point of reference. Inevitably, where comparison is the focus of attention, the measurement of quality, rather than improving it, may by default become the centre of attention and action.

STATE INITIATIVES

Governments have considered that improved quality is likely to be achieved through taking greater central control, or in contrast by decentralising control, offering a greater degree of institutional autonomy. Often in practice initiatives to achieve both are in tension. Thus, schools may have greater control over their budget, while at the same time being impelled to implement a more tightly defined curriculum.

Yin (1999, p. 18) suggests that centralised activity to improve quality has been implemented thorough three major strategies:

- the input enlargement approach
- the process improvement approach
- the integrative approach (including both input and process improvement).

He argues that the first, input enlargement, has been the dominant approach. Within this, improving the input of teachers, either through increasing their number or their competence, has been the most prevalent strategy (Chapman and Adams, 1998). Improving facilities in terms of accommodation or textbooks is a concrete action which is reassuringly visible and assumed to lead to better teaching and learning. Improving teaching, though recognised as key, is much more problematic to achieve and to measure. The means to change instructional practice, or the relationships between educators and learners, are less obvious. The visible proxy adopted has tended to be increasing the level of qualification amongst staff, primarily through initial training (Chapman and Adams, 1998). Such action is expensive and there is little evidence that increasing qualifications or the other presumed indicator of teacher quality, length of experience, necessarily increases student achievement (Hanushek, 1995). This is supported by an extensive literature analysing the failure of both initial and continuing teacher training and education to translate into improved classroom practice (Lumby, forthcoming; Peacock, 1993). Rewarding teachers with higher salaries or performance-related incentives is a further popular teacher-related strategy, but again research has concluded that there is no certainty that such action is likely to improve classroom practice (Foreman, 1997).

A second major means of influencing process is legislating for the content and delivery of the curriculum (Lumby, 2001a). In many parts of the world there have been radical attempts to introduce curricula which shape the way teachers engage with learners, by prescribing a syllabus and sometimes its means of implementation, assessment and the required learning outcomes as discussed in the preceding chapter. Much of this reform has not been evidence informed. In many parts of the world there is little relevant research or as in Hong Kong 'little tradition of using research findings in policy-making' (Yin, 1999, p. 16). Consequently, initiatives have been largely the result of the deliberation of those in power. The impact on improving process or outcomes is unproven.

A final centralised strategy has been opening education to apparent market forces. However, the belief that the advent of parental or student choice will inevitably lead to improvement as institutions compete to attract custom, is not supported by research findings. Commercial organisations, where market forces are most strongly felt, are run for their own benefit, not for that of the customer. Tang and Morrison (1998) considering the effect of marketisation in Macau, marshal a range of evidence that parents have less choice than imagined and that competition does not necessarily lead to improvements for the customer. Elsewhere, there is evidence that market forces have led not to improvements in teaching and learning, but to other tactics to improve results such as avoiding the recruitment of 'problem' students in favour of those from advantaged families likely to be high achievers (Bagley, Woods and Glatter, 1996).

In apparent contrast to these centralist attempts to improve quality, many countries have introduced school-based management, with autonomy given to institutions to make their own decisions, in the hope that this will lead to school-based initiatives that are well understood, supported and implemented by staff. School improvement research that stresses the capacity of schools to improve results supports such a strategy. There is no doubt that, for some, such autonomy has been relished and has indeed led to increased enrolment and achievement, for example in further education colleges in England and Wales (Lumby, 2001). It is equally true that the fact that autonomy is 'carefully screened by the gaze of authoritarian central controls' (Morley and Rassool, 2000, p. 173) has undermined the strategy. Staff will recognise their freedom to act is proscribed by state-defined parameters with a possible concomitant loss of motivation and commitment.

The state, then, has attempted to improve quality through a range of actions, few of which can be seen to have a proven impact as desired. What is far more certain is that the means to measure putative improvement has grown into an international industry, with pressures to achieve 'multiple accreditation' (Vroeijenstijn, 1999, p. 244), with kitemarks from several organisations seen as obligatory, the inspection and publication of education standards burgeoning, and many committees, consultancies, researchers and practitioners, devoting much activity to the goal of quality.

INSTITUTIONAL INITIATIVES

Where quality is perceived as poor this is often the result of what Chapman and Adams (1998, p. 659) refer to in the Asian context as 'the convergence of disadvantage'. Although the level of disadvantage is relative and will be much more severe in some countries than others, in both developed and developing economies, schools and colleges sited in areas of multiple deprivation will tend to produce poor educational outputs and outcomes. Consequently, the principal of an inner city high school in the USA and a township high school in South Africa may face similar problems of potential violence, dysfunctional families, malnutrition and a first language which is not the language of instruction (Lumby, 2001a). However, it cannot be assumed that schools and colleges in disadvantaged environments will de facto be of inferior quality. In terms of value added, disadvantaged schools may well achieve more than those in favoured environments.

Increasingly, the principal and heads of department are seen as key to improving quality whatever the baseline starting point. The central task is to change what happens in the classroom: 'Educational quality defined as student achievement does not change until something happens at the school and classroom level that changes the transactions between teachers and students' (Chapman and Adams, 1998, p. 646). Many states have envisaged a development in the role of the principal particularly, but also other school leaders such as heads of department, from administrator, overseeing the rubrics of local or national government, to innovator and leader of instructional transformation (Department of Education, South Africa, 1996). The enhancement of such roles is predicated on a belief that staff should have more freedom to lead decisions and innovation to improve quality at institutional level. Evidence suggests that increased school/college autonomy can increase student achievement, for example in Mexico (Ramos and Fletcher, 1998), India (Duraisamy et al., 1998) and China (Lo, 1999). However, increased institutional autonomy is not necessarily followed by improved quality. The community of teachers and other stakeholders may be deeply conservative and resist change. Teachers, given the freedom to act, may arrange matters to their own benefit, not necessarily those of learners. For example, in China, the freedom to take decisions on enrolment has led to very large classes of those students who can pay high fees, thereby ensuring teacher bonuses (Lo, 1999). Finally, the power vested in the principal and other managers has led to an international resistance to 'managerialism', that is, the perceived inappropriate level of power in managers at the cost of the erosion of the power of teachers (Morley and Rassool, 2000). Whereas previously schools and colleges may have been under pressure to comply with the dictates of state, their actions may now be delimited by an internal compliance structure, embedded in the authority of the principal. The apparent greater autonomy of educational institutions may therefore result in a greater degree of collegiality and support for change or it may relocate the imposition of change and resultant resistance to within the institution. The effect will depend on how far the prevailing culture supports a collegial approach and how far the autonomy of the institution is actually delimited by externally imposed curricula or managerial structures.

Chapman and Adams in the Asian context (1998, p. 649) see the sphere of influence of the principal in four areas: '(a) school management (e.g. ensuring textbooks are available), (b) school-ministry communications (e.g. ensuring that the national curriculum is available to teachers (c) school–community relations (e.g. raising money for the school; securing parental support for new instructional strategies) and (d) instructional supervision.' A strong emphasis in the first three areas is in the management of resources and finance, ensuring that the elements necessary for teaching are available, and particularly accessing more resources. There is considerable evidence that one of the effects of demands for improved quality has been to place a greater onus on principals to raise funds than previously. Thus in China principals spend much time seeking sponsor funds (Fouts and Chan, 1997; Lumby and Li, 1998); in the UK further education college principals are largely concerned with maximising resources (Lumby, 2001). The author's field notes from a recent trip to South Africa record the case of an indomitable rural primary principal, who took her umbrella to protect her from a searing temperature and walked several miles to the local educational administration at regular intervals to persuade them of the need to resurface the badly rutted mud road which was the only access to the school. Whether time is spent in pursuing the improvement of such basic facilities or at a computer manipulating spreadsheets of income and expenditure, the same shift in focus is apparent. The principal will spend a great deal of time on activities not directly related to instructional activity, but to ensure additional resource to increase inputs on the assumption that this will improve the learner's experience.

School staff may share a belief that a rise in inputs is the key to quality improvement, rather than any change in their own practice (Walker and Cheong, 1996). There may be a belief that smaller class sizes, more textbooks, fewer student/teacher contact hours etc. will improve learner achievement. Many of such input increases are designed to improve the teacher's lot. There is however no certain evidence that teachers who are paid better or who teach smaller groups will change their practice. They are just as likely to continue in the classroom or workshop much as they ever have. The crucial characteristic of raising quality is that teachers are motivated or impelled to change their practice, as indicated in Chapman and Adam's fourth area – instructional supervision and innovation.

The activities seen as appropriate to raising quality and, therefore, achievement, encompass both longstanding strategies, such as staff development, and improvement of curriculum materials, but also newer mechanisms such as self-assessment protocols and reference to quality assurance standards to guide practice. The role of establishing and supervising such processes is usually that of the principal or a senior manager. The responsibility of managers for ensuring quality is therefore structured through the expectation that they will ensure compliance with quality assurance (QA) procedures. The impact on quality improvement is disputed. Self-assessment can be perceived by staff as creating awareness of current strengths and weaknesses and commitment to improvement (Lumby, 2001). However, the process may also be seen as having minimal impact, particularly where the quality of provision is satisfactory or better. For example, Munton, Mooney and Korintus report that a study assessing the impact of the use of self-assessment materials in 119 early years day-care centres in the UK concluded that 'the materials were found to have little significant impact on the quality of care provision' (Munton, Mooney and Korintus, 1999, p. 177). A further study implemented and assessed the use of the materials in 76 Hungarian day-care centres. The findings were consistent with that of the earlier study. Quality was not influenced by the use of the self-assessment materials. It may of course be the case that the materials were not well designed. The researchers themselves believed differently. They concluded that the standards in Hungary were very high and therefore self-assessment did not lead to any significant improvement. Where quality is good or excellent, time spent on self-assessment, devising manuals and monitoring compliance may actually rob teachers of time which could be spent on activities with students.

An interesting feature of this example is the fact that evidence that use of the materials did not improve quality did not deter their further use. The materials were shown to be not very effective in the UK but nevertheless were then used in Hungary. Internationally, there is little rigorous evaluation of how far the adoption of quality assurance procedures actually leads to improvements in quality. Rather the use of QA manuals and self-assessment materials is seen as a requirement by funding bodies, sometimes enshrined in legislation. Questioning their use may be seen as evidence of a lack of commitment to quality improvement. The adherence to quality assurance processes has become something of a dogma. There is still much to be done internationally to research how far the overlay of such QA procedures on more traditional quality improvement strategies, such as staff development, actually improves quality.

QUALITY, CULTURE AND EXPECTATIONS

Few would disagree with the aim of improving the quality of school and colleges. However, the enactment of such agreement draws on a variety of discourses, each of which has limitations, relating not only to educational practice, but also to the wider context of political relations, economic advantage and disadvantage, and societal expectations. The discourse of school effectiveness, which attempts to link measurement of student achievement or outputs to school factors does not engage with the struggle for control embodied in part in quality initiatives. The discourse of international comparison often avoids the cultural tensions in assuming that outcomes in different cultures can be directly compared. The problematic conceptualisation of quality persists. All over the world are elite schools where those who can pay secure what they perceive as a good education for their children or themselves (Lo, 1999). Quality is therefore relative to resources. Quality is also relative to cultural norms. What appears a quality provision for pre-school children in China will look very different to western eyes and vice versa. Measures of quality by definition are dependent on numeric values in relation to, for example, examinations passed or expectations met, but such values do not necessarily capture the variety of outcomes expected of education or the dynamic changes in expectation in the experience of even one learner, let alone all those of an institution. Quality will therefore remain a fluid and nebulous concept, interpreted variously in practice, an orthodoxy to which many feel obliged to subscribe. No single prescription will secure improvement in quality in a context as complex and animated as a school or college. The most that an educational manager can do is to remain aware of the imprecision of the concept and be sensitive to both the educational and micropolitical forces which will affect its achievement, choosing with care from the plethora of taxonomies, philosophies, 'good practice' and recommended processes that are on offer.

Section C: People and communities

This section explores the interface between leaders and managers in education with the individuals and groups with whom they come in contact, moving in concentric circles from the staff with whom there is daily contact to those members of the community, parents, employers, regional and national administrators and policy-makers, with whom contact may be less frequent but is equally vital.

5

MANAGING PEOPLE IN EDUCATION

PEOPLE MATTER

In every continent practitioners and writers on leadership and management proclaim the belief that people are the bedrock of success in schools and colleges, as in all other organisations. The instinctive belief that people are key has been reinforced by a number of factors leading to a greater emphasis on the effective management of people. First, the greater degree of devolution in many parts of the world means that staff in educational organisations must carry more of the responsibility for achieving appropriate teaching and learning for their students. Secondly, the percentage of the education budget spent on staff salaries is universally high, up to 90 per cent in some countries (Coombe, 1997), leading to a determination to ensure that this high proportion of the available resource is used to the greatest effect. In many countries the need for a cost-effective use of staff is also linked to the aim of increasing the numbers of children and adults receiving or staying longer in education. Given limited resources, efficient use of staff to ensure maximum capacity is high on the agenda (Gottelmann-Duret and Hogan, 1996). For example, in Mexico, Bray (2000) explains that teachers are known as 'taxi teachers' because many have to jump into a taxi after teaching a morning session in order to teach elsewhere in the afternoon, in order to make more school places available within budget constraints. Thirdly, the indigenisation of education in ex-colonial countries has placed the need for the training and development of staff in sharp focus (Akinnusi, 1991). However, the most significant factor is simply the conviction that the quality of staff and of their professional life influences the quality of the learner's experience (Menlo and Poppleton, 1990).

The near universal rhetoric of commitment to people as key in policy documents or fine-sounding speeches hides the reality of the working life of educators and the wide variety of practice in their management. The Minister of Education for South Africa in a speech on World Teachers' Day to the National Assembly in Cape Town took the opportunity 'to acknowledge the worth of our nation's teachers, to recognise and applaud the important work they do', speaking of the nobility of their work, but also recognising that 'these are good sounding words, but somehow without life or meaning in so many of our schools' (Asmal, 2001). The very poor conditions in which many work, and the failure of many staff to live up to even the basic requirements of attendance, are also acknowledged. Any glib dependence on the development of 'human resource management' does not necessarily address the profound difficulties faced by those who manage staff.

Emphasis on human resource management (HRM) is a 'fashionable nostrum' (Rowley, 1998, p. 1). There has been relatively little rigorous research into the nature of managing people in education compared with that undertaken for business and industry. Though the latter is often characterised as using people merely as a disposable resource like any other, generic research has sought to delve with some vigour into the ways in which people are led and managed, and the consequent business results. It may be that educators have assumed the existence of strong 'people' skills working in a field which is centred on the development of people, that is learners. How far such beliefs may be justified is a central question. This is the first of two linked chapters on the management of people in education which will explore how far and in what ways the rhetoric of the centrality of people is translated into practice. The first will set the parameters of activity in this area and the second will focus on issues of performance. This chapter will address the questions:

- What are the working conditions of educators?
- What goals and tasks does their management involve?
- What are the dominant paradigms in this area?
- How can we understand the impact of culture?

THE WORKING LIVES OF EDUCATORS

The nature of educators' professional life is often bleak. In many parts of the world teachers function in very poor conditions, their professionalism undermined by an absence of basic facilities (Avalos, 1998; Coombe, 1997; Gounden and Mkize, 1991). Salaries are often inadequate, forcing staff to spend time working at another job, or raising funds through entrepreneurial activities and donations within the school or college (Fouts and Chan, 1998; Lumby and Li, 1998). The hours that staff are expected to work vary across a wide spectrum. In Chile, teachers may work as many as 60 hours a week, contracted to two schools (Avalos, 1998). In Hong Kong, the expectation is that teachers will teach six hours a day with one free period, but that this will be supplemented by considerable preparation and assessment activity over and above these hours. In English colleges of further education, the amount of face-to-face contact between lecturers and students has grown steadily in the 1990s from 21 hours a week to 27 or more. Hours may be greater for those teaching older students, as in Malawi (Gottelmann-Duret and Hogan, 1996). Staff–student ratios also vary with the prescribed maximum class number as high as 1:60, though even this may not reflect the actual number of students in any class, which may exceed the official maximum. Teachers generally perceive themselves to be overworked and often poorly paid. The mandating of the curriculum in many parts of the world has also led to dissatisfaction, with teachers obliged to implement curricula, for example the Target Oriented Curriculum in Hong Kong or Objectives Based Education in South Africa, on which they were not consulted and with which they may disagree (Morris, Chan and Lo, 2000). Poppleton (1992, p. 225) describes 'an international culture of discontent' as a result of a five-country study, which included only developed economies. Amongst teachers working in much more disadvantaged conditions, dissatisfaction may be more profound still (Holman, 1998). The recruitment and retention of staff has become a critical issue. The task of managing people in such a climate is challenging indeed.

The management of staff is also shaped by the degree of economic, political and educational development in their country or region. The national/regional context may dictate the goals of the school/college, thereby influencing the agenda of those managing educators. At the most fundamental, Chapman and Adams (1998, p. 606) speaking of the developing states of Asia, suggest that indicators of the successful management of staff include:

- teachers come to school on time.
- teachers have copies of the curriculum.
- teachers receive instructional supervision.

Having teachers in the classroom for the required hours, for the required number of days and with a minimum understanding of what they are to achieve is a real challenge for some countries. In South Africa, a long-standing culture of teacher absence and disaffection has led to setting targets which reflect these basic aims to get the teachers into the classrooms for a specified number of hours and days, and to increase their instructional competence. The Deputy Education Minister describes the goals: 'We must make sure that educationists actually do their jobs, prepare properly, are well qualified, know how and what to teach, can manage a class, and teach for 200 days a year' (Department of Education, South Africa, 1996). Achieving a minimum attendance and basic competence is therefore the aim of staff management in some countries. In others, staff may be well qualified and a high level of professionalism taken for granted. There the aim may be, as in China (Paine and Ma, 1993) or Japan (Shimihara, 1998), to continue to build on long-standing traditions to maintain and improve performance.

ANALYSING ENVIRONMENT

Sparrow and Hiltrop (1998) identify four major sets of environmental factors upon which the appropriate approach to managing people is contingent: cultural factors, the legislative framework, the structure of the system within which they work, and the roles/competence of those who manage people. The relevance of each of these to education is immediately apparent. The explosion of books on 'international' human resource management registers the intense interest in understanding the profound influence of culture on relations between people and on organisational behaviour. Some writers have suggested that there are unique styles of managing people, for example in Africa (Akinnusi, 1991) and Japan (Gill and Wong, 1998). Certainly there are underpinning attitudinal orientations which are a critical factor. For example the reasons why people work will shape the appropriate ways of managing them. Poppleton (1992, p. 217) in a study of teachers in five countries, England, the USA, Japan, Singapore and Germany, defined three attitudes to work: 'An *instrumental* pattern in which work is largely an instrument to obtain income, an *expressive* pattern where work is an instrument of self-expression, and an *entitlement and contact* pattern where emphasis is placed on work as a means of social contact and as a duty rather than a right.' Poppleton links these different approaches as much to the specific work setting as to national culture. In other words, how teachers feel about their work, whether it is primarily to earn a living wage or whether it is intimately bound up with their ideals, beliefs and self-image, is shaped at least as much by the particular circumstances in which they must function as to any national predilection or history. When the reasons why educators work are diverse, there can be no single approach to managing them which is likely to be equally successful in all contexts.

Sparrow and Hiltrop's second point on local legislative and work structures can be illustrated by reference to South Africa. The trade unions and legislation relating to affirmative action exert powerful positive and negative forces shaping the relationships between people in education and the courses of action which are open (Kraak and Hall, 1999; Kaabwe, forthcoming). The requirement to address a history of oppression and inequality dictates so many aspects of staff management, for example, how recruitment and selection may be undertaken, the negotiation of conditions of service and the democratisation of school management structures.

The third point draws attention to structural issues. The division of responsibility between national, regional and local managers/administrators will inhibit or free the range of activities open to those managing staff. The Commonwealth Secretariat and World Bank (1992) offer a model for the range of activity, assuming the following division of responsibility. There will be agreement at national level on:

1) Conditions of service: policies and procedures for

(1) appointment
(2) deployment
(3) appraisal
(4) promotion
(5) discipline.

2) Benefits:
(1) salary scales
(2) pension schemes
(3) health insurance
(4) housing.

Although, as the model suggests, it is likely that decisions on these will be taken at national level, in some schools and countries a degree of local decision-making will also be possible. Teacher salaries and other benefits such as housing may be supplemented by funds raised through entrepreneurial activity. Deployment and promotion may also be subject to institutional decision.

Within the institution, it is suggested that the management of staff should include:

• involving staff in setting aims and objectives for the institution
• involving staff in management
• implementing agreed procedures on recruitment and selection, induction, appraisal and retirement
• maintaining staff records
• ensuring staff access to relevant written information on conditions of service, complaints procedures, etc.
• providing development opportunities for staff
• providing/implementing a structure for promotion
• dealing with individual staff problems/difficulties as they arise
• evaluating and supporting staff performance in teaching and learning (adapted from the Commonwealth Secretariat and World Bank, 1992, pp. 21–2).

This is an inclusive framework which, in its insistence on involving staff, is clearly predicated on a human resource management approach. As such it will not be universally applicable. Some educational managers will have no control over some of the responsibilities outlined. The degree to which responsibility for each of these areas is located at institutional level will shape the management of people.

Whatever the context, the importance invested in the management of people demands the support of a well-developed foundation of research and writing that can inspire and guide leaders and managers who bear responsibility for staff in schools and colleges. While there is undoubtedly much of great value, the literature also promulgates a number of mythologies, particularly in the unthinking promotion of human resource management strategies that emanate from particular dominant cultures:

Myth 1 – that there is a march from previous old-fashioned personnel approaches to a future of strategic human resource management.

Myth 2 – that such an approach represents the appropriate way of managing staff.

Myth 3 – that improving teachers' pay and conditions will improve their performance.

Myth 4 – that performance review/appraisal systems improve teachers' performance.

This chapter will examine the first two of these myths, while Chapter 6 will move on to explore myths three and four.

HUMAN RESOURCE MANAGEMENT

The management of people in schools and colleges can be seen both as a set of technical requirements – understanding local legislation and regulations in relation to the hiring of staff, implementing the pay system, conducting reviews, etc. – and as requiring social/emotional skills to create and maintain a successfully functioning set of relationships within a school/college community. The balance between these two is at the heart of the debate on the nature of managing people in education in the twenty-first century. The debate has largely been framed by discussing the nature and relative merits of two approaches, personnel and human resource or strategic human resource management. In South Africa, Van der Westhuizen and Theron (1994) refer to reports from the National Training Board/Human Sciences Research Council, the African National Council and the Congress of South African Teachers' Unions which all stress human resource management as of crucial importance in achieving political, social and economic progress in South Africa. Human resource management is characterised by them as the way of the future, moving from previous personnel approaches which are identified with slow and ineffective organisations. The personnel function tradition is depicted as emphasising a bureaucratic approach, keeping the management of staff largely in the hands of specialists at organisational and regional level and focused on consistent procedures (Middlewood and Lumby, 1998). This is contrasted with human resource management which is associated with a more responsive approach, placing responsibility and authority for change at the location where change is needed, the individual organisation. Human resource management approaches are predicated on placing responsibility for staff management with line managers, evolving individualised activity according to the strategic needs of the school or college, and substituting individual negotiation for system-wide procedures.

The main criticism of the personnel approach is that consistency is achieved at the cost of adaptation to individual context. Additionally, the approach is criticised for attempting to deal with the increasing ambiguity and paradox of managing schools by creating ever more tightly delineated controls, a strategy doomed to failure in that endemic and potentially infinite change cannot be brought within the bounds of finite agreed procedures. It is argued that personnel approaches have failed to deal with the complexities of managing people in the past and will certainly fail in the twenty-first century.

However, personnel management may have a long history, for example in the armies and administration of African kings (Akinnusi, 1991), and as such reflects a number of strengths and relevance to particular cultures. For example, locating the responsibility for staff management with 'personnel' is predicated on the latter having specialist skills and knowledge. Certainly in the area of the technical aspects of people management, handing wholesale responsibility for staff management to principals and others who are untrained and have little time may not be an unalloyed move for the good. Equally, the emphasis on negotiation with representative groups such as unions, rather than the individual negotiations suggested by HRM, may offer protection of professionalism and conditions of service that are a valuable foundation for the way people are managed.

Human resource management as characterised above, with its emphasis on individual relations between leader and led, may also stretch back for millennia, for example in the Chinese Confucian tradition (Satow and Zhong-Ming, 1994). It is argued to have great strengths and a particular fit to the endemic change of the twenty-first century. It is more concerned with individual organisational fit than with overall consistency throughout education. The strategic aims of the organisation are the basis for deciding issues of people management. If this is a different administrative starting point, there is also a difference in psychological premise. Personnel approaches seek to assure compliance with the standards and regulations established centrally. Human resource management assumes that this is unlikely to lead to a sufficiently motivated workforce and emphasises the need for a psychological contract and commitment rather than mere compliance. It is also assumed that to achieve this, many staff will need to be involved, not just personnel specialists. Managers are able to agree goals for their institution and to negotiate and agree goals for their own contribution and that of the staff they manage. The management of people becomes of central strategic importance to all managers and the focus moves from compliance with policy to motivating human beings to give of their best in a direction aligned with the strategy of the organisation.

Human resource management appears to be gaining ground as the preferred system and the goal to attain (Van der Westhuizen and Theron, 1994) yet there are many difficulties in implementing the approach. It is very dependent on the capacity of line managers in the double sense of their ability and their time. Even in countries where educators are highly trained, their ability to take on the HRM role is problematic along both dimensions (Lumby, 1997). Given the context in many parts of the world, it may be unrealistic to expect beleaguered, overworked and underpaid staff to take on an enlarged staff management role over and above their teaching responsibilities.

The removal of traditional bureaucratic processes may liberate managers to arrive at individually shaped ways of working, but it also removes the safety net of agreed practice and specialist expertise ensuring compliance with agreed codes. In this sense, HRM provides little protection for those in the system. Finally, there is little empirical evidence on how the management of staff in a flexible and strategic manner might actually happen in practice. Much of the writing is at the hortatory level, with an absence of detailed empirical research. Extolling the virtues of HRM to managers who have little time, training or resource, and who work within a tradition which has not placed responsibility for staff management at the institutional level, may have a wonderful aspirational and inspirational ring, but may not offer much practical help on how to proceed.

Rowley (1998) explores how far there is convergence towards HRM practice in business in the Asia Pacific region. He concludes, first, that the concept itself is contested, and that even were there a universally agreed model, the extremely varied practice in the region, reflecting cultural differences, could not be constrained into a monolithic prescription. He suggests that:

> There is not just 'one best way' or magic elixir. While such conclusions may not be welcomed by many parsimonious managers (and, it must be said, some academics), who have become addicted to a diet of simple lists, naive nostrums and pleasing platitudes, such complexity and diversity remains prevalent in the modern, still murky, world of HRM.
>
> (Rowley, 1998, p. 207)

Education is equally enamoured of prescriptive lists, and virtuous calls for empowerment of staff. However, it is either disingenuous or foolish to assume that systems based on centuries of evolution of culture could be quickly replaced. For example, millennia of seniority-based promotion will not be quickly overturned. This is not to suggest that existing personnel approaches are not beset with problems. Chapman and Adams (1998, p. 611) paint the situation in many developing countries of Asia, where teacher supervision is the responsibility of district or regional officials:

> This removes it from the administrator most aware of a teacher's pedagogical skill (e.g. the headmaster) and assigns it to individuals removed from the school context, who visit the school only inter-

mittently or not at all, and who often view their role more as one of enforcing rules than of demonstrating to teachers how they could improve their teaching.

He provides examples of the results of such a policy in the Philippines, where supervisors may have responsibility for 600 teachers yet are largely unable to physically visit them, and in Nepal, where visits may be three to four years apart. Even when schools and colleges are not so inaccessible, the delay in decision-making when decisions must be referred can undermine any attempt at being responsive to changing circumstances. For example, in technical colleges in South Africa, a national decision to offer severance packages followed by lengthy delays in replacing staff virtually paralysed the planning capacity in many colleges (Lumby, 2000). Adherence to one or other approach as universally preferred ignores the importance both of local environmental and cultural factors. Both personnel and human resource management approaches have valuable aspects, and where some literature, for example Van der Westhuizen and Theron (1994), presents the two approaches as alternatives, usually with personnel management as the less satisfactory option, it may be more productive to consider them as parallel, with what is valuable in both combined. Given the cultural diversity of the contexts within which schools and colleges function, any debate which is polarised into two approaches is simplistic in the extreme. The fusion of cultural, technical, social and emotional requirements within a legislative framework will demand creativity in moulding a unique approach contingent on the specific environment.

RELATING CULTURE TO THE MANAGEMENT OF PEOPLE

Such creativity will certainly involve a consideration of culture. A number of frameworks have been suggested to underpin the analysis of culture and its implications for management. The most celebrated is that of Hofstede (1980). His analysis of national culture has been applied simplistically at times, resulting in stereotypical views that, for example, western cultures expect and value a far narrower range of power distribution than do those of Asian cultures, that western cultures place far more emphasis on the individual than the group in contrast to Asian cultures. In fact, Hofstede's later work (1993) showed that within Europe there was massive variation. '86% of the worldwide variance on individualism-collectivism and 70% of variance across power-distance are found in Europe' (Sparrow and Hiltrop, 1998, p. 73). Ignoring the wide variation in culture, assuming homogeneity, gives rise to notions of the appropriate way of managing people which assume mythic status. The process of the recruitment and selection of staff can serve as an example.

Recruitment can be defined as the process of attracting applications from an appropriate number and range of people who have the ability or potential to perform the job in question. Selection is the process of choosing from the applicants the best match to the vacant job requirements, including not only hiring people for the first time, but internal appointments also. Two apparent approaches to selection can be discerned, what Akinnusi (1991, p. 167) describes as 'particularism' and 'universalism', terms which relate strongly to the cultural dimensions of Hofstede (1980) and Trompenaars and Hampden-Turner (1997). In particularist approaches, selection is shaped by the personal affiliation of the players, for example kinship, religion, ethnic or political similarities. The particularist approach of appointing people to posts as a reward for support or in recognition of an affiliation can be adopted both by government agencies or departments, and by individual managers in schools and colleges:

> Reasons for this are not difficult to find. In settings where paid work is scarce, and where there are strong pressures to allocate jobs in a particularist fashion, the selection process constitutes a prime means of fulfilling one's obligations to kin and other personal contacts. Moreover, in many African societies, this behaviour is virtually regarded as compulsory.
>
> (Blunt and Popoola, 1985, p. 51)

Although this argument is here applied to Africa, it is clear that in other societies, appointment may depend upon matching affiliation criteria. For example, in China, holding a role within the Communist Party may influence success in promotion. There may be specific circumstances which lead to consideration of characteristics other than how far candidates match a job specification. In South Africa affirmative action has resulted in ethnicity being a highly significant factor in selection. This is a long way from the personal affiliation discussed by Akinnusi, as it is an attempt to rectify decades of discrimination against black people. Nevertheless, the result is a similar process of selection which rewards characteristics not connected with the job specification.

From the perspective of the appointing individual or authority, the result of this process may be highly satisfactory, with posts filled by people with the 'right' political views or ethnic background, or simply those who will continue to offer support as a quid pro quo for the reward of a post. There may be also a strong moral component to this approach in that those with the power to offer a post are seen as obligated to use this power to support and protect the interests of family and friends. What may be labelled as corrupt, nepotism or simony by universalist cultures may embody for those in particularist cultures a moral stance which values people above rules.

There is an assumption in western literature that the universalist approach, that is, using a selection process which attempts to match applicants to objective criteria, is the preferred approach because it is both more fair, and therefore more motivating, and also more successful in identifying the best match to the vacant post. In this approach a detailed description of the post is defined and a variety of instruments used to measure the match of applicants to the post. Lundy and Cowling (1996, p. 232) describe a typical sequence of instruments:

- application blank
- interview/s
- test/s
- medical examination
- references.

The tests might include asking staff to participate in leaderless discussion, to teach a real or artificially convened group, to undertake an in-tray exercise, to complete a psychometric test, or might involve a whole phalanx of tests at an assessment centre. The most universally applied method, the interview, is reported by many to be of dubious value with low validity coefficients (Hackett, 1992; Middlewood, 1997; Robertson and Smith, 1989). It is suggested that the universalist approach is effective in selecting the best match to a job, and that the degree of effectiveness can be increased by a systematic approach to the process and by staff training. However, the assumed much greater degree of effectiveness may not be of the scale assumed. Nor does the theoretical ideal type of a universalist approach offer a convincing description of why the appointment of people in universalist cultures appears nevertheless to be in part dependent on factors not related to the job specification, such as race or gender. There are suspicions that less obvious factors may also be at play, that those appointing may be consciously or unconsciously influenced by class, religion or membership of networks such as the freemasons. Researching the degree to which such factors influence selection is, of course, highly problematic. What is clear is that, as Trompenaars and Hampden-Turner (1997) argue, rather than cultures being particularist or universalist, the two approaches ride in tandem, individuals being influenced by the systems and rules laid down and by personal affiliations. The two apparently divergent systems actually work together: 'The universalist approach at best helps us to avoid the pathologies of particularism taken too far; and the particularist position needs to be taken to avoid the pathologies of universalism taken too far' (Trompenaars and Hampden-Turner, 1997, p. 43).

The particularist approach to the selection of staff if taken too far could paralyse an organisation by creating a staff which, chosen for affiliation reasons, have no competence to carry out the required roles. Similarly, the universalist approach if too rigidly applied can discount important aspects of the relationships which will be part of the successful creation of staff who can work together. It follows that some of the mythology emanating from western literature, that universalist approaches are morally superior and practically more effective is discredited. It also follows that any simple division by country of universalist or particularist approaches is prob-lematic. The pure approaches are unlikely to exist in practice, and cul-tures which claim to adopt a universalist approach might more honestly admit that this is not the case, and that particularist factors covertly influence selection.

The case of selection is but one illustration. Whichever framework of cultural dimensions is selected to guide leaders and managers, whether suggested by Hofstede (1980), by Trompenaars and Hampden-Turner (1997) or by any other writer, there will be implications for every aspect of managing people. Consequently, it is unlikely that any prescription will have universal application, despite apparent similarities across systems in the world. For example, once staff are appointed, one of the chief strate-gies for managing them is to place them within a structure which delin-eates their responsibilities and relationships, and so provides a framework for the contract of what is expected in exchange for what reward. In both schools and colleges, structures are generally based on either subject areas or groupings of students. Thus in China, the group of subject teachers who work together collectively, 'the *jiaoyanzu* . . . looks very much like a department in a U.S. high school' (Paine and Ma, 1993. p. 678). There is also a director for each class of students with responsibility for their progress and welfare. The pastoral and subject structure is therefore very similar in China, the USA and in many other parts of the world. However, this apparently universal similarity in approach rests in reality on great differences in how the organisational structure is understood and func-tions in practice. The extent to which the roles within the organisational structure relate merely to function or to power within a hierarchy, the extent to which the most senior positions are seen as administrative or leadership roles, the degree of autonomy or interdependence invested in the roles will all be culturally shaped (Adler, 1997). Any mirage of uni-versal practice soon vanishes.

DISCERNING THE THREADS

In all the variety of philosophy and practice reviewed, only one true uni-versal emerges, that people matter. Who is recruited to the range of roles within schools and colleges and the way in which they are subsequently managed is the single most significant factor in assuring the best experi-ence possible for learners. Every policy decision, every plan, every resource is ultimately transmuted through the practice of an individual educator in his or her classroom, workshop or laboratory. The way staff are managed influences the process of transmutation. The responses to the fundamental conviction that people are key vary, but perhaps not as sig-nificantly as imagined. The expectation of teachers may be for a high degree of autonomy or for a close degree of supervision. In some ways in whatever part of the world they work, they will get both. Even in cultures where a collective approach or a tight bureaucratic supervision is the norm, the technology of teaching, which involves interaction usually in a physically isolated space of a single room, secures a degree of autonomy for the individual who essentially shapes the interaction between the teacher and the group of learners. Equally, there appears to be a ubiquitous regulatory system, which may emanate from the institution itself and/or from regional and national administration, which scrutinises action and limits the power of choice. The role of leaders and managers, therefore, cannot be to influence directly the quality of teaching and learning. That depends on the teacher's interaction with learners. However, they can indirectly influence it by their management of staff. They can never completely control development, and many would not to wish to, but they can nudge it in a desired direction along a number of spectra. For example, questions which might be asked include:

1) Are the priority aims to be centred on the fundamentals of getting teachers into the school for the required hours, or are they to be towards the other end of the spectrum, a focus on improving pedagogic effectiveness?
2) How do managers assess the current position in the recruitment and selection of staff along a particularist/universalist spectrum? Are particularist criteria overt or covert? Is the current position the optimum one and, if not, how can the process be moved along?
3) In terms of staff rewards, is the current system offering a clearly delineated structure of pay dependent on qualifications, position in the organisation's structure and length of service, or is it largely framed in terms of individual rewards related to performance?

In all these areas, managers may have little room for manoeuvre, but there is usually some. Managing staff is dependent on the same strategy as any other area of management, deciding the goals and finding the leverage to race or to nudge painfully in the desired direction. Whatever the plan, fine-sounding commitment to people as central signifies nothing if the reality of educators' working lives and the reality of their culture is not taken as the starting point rather than the latest clarion call for the current favoured approach.

6

PEOPLE AND PERFORMANCE

THE MYTHS OF PERFORMANCE MANAGEMENT

The previous chapter explored the management of people, particularly the culturally bound nature of current perceptions of appropriate approaches and processes. It proposed the existence of myths including:

Myth 3 – that improving teachers' pay and conditions will improve their performance.
Myth 4– that appraisal systems improve teachers' performance.

This chapter will explore the management of performance, bearing in mind these two myths which reflect the different perceptions of two main stakeholder groups. Teachers themselves tend to argue that improving their pay and conditions and/or improving the resources available will improve teaching and learning by increasing their motivation (Walker and Cheong, 1996). National and regional administration may take a different approach, seeing the management of performance as key. This chapter will explore the evidence that exists on the effectiveness of both the means of motivating staff and of managing their performance, ultimately to improve teaching and learning.

SUPPORT OR CONTROL?

The last decade of the twentieth century saw an 'intensification of teaching' (Shimihara, 1998, p. 460) with an unremitting demand for changes, for improved teaching and for improved outcomes. Teachers have been subject to requirements which for many have become overwhelming. The incidence of stress has become epidemic and stress-related illness an ever present hazard, to the extent that Nimomaya and Okato (1990), writing about Japan, claim that ensuring psychological health is one of the most important tasks of school leaders.

These phenomena have been the result of an apparently commendable drive to improve education. Governments, and to some extent educational leaders, in their determination to reform education, have adopted many different strategies in their approach to securing improved outcomes. Two contradictory trends can be discerned, one for greater regulation and conformity and one for greater supported devolution and autonomy. The underlying assumptions in these two approaches conform to McGregor's (1970) X Y theory. Theory 'X' suggests that people generally seek to avoid work and must be pressured by managers and/or driven by the need to make a living. Theory 'Y' views people as wanting to take responsibility for themselves and be self-directed. Thus, centrally directed curricula, employment frameworks and performance management systems assume a need to control the activity of educators, Theory X. Devolution of funds and decision-making powers to educational organisations assumes that greater autonomy will bring results, Theory Y. Overall, educators perceive a dominance of the former, with a concomitant widespread discontent. Delving deeper still, beneath the underpinning assumptions lies a struggle for power, with teachers, in common with other professional groups, subject to challenge from governments and other stakeholders who are attempting to wrest more control of education from educators. In her study of five countries, Poppleton (1992) found in all that teachers were unhappy with their status as professionals and how they were viewed by the community. In all continents, teachers believe the community has lost respect for them as professionals and, sometimes, for the value of education (Coombe, 1997; Gershunsky and Pullin, 1990; Poppleton, 1992). In response teachers resist what they may perceive as attempts by government or others to further restrict their power. Governments carry on with their reform agenda regardless. Resistance or failure of existing initiatives are no deterrent to further attempts at change. Despite a history of state initiatives which fail and quietly vanish or are curtailed, governments remain stubbornly surprised when their plans remain unimplemented and move swiftly on to the next policy change (Coombe, 1997; Timperley and Robinson, 1997). Nowhere is this scenario seen more acutely than in the area of managing teacher performance.

In many countries the management of teachers' performance has negative connotations. For example, in New Zealand (Cardno, 1995), India (Rajpu and Walia, 1998), many parts of Africa (Makau and Coombe, 1994) and in Russia (Gershunsky and Pullin, 1990) managing performance is associated with a punitive and often inefficient inspection system. In considering how to support teachers to achieve a satisfactory or better performance, governments and individual educational managers have striven to move forward by balancing the strong accountability element of previous inspection regimes with a more positive determination to provide support. Performance management as a phrase may be very specifically defined within any one country (DfEE, 1999a) but this chapter deals with managing performance, that is, rather than any formal national system, the actions which can be taken by school and college leaders to ensure that staff are managed in a way which gives them a framework to make their optimum contribution to the effectiveness of the organisation and to help learners achieve. The framework will involve making sure staff know what is required of them, receive feedback on how they are doing and are supported to achieve expectations (Middlewood and Lumby, 1998). Three interlinked and mutually reinforcing elements provide such a framework:

- motivating staff
- providing a means for staff to review and plan to improve their performance
- providing development opportunities to support the planned improvement.

These elements are all positive. There may be other elements such as capability and disciplinary procedures which are used as a last resort when the above have not succeeded. The chapter will focus on the fundamentals of positive management, achieving a motivated, self-aware and developing staff.

MOTIVATING STAFF

Motivation is a concept which has attracted a plethora of definitions and theoretical explanations, some of which appear to have similarities and some of which appear not connected at all. Turner (1992) charts the several processes involved in motivation: 'Motivation has more than one aspect; it involves arousal, direction and persistence. People have to be activated in some way; having become activated, they have to choose a particular line of action; having chosen that direction, they choose to maintain that behaviour for some period of time' (Turner, 1992, p. 2). Turner further points out that educational managers do not have to motivate staff. The latter are motivated. The question is whether managers can in any way influence the direction and strength of the motivation. To do so, they must have some understanding of how motivation can be aligned with the organisation's objectives. Managing motivation is therefore concerned with ensuring staff are committed to achieve organisational goals over time.

An additional conceptual complication is the fact that some theorists refer to job satisfaction as if it were synonymous with motivation. In fact satisfaction and motivation are quite different. Motivation describes the impetus to take action, the direction and persistence of the action (Turner, 1992). Satisfaction is 'a function of the gap between the rewards actually granted and the rewards an individual thinks he/she deserves' (Kremer-Hayon and Goldstein, 1990, p. 287).

International studies have attempted to measure the degree of motivation, morale or more usually job satisfaction. The fact that different concepts are in use makes cross-cultural comparisons problematic. Additionally, as most research is based on self-reporting, differences in the process of reporting will affect the results. For example, Nimomaya and Okato (1990) suggest that the Japanese habitually hesitate to make themselves clear and may be underplaying the degree of satisfaction in responding to questions. At the other end of the spectrum, Arabs may inflate feedback, habitually seeing the ideal as synonymous with reality (Ali, 1996).

Despite the conceptual confusion and the weakness of self-reported data, attempts continue to arrive at comparative lists indicating the degree of importance of various factors in motivating staff in different countries (Kremer-Hayon and Goldstein, 1990; Mwamwenda, 1995; Poppleton, 1992). Additionally, some studies have attempted to find correlations between the degree of satisfaction felt by teachers and national factors such as economy or culture. For example, Harrison (1995) in a study of Singapore and Australia, attempts to demonstrate that satisfaction is adversely affected by high power–distance cultures. Hofstede's (1980) cultural model suggests that in high power–distance cultures, inequality is accepted and institutionalised in organisational hierarchies, whereas in low power–distance cultures, the norm is that inequalities should be minimised as far as possible. If Harrison is correct, then the adverse effect of high power–distance societies on satisfaction would appear to support theories which link individual autonomy to higher levels of satisfaction. Harrison further builds on Hofstede's work to suggest that there is a connection between the country's wealth and the degree of individualism, that is, the assumption that people should function independently, rather than as one of a collective. He argues that, as an economy develops, the degree of individualism will increase and the degree of autonomy expected and, therefore, needed to achieve satisfaction would grow.

The argument seems persuasive but is undermined by the many contradictory conclusions in published studies. While there seems often to be a connection between the degree of autonomy afforded and satisfaction, this does not appear to be a universal. What emerges most clearly from the studies is that the factors which appear to be of greatest importance to people vary considerably from culture to culture. In a study of Chinese, Taiwanese, Russian and US employees, Fisher and Yuan (1998) found that each group ranked factors leading to satisfaction differently. The most important factor for each was found to be as follows:

Chinese   Good wages.
Taiwanese   High job security.
Russians   Promotion and growth of my skills within the organization.
USA   Interesting work.

Being well informed and involved with decisions was important to the Russians and Americans, but of least importance to the Chinese and ranked seventh by the Taiwanese. Such research is linked to the Discrepancy Model (Wanous and Lawler, 1972) – that satisfaction is a result of the congruence or discrepancy between what the job offers and what one wants. Thus study after study attempts to identify the key factors that lead to teacher satisfaction with the hope of providing some clue for principals and other managers on what is most important in motivating staff. However, no universals emerge and the overriding message is that the factors which are important in leading to job satisfaction in teachers vary not only by nation, but sometimes by age, length of service, gender and economic position (Davies and Gunawardena, 1992; Ninomaya and Okato, 1990; Sim, 1990; Wisniewski, 1990).

Theorists have tried to impose some order by categorising factors in order to assess whether particular types of factor may be more likely to be important in different cultures. One such categorisation is the division between intrinsic and extrinsic motivation. Vandevelde explains it in this way:

> Intrinsic motivation is characterised as deriving from an individual's need to be competent and self-determining: it operates in relation to tasks which are interesting and enjoyable to perform in themselves irrespective of pay or other external rewards; by contrast, extrinsic motivation refers to behaviours which are motivated by factors external to the individual, such as pay ... a person in effect rewards himself with intrinsic outcomes, whereas he is dependent on other persons for extrinsic outcomes.
>
> (Vandevelde, 1988, pp. 34–5)

Teaching is rich in intrinsic motivation, to the degree that some have claimed that teachers 'remain motivated to get on with the job no matter what their circumstances are' (Holman, 1998, p. 7) and that the need to motivate which is necessary in commercial organisations is not relevant in the profession of teaching. In contradiction Kremer-Hayon and Goldstein (1990, p. 287) believe it to be 'naïve' to assume high levels of dedication and commitment in all teachers. What is incontrovertible is that much evidence exists that large numbers of teachers are not satisfied with their job and that provision of a good salary and working conditions does not necessarily correlate with satisfaction. In Poppleton's (1992) study Japanese teachers who had the poorest working conditions and salary had only slightly lower job satisfaction than German teachers with excellent salary and conditions.

This bisection of motivation into the two categories of intrinsic and extrinsic motivation is echoed in Herzberg's list of satisfiers (related to job content, interest, challenge, autonomy) and dissatisfiers (related to the job environment, pay, physical conditions, etc.). Herzberg (1966) believed that the effects of these two were independent and that removing dissatisfiers by providing good pay and working conditions would not necessarily lead to greater satisfaction. This seems borne out by many of the studies of teachers' job satisfaction. However, it is also clear that extrinsic factors such as pay and security are considerably more important in motivation in some cultures than others and where a living wage is not provided, as Maslow (1943) suggests, intrinsic motivation may be set aside by efforts to survive economically. Equally the job enrichment strategies suggested by Herzberg to increase motivation, such as increasing autonomy, may be inappropriate in cultures where there is no expectation or desire to be involved in decision-making. Expectancy theory may be helpful in suggesting that employees calculate the results of their actions, and that motivation relates to how attractive the likely results will be. The extent to which employees believe they can control or influence results, and, therefore, how motivated they feel, will vary by culture and by context (Neider, 1980). While this has an application across cultures unlike some other theories, it provides no specific agenda for action.

The only universal is that motivation is intensely personal, and that managers who seek to increase staff commitment and align their goals with those of the organisation need to do so in the context of understanding what motivates each individual with whom they work. Employers are often not skilled at such understanding. Fisher and Yuan (1998) found that American and Chinese superiors had inaccurate perceptions of what was important to their employees. As Adler (1997, p. 166) asserts:

> Most motivation theories in use today were developed in the United States by Americans about Americans. Of those that were not, many have been strongly influenced by American theories ... Unfortunately many American as well as non-American managers have treated American theories as the best or only way to understand motivation. They are neither.

Leaders and managers in education are equally prone to assuming a knowledge of what will motivate. Teachers often argue that pay and conditions are key. The evidence of the surveys referenced above suggests that this cannot be assumed to be the case. Equally those who adopt a Herzbergian (1966) approach, believing that intrinsic motivation is sovereign, will be quite wrong in many cases. However, despite the lack of a satisfactory universal theory, managers can seek to influence the factors which impact on motivation at different levels, predicated on efforts to understand what each employee values. Where extrinsic factors are important, the manager can try to provide the conditions and rewards desired. In severe resource constraint, or where national systems dictate conditions, this may be difficult, but some creativity may be possible. In a Moscow school, a principal short of a mathematics teacher, shared the fourth salary out between the existing three teachers to boost their pay and motivation (Gershunsky and Pullin, 1990). Many schools and colleges can use funds achieved through enterprise activities to provide a range of rewards and incentives (Lumby and Li, 1998). It is, however, in the range of intrinsic motivation where all educational managers have the potential for action. Staff may appreciate the opportunity to agree goals, to have the freedom and support to experiment and improve their teaching, to enjoy good relations with learners, colleagues and parents, to be a member of an improving organisation. It is in these areas that managers have the potential to make an impact on motivation.

REVIEWING PERFORMANCE

The fourth myth concerns a widespread belief in the efficacy of performance review in improving teachers' performance. Certainly a vehicle to discuss issues which are important to staff and to agree goals may be needed. The widely accepted model is a performance review or appraisal system, but unfortunately the latter has an uninspiring track record. In many parts of Africa the association between appraiser and appraisee seems based on a master–servant relationship. As a consequence, Keitseng (1999) found that 70 per cent of teachers he surveyed in Botswana were either dissatisfied or unsure of the benefits of the system. Systems elsewhere may be at the other end of the spectrum, where teacher autonomy is so powerful, that principals feel unable to take action to address unsatisfactory performance, as in an example given for Norway (Moller, 2000). A further widespread concern with review systems is that where appraisees do have the potential to address unsatisfactory performance, they are unlikely to do so. As Cardno (1995, p. 119) puts it, 'the literature dealing with dilemmas in appraisal consistently shows that leaders avoid dealing with dilemmas', and that their behaviour is governed by a desire to avoid unpleasantness. If one of the defining characteristics of professionalism is self-regulation, then appraisal systems at the end of the twentieth century were not predicated on professionalism. Either staff were treated as servants and not involved in decisions about standards and performance, or appraisees avoided addressing difficult issues in order to escape a situation which might lead to strained relations and unpleasantness. The net result was that performance review did little to regulate the profession and much to demoralise it.

Internationally the response has been widespread reform of national systems (Middlewood and Cardno, 2001). Many countries have mandated systems designed to achieve the elusive combination of supporting improvement but also achieving a degree of accountability. Most select an apparently optimum prescription from a range of options to assemble evidence on teacher performance. The USA has a variety of state legislated regulations using a wide range of instruments including: 'Classroom observation reports, evaluation interviews, supervisors' ratings and rankings, checklists, annual ratings, peer or colleague evaluation, self-evaluations, narrative or anecdotal reports, work portfolios, occasionally even pupil evaluation or ratings, and even pupil test scores' (Parry, 1995, p. 22). This list is not exclusive. Additional instruments are in use elsewhere. For example, in India, teachers must keep diaries noting achievement or short-fall against agreed targets in three areas, teaching and learning, extra-curricula activities, and relations with parents and the community (Rajpu and Walia, 1998).

The intention of often elaborate systems is to elicit valid and sufficient evidence on teacher performance so that teachers receive detailed feed-back on their performance, allowing both supported further development and accountability in relation to performance. However, the rationally pre-scribed process is overlaid on entrenched culture. 'The way we do things around here' may not be in accordance with what designers of review systems planned. Consequently the results of awesome national systems may be far from what was intended. In many parts of the world, insuffi-cient attention to the capacity of schools and colleges to implement systems has led to a fair degree of chaos. In Africa, many managers are untrained and have not the time, skills or administrative back-up systems to implement the new regime (Thurlow with Ramnarain, 2001). In Russia there has been great confusion, with appraisal conducted differently by school administrations interpreting the law variously, leading to perceived inequities in results. In New Zealand, schools have been very slow to implement systems. Where systems are implemented, they are often chal-lenged by staff. In the USA teachers are increasingly challenging appraisal outcomes through litigation (Parry, 1995). In New Zealand, minority ethnic groups and women are questioning what is perceived as the male, white dominance embedded in the system. In South Africa the involvement of people from local villages in the appraisal process, though intended to involve and empower the community, has led to women particularly feeling threatened and disempowered by male dominance (Sebakwane-Mahlase, 1994). Internationally, there is considerable evidence that staff are demoralised and made anxious by systems designed to support them. The signs of success in achieving intended outcomes are rare. Timperley and Robinson report on one school that worked through their implemen-tation of the new review system to ensure that a number of requirements were met: 'The five nominated constraints were that the system made a difference to teaching and learning, it linked to professional development, it respected and supported staff, it held all levels of staff accountable for performance and was practical and efficient' (Timperley and Robinson, 1997, p. 338). The internal debate and resulting accommodation demanded new skills of all involved to think through ways of integrating the tensions within the requirements. This contrasts with Cardno's case studies of two principals in New Zealand schools who found it very dif-ficult to resolve the dilemmas of wanting to be both effective, accountable managers and caring colleagues, resulting in the phenomenon of 'vanish-ing appraisal' (Cardno, 1995, p. 126) where 'being nice' to people effec-tively negated the appraisal process.

When governments issue complex plans for new performance review systems, they present them as rational strategies to achieve improved teaching and learning. Underlying the rational surface lies a micropolitical intent, to take more power to themselves and to increase control. Having presented new policies as a rational development, governments persist in expecting a rational response. Instead they are often met with a micropolitical one, matching the hidden agenda in the policy. Thus teachers will feel disempowered and demoralised by attempts to limit their professional freedom, and will challenge. They are likely to mirror the government by presenting their micropolitical objections in a rational cloak. Thus what is essentially a power struggle is enacted in terms of a formal debate about improving teaching and learning. Performance review systems therefore founder on the twin rocks of insufficient care in implementation strategies, with staff not trained or supported sufficiently to implement policy, and micropolitical resistance. The hope to move forward lies with school and college managers recognising these impediments and attempting to resolve issues internally, to achieve an agreed system which balances support and accountability. Such activity is likely to require deep learning for all, and will be discussed in Chapter 13 on the learning organisation. If governments impose regimes which are too prescriptive or insufficiently resourced, there may be little school and college managers can do to manage a performance review system which achieves what is intended, that is, contributes to improving teaching and learning.

DEVELOPMENT – CLOSING THE CIRCLE

There is little point in establishing an effective performance review system if the needs identified by the process are not met. Thus, providing staff with opportunities to develop is the final step which closes the circle of managing performance. Tam and Cheng (1996, p. 17) describe the nature of staff development as: 'Different types of programmes and activity which aim to empower teachers and administrators to develop positive attitudes and beliefs about education and management, become more effective individuals and teams, be competent in teaching students and managing the school process, as well as helping the school adapt to its changing environment'. Such support is required because the initial training staff may receive prior to joining the profession may be of poor quality (Mutshekwane, 1995) or largely theoretical, as in Japan (Lamie, 1998). Ubiquitous change also demands ongoing development. A review system can provide a mechanism for reflecting on the attitudes, knowledge and skills that may need adjustment and for planning to achieve change through activity.

Considerable effort is often expended in securing appropriate development opportunities, but there are a number of issues which appear to be widespread internationally. First, there is a tension between the priority placed by individuals on activity which may enhance career progression and the priority placed by managers on activity which meets organisational objectives. Individuals may favour certificated programmes which provide currency for promotion. Schools that sponsor staff in such programmes may feel that little is gained by the organisation, that staff 'come back empty' (Mutshekwane, 1995, p. 157). Bahar, Peterson and Taylor (1996) place such a tension explicitly within Arab culture in Bahrain, characterising the different pressures at work arising from the existence of both an organisational rationale and a social rationale. The latter reflects a particularist approach, as discussed in the last chapter, where there is an expectation that attitudes and decisions are formed within and influenced by a social structure of friendships and family. Bahar, Peterson and Taylor's analysis discovered three types of organisation: one where the needs of the organisation are dominant, one where the wishes of friends and family dominate, and a final type where the two are held in synthesis. In the latter, the need for a rational system of identifying and prioritising training is acknowledged but accommodated within a traditional culture that is people centred. This seems to provide a model for progress in resolving the individual–organisation tension. It is reasonable for managers to feel that if resources are given to staff development, then the school should benefit in some way. It is reasonable for a member of staff to feel that if additional time and effort is put into development activities, then they should benefit personally. The tension between these two different perspectives cannot be resolved in any mechanistic way, but only by on-going discussion at both individual and organisational levels.

Secondly, there is much evidence that staff training programmes may be of insufficient quality. In Russia, in-service providers 'have themselves not yet formulated ideas and materials to match the new concepts of individualised, humanised, interdisciplinary and differentiated teaching' (Gershunsky and Pullin, 1990, p. 314). The Japanese mentoring system has a tendency to 'perpetuate the methodological status quo' (Lamie, 1998, p. 522). The palliative to unsatisfactory initial training and the response to preparing people for on-going change or meeting an identified development need is generally workshops and short courses offered by providers external to the school or college (Walker and Cheong, 1996). This is universally the favoured approach despite the fact that there are considerably more methods of developing staff. O'Sullivan, Jones and Reid (1997) provide a much wider list of options which include:

- external short courses
- in-school short courses
- external or internal one-day (or less) one-off conferences/ seminars/workshops
- contracted training/consultancy programmes

- attendance on degree/certificate/diploma or other award-bearing programmes
- job enrichment schemes
- job rotation
- private study or sabbaticals
- open learning or flexistudy
- distance learning programmes
- lectures
- coaching/on-the-job training
- special assignments
- research projects
- internal and external secondments
- industrial or commercial links/joint ventures/secondments
- self-help staff meetings ('quality circles')
  (adapted from O'Sullivan, Jones and Reid, 1997, pp. 186–7).

This full range of options will probably not be considered at appraisal interviews or as follow up, the habitual response being to look for an appropriate one-off course, despite the fact that such training frequently has minimal impact on performance (Peacock, 1993). Closing the performance review circle implies that a process is devised which best matches the needs and circumstances with the appropriate development tool and, above all, ensures not only the acquisition of new ideas, attitudes, knowledge and skills, but also their application. Peacock (1993, p. 24), writing of the training of science teachers in Namibia, outlines the stages involved:

Stage 1   Awareness/orientation/acquisition of information on new ideas/skills.
Stage 2   Organisation and 'mechanical use' of new ideas/skills.
Stage 3   Refinement/restructuring of skills and techniques.
Stage 4   Application/integration of new skills into everyday practice.

In this model, the acquisition of new ideas, knowledge or skills is merely the first step in a process of reworking what has been learned and making it one's own, of achieving a reshaping which will match what is new to the specific context of the individual and to his or her own school or college. It involves reflection, practice and on-going support. Where the process stops at Stage 1 there is 'tissue rejection' (Ingulsrud, 1996, p. 176), where what has been learnt fails to lead to any change or improvement.

There is an irony in the fact that state and organisation will exert themselves to achieve an impressive-seeming appraisal system and then fail to ensure that the foremost point of the exercise, which is to improve performance, is not achieved because the focus slips when the review is complete. Instead of seeing the review as merely the first step in a series of stages leading not only to development but also to implementation of what has been learned, the review is seen as a triumph in its own right.

Schools and colleges in many parts of the world are obliged to establish an appraisal system but perhaps the lack of follow-through is partly due to a lack of conviction that staff development is key. In their study of Hong Kong primary schools, Walker and Cheong (1996, p. 202) found that staff believed that school improvement depended on what they referred to as 'the technical solution', that is greater resources leading to more materials, lower staff/student ratios, better salaries and more clerical support. The development of staff was seen as a relatively weak force. In this conclusion they may have been entirely correct, given that one-off events, just those likely to produce very little impact, were the most frequent method of development. Staff development has the potential to transform schools, but only if the process becomes more than a bureaucratic process to successfully arrange attendance on courses. The staff must work at learning, that is, not only acquiring input of value but also working to translate that into their own practice in their specific context.

MANAGING PERFORMANCE

In the international efforts to increase accountability and improve performance much effort has focused on putting systems into place. Elaborate national review structures exist in many nations, including India, South Africa, Singapore, New Zealand and the USA (Middlewood and Cardno, 2001; Rajpu and Walia, 1998). The superficially rational process has disguised the underlying micropolitical struggle and overall has led to a diminution of teacher motivation. Different stakeholders argue for different solutions, but the evidence reviewed in this and the preceding chapter suggests that there are no universal panaceas, and that those currently in circulation reflect bounded, often western, views. Thus, suggestions that improving teachers' pay and conditions or managing their performance more tightly will improve the experience and outcomes for learners are far too simplistic. First, motivation and development are intensely personal and individual, and no formal process will succeed in improving performance if the individuality of each member of staff is not recognised as an essential element. Secondly, appraisal and review give an account of performance that is a prelude to development. The latter involves staff learning, defined as the transformation of information or activities into new or renewed emotion, thinking and skills. Managing performance is, therefore, a holistic process, part of the overall approach to managing people and predicated on learning, that is, staff at all levels constantly reviewing and changing in the light of their own goals and culture. If leaders in education have the courage to do this, rather than accepting off-the-shelf theory from the West, they will be providing a model of lifelong learning relevant to all learners and to the wider community.

7

MANAGING EXTERNAL RELATIONS

LOOKING BEYOND THE BOUNDARIES – THE EMERGENCE OF THE EXTERNAL RELATIONS PRIORITY

Management of institutional and personal relationships is a key aspect of educational leadership. Chapters 5 and 6 have examined aspects of managing the staff within the institution as the most important resource. This chapter and the next one look outward from the school or college and examine the management of relationships with people beyond the institution's boundaries – Chapter 7 is an overview of external relations management while Chapter 8 specifically focuses on parental and community links.

As part of the social and cultural infrastructure of their local and national communities schools and colleges have always managed external relations as well as the internal activities of learning and teaching. The scale and scope of that management challenge, however, has not traditionally extended far beyond the supply of essential services to the school, the administration of command and dependency systems for the provision of resources from national or local government, and the handling of relationships with parents usually in terms of essential administration or pupil behaviour. Although never entirely closed systems, the degree of openness has often been limited, for schools have been seen as serving the needs of the state or of other sponsoring organisations (for example, the churches) rather than the immediate communities they serve.

In any international perspective such partially closed systems still have a strong presence. However, during the final two decades of the twentieth century we can identify the growth of responsiveness to external environments as one of the global metatrends that characterises economic and social policy development across a wide range of political and ideological settings. At all operational scales, from national government to regional authorities to individual service providers including schools, two accountabilities have achieved ascendancy through a recognition that education is essentially a service function – first, a macro-scale accountability to society and community for the nature and standards of its outputs, and, secondly, a micro-scale accountability to the direct consumers of the service (parents and pupils) to identify and meet their individual needs and wants. To operationalise these accountabilities, some governments have instituted varying forms of market-based resource allocation models. This movement from resource allocation models based on centralised planning to models founded in the accountabilities of the market and competition began with the economic strategies of Ronald Reagan in the USA and Margaret Thatcher in the UK during the 1980s, but has been adopted or retained to varying degrees in the public sector policies of many countries, irrespective of broad political ideology. As a result, those with responsibility for leading and managing schools and colleges, therefore, must increasingly take account of the external environment in their day-to-day activities.

As a new field, external relations management in education has yet to establish a range of common conceptual ideas. As a basis for understanding and reflection, therefore, a number of key questions can be identified:

1) What is external relations management?
2) What factors promote or constrain the growth in importance of external relations management?
3) What patterns and models of external relations management can be identified globally?
4) What are the management and leadership issues for schools and colleges that arise from the growth of external relations management?

We shall consider the questions below in the context of a number of prevalent myths and partial conceptions. Amongst these myths are three that have significance in understanding the field:

Myth 1 – that external relations only concerns processes and actions outside the institution, and is not linked to the key activities of learning and teaching.
Myth 2 – that external relations management equates only to marketing.
Myth 3 – that marketing equates only to selling, and is, therefore, only of importance to schools or colleges facing recruitment issues.

THE NATURE AND GROWTH OF EXTERNAL RELATIONS MANAGEMENT

External relations management is the management of all those activities of a school or college that have an external dimension (Foskett, 1992). However, their significance lies in their relationship with the experiences of those *within* the school, in the daily round of learning and teaching. The planning and delivery of the curriculum, therefore, is the primary arena in which external relations management is effected. Hence, external relations management has two important vectors – managing the flow of external influences and their impact on internal processes, and managing internal processes to meet the requirements of the external world.

The second myth identified above, that external relations management equates only to marketing, is founded in the shorthand description of increasing accountability linked to resource management as 'marketisation'. The term is useful in that it emphasises the interactions of providers and consumers that characterise the new operational environments. However, Foskett (1999) has shown that the rise of the external focus has introduced a range of accountabilities and a variety of external relationships that must be managed, only some of which might fall within any broad definition of marketing. These are:

- transactional relations, in which the school is a buyer or seller of a service or commodity, for example, in the 'selling' of education that is seen as pupil recruitment, or in the purchase of supplies, or in bidding for funding from central government funds
- relationship-based relations, in which the school is managing its ongoing professional links in support of the education service it provides. This is the emphasis, for example, in linking with parents of current pupils, in liaising with professional services such as educational psychologists, or in relating to community groups such as churches
- public accountability relations. These involve managing the accountabilities that operate, including for example, inspection systems or financial management systems.

All these relationships require effective communications management, and it is important to recognise that managing external relations requires key communications skills both internal and external to the school. Furthermore, for any individual school within its own context the precise combination of these relationships that must be managed, and the priority that must be accorded to each, is unique. Hence a key first task in the management of external relations is the determination at local level of what the priorities must be.

The third myth, that marketing equates to 'selling' and is therefore only of importance to schools struggling to recruit pupils, is a common misconception not only in the world of education (Kotler and Fox, 1995). While selling may be an important aspect of marketing in some circumstances, the key principle underlying the term is that of managing the relationships that bring together the institution and its 'service', on the one hand, and those clients who will use or benefit from the service, on the other. Hence marketing includes a wide range of activities from market research to service design, quality assurance and communications management, and the balance between these activities will depend upon local circumstances and needs. The ideological shift we have seen in the last two decades which introduces responsiveness and accountability inevitably draws schools into activities that may be described as marketing, but does not necessarily prioritise or even include a 'selling' function.

The growth of these accountabilities has generated a very wide spectrum of change. Although representing a response to a number of internationally recognisable forces, the precise form and impact of change are determined principally by local or national political, economic and sociocultural circumstances. No two countries have adopted identical views of what marketisation means, and no two countries have started the process from the same point of departure. Even within individual states, changing political and ideological perspectives have meant that marketisation has been an evolving concept, differing in nature over time, sometimes raising the profile of market forces, sometimes constraining them or retreating from them. Marketisation, therefore, can only be defined at a high level of abstraction as being a change in the socio-economic and cultural environment of schools and colleges that increases the role of choice or market, rather than command processes in their operation or organisation, requiring them to be more responsive to their external environment.

But what are the forces that are promoting these changes? Any commitment to marketisation by governments is driven by a number of social and economic perspectives, dominant amongst which is the pursuit of national economic competitiveness in global markets. Such competitiveness is seen to require a well trained and educated labour force with high levels of personal skills and competency, for there appears to be a marked economic advantage for societies with skilled, adaptable and learning workforces in an increasingly global economy (Tuckett, 1997, p. 1). This in turn requires increased participation rates and output levels of achievement from the education/training system. Such expansion of education and training, however, needs to be undertaken alongside a commitment to limiting public expenditure to sustain overall economic competitiveness, and the pursuit of the three 'Es' of economy, efficiency and effectiveness within public sector finance models. Reagan/Thatcher economics were driven by the view that markets provide the mechanism for the most efficient use of resources. Although originating with the economic models of Adam Smith, it is in the ideas of Milton Friedman (Friedman and Friedman, 1980) and Friedrich von Hayek (1976) that modern market models are to be found. Broadly they propose that competition forces providers in the marketplace to compete for resources by enhancing the quality of provision and making more efficient use of resources, thereby raising standards and lowering unit costs.

The economic pressures towards marketisation have been strong, therefore, but are reinforced by key libertarian views of the rights of individuals, personal liberty and autonomy, and the drive towards the empowerment of the consumer. Indeed, it is in the persuasiveness of a commitment to liberty and choice that the economic imperatives are frequently dressed. The individual's right to choose in relation to all aspects of their personal lives sees power 'wrested from professional protectionism and producer capture' (O'Hear, 1991, p. 56), and makes consumer choice and the operation of 'market forces' central to the shaping of society and the economy. Such rights are enshrined in education in the United Nations 'Universal Declaration of Human Rights', which gives to parents 'the right to choose the kind of education that shall be given to their children' (Almond, 1994, p. 14). Such a libertarian perspective, however, generates two tensions in public sector service provision. First, liberty may in fact be in conflict with issues of equity, for choice-based systems do not necessarily allow the protection of individuals from the negative consequences of choice. Intervention in the market by government may be necessary to ensure equity goals are not compromised. Secondly, the outputs of markets are by definition outside the control of government, yet the requirement to ensure other policy objectives are being met requires governments to intervene and control public sector markets, and to impose the sort of market system which will produce the shape and structure of society they desire. Governments have, therefore, consistently intervened and controlled the markets they have created in public sector services such as education, and as a result such markets must be seen as 'quasi markets' (Bartlett, 1992).

Marketisation results inevitably in the movement of schools and colleges from an inward-focused, protected and closed operational environment to one which is open and focused on the external world, which is highly accountable both in political and market terms and which is increasingly competitive. Carlson (1975) has described this change as being from a domesticated to a wild environment, in which the organisation's long-term survival is dependent on its own ability to manage its activities, acquire and harness its resources, ensure the provision of a high-quality service, and interact and respond to the constituencies it serves. While acknowledging the diversity of emerging patterns of organisation and practice, on a global scale we can identify a number of elements requiring external relations management that have arisen from marketisation:

1) Decentralisation and the delegation of management responsibility. The increasing autonomy of schools and colleges has arisen from the delegation of responsibility for resource management. Individual heads or governing bodies may be expected to take responsibility for some or all aspects of staff recruitment, retention and development, financial management, curriculum organisation, and the identification and achievement of output targets in relation to the institution's management (Bullock and Thomas, 1997).

2) Increased accountability. With delegation of responsibility comes accountability (Scott, 1999), the requirement to demonstrate not just

probity and honesty but the achievement of expected performance standards for the institution. This may be in terms of political accountability, in that audit or inspection by government may examine institutional performance, and/or in terms of market accountability, in that information provided to the community and the public may be used as the basis of students' or parents' choice of institution.

3) Competition for resources. Resource allocation may be driven through the mechanisms of accountability. This may be through linking resources to planning processes that demonstrate the pursuit of externally defined aims and strategies, or to market processes and consumer choice through the connection of resources to pupil numbers.

4) Managing the boundaries. Delegation, accountability and competition all require the school or college to seek to interact with the environment beyond the school gates. Developing responsiveness to political and community stakeholders and implanting the mechanism for sensing and responding to the environment and, where possible influencing and shaping it, are important components of external relations management.

The interaction of the economic and the libertarian arguments with existing politico-cultural environments has resulted in the generation of the full spectrum of responses that we can observe internationally. As a result, the management of external relations is quite variable in its significance within education, and we shall examine some of the patterns in the section that follows.

CONTEXT AND PRACTICE IN EXTERNAL RELATIONS MANAGEMENT

Analysis of markets in education demonstrates their variability in form and nature. Each of the four components of a marketised system outlined above may be present or absent, or developed to differing degrees in each particular setting. While the international pressures towards marketisation may be identifiable, their translation into operational outcomes is filtered by a complex of social, economic, historical, cultural and ideological perspectives at the national scale. Bowe, Ball with Gold (1992) and Woods, Bagley and Glatter (1998) stress, too, how national market systems are themselves operationalised at local level in highly varied ways. The idea of the 'micro market' is important, therefore, with Foskett and Hemsley-Brown (2001, p. 17) indicating that 'markets are dynamic and individual, defined as much by geography and history as by the over-riding principles of the economics of supply and demand'. Gorard (1997), also stresses that markets change over time, in response to the feedback effects of the market forces themselves, and also as governments, local and national, modify the operational structures of the quasi-markets in response to changing national priorities and perspectives.

In some countries there has existed a long tradition of significant community engagement with schools, and the idea of partnership with and responsiveness to a wide range of external stakeholders is well established, as in the USA or Denmark (OECD, 1997). This may or may not be linked to the main resource allocation system that is applied. In others the traditional perspective has been one in which schools and colleges are largely closed systems. In Spain and Sweden, for example, the introduction of enhanced responsiveness has led to only a limited extension of competition, particularly between state and private schools (Agudo, 1995; Van Zanten, 1995). In Germany parental choice has been adopted in only one of the Länder, while in France Ambler (1994) reports that some degree of parental choice has been adopted for almost half the schools. In contrast, in some parts of the USA (notably Chicago, California and Kentucky) and Israel there has been encouragement for experimentation with less constrained market forms, including the development of 'magnet schools' with a specialised focus in their provision. More radically, in the UK, Australia and New Zealand the establishment of parental choice as the critical factor in determining resource allocation has pushed schools both towards increased responsiveness and quite aggressive competitiveness in school and college markets (for example, Waslander and Thrupp, 1997). Despite these global trends, however, there are still many countries where such developments have had little or no impact, and a strong centrally controlled system remains. Japan retains such a system which is so embedded in the national culture that the prospects of change are small (Thrupp, 1999), and even in countries fundamentally restructuring their educational system, such as Namibia (Auala, 1998), adoption of a market system has not necessarily been prioritised.

These contrasts will be examined through three case studies of external relations management. The case of Tanzania, in East Africa, illustrates a country where delegation is just beginning and where the notion of the market is only little developed, even though the pressures to manage external relations by schools are growing. The second example, Israel, has adopted the canons of parental choice in some localities but not others and so presents a 'mixed economy' from the perspective of marketisation and the challenges for external relations management. The third case study, New Zealand, represents strong adoption of the markets experiment, and illustrates the external relations demands of such an environment and the impacts on the system of a strong emphasis on choice and markets.

Tanzania's education system changed radically from a traditional colonial system through nationalisation of the school system in 1969 to provide a single centralised operational model with an explicit aim of replacing a European/Christian cultural model with an African cultural model. Economic problems and the inflexibility of the system (Babyegyega, 2000), however, resulted in difficulties within the system during the late 1980s, and the gross pupil enrolment rate fell from 98 per cent in 1981 to 56 per cent in 1993. Following a presidential Commission on Education and a UNESCO report on the Tanzanian education system, a National Task Force on Education (in 1993) recommended the implementation of a decentralised system by a gradual process through to the year 2000. The model of decentralisation adopted retains policy-making, curriculum and overall strategic planning and monitoring with central government, but delegates to secondary schools some 90 per cent of their budget. Primary school budgets and staff management remain the responsibility of District Education Authorities. The key aim of the model is to move schools to being more responsive to their local communities. Babyegyega (2000, p. 5) describes this process as one in which:

> District authorities are supposed to collaborate with school committees to build confidence in school services by raising enrolment and completion rates of students. Various operational strategies to improve attendance and performance are stipulated ... One of the strategies is to increase and guarantee instructional hours, through supervision and curriculum reform, and making school committees and headteachers watchdogs in regulating teachers' behaviour, especially the problem of absenteeism ... Another strategy is the improvement of the school learning environment by involving parents and the community in planning for the development of the school.

To support the decentralisation process government has established a project called the Community Education Fund (CEF). This requires participating schools to produce a three-year development plan in conjunction with the local community. Government matches funding raised by the community, and the project involves the school committee and the headteacher working with parents and village councils to develop the plan, make financial contributions, and send their children to school.

Of the four components of a marketised system outlined earlier, all are present to some degree. Delegation and self-management are central elements of the system, bringing with them accountability and an increasing requirement for external relations management. It is only in the arena of competition and choice where the market has not been developed to the point of providing parents with choices between schools. Rather, the pressure is to push parents and communities to choose schooling and participation in education as the preferred option for their children, with an emphasis on relationship-building in the community. Both the generic decentralisation plan and the CEF make considerable demands on headteachers in terms of external relations management responsibilities. The recruitment and in-service training of teachers falls within their remit, as does recruitment of pupils, together with fund-raising from local donors for buildings and resources. Babyegyega (2000) suggests that considerable variability in patterns of activity are emerging, and that the government is using a process of incremental decentralisation in which responsibility is delegated as schools show their readiness culturally and managerially to take on the management challenges. Critical within this is the capacity for effective external relations management, and this represents a priority for training.

In Israel a range of market forms exists (Goldring 1991; 1997), from strongly centralised resource allocation models with very limited parental choice in much of the country to the promotion of parental choice and a more strongly 'marketised' system in Tel Aviv and, to a lesser degree, in Jerusalem. Decentralisation and school autonomy have been promoted by the Ministry of Education since the early 1980s, with a recognition that pluralism in provision is both inevitable and desirable. Goldring (1997, p. 88) suggests that 'parental choice is being promoted to move the highly centralised system away from uniformity towards more local school autonomy in an attempt to meet the diverse needs of parents and students'.

Despite this pressure the strength of the existing public school system means that choice is not widespread, but Shapira, Hayman and Shavit (1996) identify four models of school choice that have arisen within Israel:

- autonomous neighbourhood schools, which define their own character, but which serve the local community needs
- autonomous selective schools of choice, similar to US 'magnet schools' in which a specialism (e.g. music) is the basis of choosing pupils who may enrol
- autonomous non-selective schools of choice, which focus on particular ideologies e.g. Judaism or social participation as their basis for entrance
- non-autonomous, non-selective schools, where there is explicit parental choice between schools across a wide district, such as amongst the 15 high schools in Tel Aviv.

Shapira, Hayman and Shavit (1996) suggest that there is evidence that the autonomous schools of choice have led to an improved quality of education and enhanced parental satisfaction where such schools have been created. In the school districts where non-autonomous non-selective schools of choice have been established, a number of distinctive key features have emerged. In Tel Aviv the local education authority instituted market-based reforms in the city's education system in 1992, with the explicit aim of raising the standard of student achievement by creating choice for students and parents, but with a sub-theme of reducing the contrasts in school quality between schools in the high socio-economic status (ses) north of the city and the low ses south. Schools were given enhanced autonomy in terms of decision-making, curriculum and approaches to learning and teaching, while parents were enabled to identify up to five preferences for high schools for their children, with the education authority providing a central information centre to facilitate choice and paying for transport to school for all children.

Goldring (1997) and Oplatka (2002) have described the impact of marketisation in the Tel Aviv education district. They believe there is as yet little evidence in relation to overall pupil achievement, but the raised profile in the schools of communication, school image development and external relations management has emerged quite clearly. The principal's role has moved away from the traditional one of 'leading professional' towards a new emphasis on entrepreneurial skills and resource management in an environment dominated by competition, instability and uncertainty. Goldring (1997) has examined the impact of choice on socio-economic segregation in Tel Aviv schools and the changing nature of parental engagement with the schools. She shows how there is some evidence of a 'creaming effect' in which the more attractive schools emphasise their advantages and attract increasing numbers of better motivated children. Their oversubscription means that such schools rely strongly on low-level promotion through word of mouth, in contrast to the less attractive schools in southern Tel Aviv which are undersubscribed and are resorting to active promotional campaigns. The external relations priorities for the northern schools, therefore, lie with relationship management rather than transactional relationships, while the southern schools have become more focused on 'selling' and recruitment processes. In relation to engagement with the schools, Goldring shows an interesting contrast to patterns observed in the UK and New Zealand, for it is parents of low socio-economic status who are both more active in the choice process in seeking schools further away from home, and also more engaging with the schools once their child is enrolled.

In New Zealand (Cardno, 1998; Lauder and Hughes, 1999; Thrupp, 1999; Waslander and Thrupp, 1997) parental choice has been placed at the heart of the secondary school system. Prior to 1987 New Zealand operated a highly centralised education system, as with other public sector services. In the wake of 'new right' thinking in the UK and the USA, however, the government made a large-scale commitment to marketisation of the public sector, to the extent where 'the new social experiment of creating a market society gave the nation the soubriquet of the New Right laboratory of the world' (Lauder and Hughes, 1999, p. 36). Following a substantial period of political debate, the 1991 Education Amendment Act put in place a market system for schools with the abolition of 'school zones' (catchments) and the promotion of enrolment schemes by which oversubscribed schools can select pupils for admission.

The New Zealand education system has been regarded by many writers as a 'natural experiment' (Lauder and Hughes, 1999, p. 41) in school markets, and a number of substantial research projects have examined the evidence of impact, for example the Smithfield Project (Thrupp, 1999) and the Wellington Schools Project (Lauder and Hughes, 1999). This analysis shows a number of emerging findings:

1) 'Circuits of schooling' (Gewirtz, Ball and Bowe, 1995) have developed. The school market has become segmented along socio-economic, class-based lines, with differentiation between groups of schools with distinctive ethos and approach which recruit predominantly from clearly distinguishable sectors of the community.
2) All schools have adjusted to the challenge of the market by adopting internal organisational systems and external relations strategies to seek to meet parental choice priorities. However, the balance between transactional and relationship-based relations in each school's prioritisation varies considerably between schools.
3) The management challenge of responding to the market is much greater for disadvantaged schools. Disadvantaged schools must work much harder than advantaged schools on innovating the curriculum, establishing strongly supportive pastoral and guidance systems and proactively engaging with the outside world in terms of marketing and external relations management. As Thrupp (1999, p. 102) suggests, 'by comparison [with working-class schools] organising and managing the middle class schools was relatively straightforward because they were cushioned by the social characteristics of their students'.
4) Generally, the effect of school choice is to emphasise the polarisation of schools according to socio-economic status. Schools with low achievement, usually working class or with high Maori or Pacific Island pupil numbers, experience 'middle class white flight and in some cases brown flight as relatively advantaged students exit their local working class schools' (Lauder and Hughes, 1999, p. 132), leading to a downward spiral of achievement. The external relations management challenge here is a strong dimension of the school, for the instability of the external environment makes constant vigilance to change and high levels of responsiveness to that change essential for the school's survival.

The general issues that emerge from these three contrasting case studies will be considered below.

EXTERNAL RELATIONS MANAGEMENT – THE COMMON THEMES

The rise of the importance of external relations management goes hand in hand with marketisation, as engaging with the external environment is a key feature of the market place. The case studies presented here have demonstrated both the common pressures towards enhancing school's responsiveness to their external environment, but also the substantial contrasts that exist in the responses that can be observed. The common themes, though, enable us to identify a number of emerging issues and implications for school managers and for policy-makers in education.

First we must recognise the challenge to values that the pressures towards responsiveness and external relations management can engender. Although we have shown how external relations (ER) management has become prioritised in a range of market settings, the strong perceived link between ER and marketing can create conflict between the aims and values of policy-makers and those of professional educators, whether managers or teachers. Educators typically are from a personal orientation that emphasises equity, individual need and a focus on personal development, with personal autonomy and professional collaboration as an important aspect of their work. Gewirtz, Ball and Bowe (1995) demonstrate how marketisation challenges these 'comprehensive education' values and begins to replace them with a suite of values more based on competition, output measurements, external attention and reduced professional collaboration. Marketisation, therefore, demands a process of cultural readjustment within schools, which provides a significant management challenge. Maguire, Ball and Macrae (2001) have considered these changes in the context of a single school within the UK, Northwark Park, and have identified the slow but developing acquisition of market-driven values. Here a process of 'internal marketing' has moved both senior staff and class teachers to be more aware of the need for responsiveness and of issues such as image and perceptions.

Secondly, the emergence of the 'external dimension' to a range of internal processes, with an emphasis on personal and institutional accountability diversifies, intensifies and expands workload demands on staff. Decentralisation, responsiveness and the increase in autonomy for individual schools brings with it an increased level of accountability, which in turn demands the shouldering of responsibility both for successes and failures by senior managers and by teachers. The underlying premise is that it is schools that make the difference to pupil performance, and that pupil achievement or failure is therefore the result of the way the school or college operates to match environmental demands with internal processes. Policy-makers and government can in this way, distance themselves from negative achievements by schools. As Thrupp (1999, p. 13) suggests, the 'politics of blame' is built on the view that 'schools which lose . . . are seen as those whose teachers and principals have not been able to improve enough to boost their reputation and hence the size of their intakes'.

This changing nature of the workload has been identified by the New Zealand studies, for example, where, particularly in the less favoured schools, staff morale was seen to have declined in response to increased workloads and public perception and status. This creates staff development and motivation and morale issues for senior managers that spread the impact of ER management into the arena of human resource management.

Thirdly, an important component of an increasingly external focus of schools is the changing role of management, and hence of the headteachers and principals who lead schools. In highly centralised systems the role of headteacher is one of intermediary between external authority and the classroom processes, often with little autonomy for decisions other than minor operational processes, and a role which is that of passive implementer. Simkins et al. (1998), for example, show that headteachers of government schools in Pakistan 'feel acutely powerless in general terms' (Simkins et al., 1998, p. 144) and have little proactive engagement with the external environment beyond meeting with parents over control and disciplinary issues. Where devolution of responsibility is occurring the external roles of headteachers become more demanding. In Tanzania headteachers of secondary schools in the Community Education Fund Project are given responsibility for leading the local community in developing the school plan, in collecting fees and donations and in monitoring, reporting and accounting for pupil enrolment, attendance and performance. A key priority within the Tanzanian government agenda for schools, therefore, is the identification and training of teachers able to take on the new role of headteacher in a devolved system.

These changing demands of headship have been described in the context of British schools by Clarke and Newman (1992) as 'new managerialism'. This is characterised as emphasising individual performance and management based on the culture of the market, of competition and of business and an external focus rather than an inward-looking school focus. Gewirtz, Ball and Bowe (1995) describe how headteachers in their study have enhanced the attention they give to the external relations implications of all decisions, and how their activities are increasingly focused on scanning and monitoring the external environment rather than the world within the school. Heads are expected to have entrepreneurial skills and to be 'bilingual', speaking the languages of education and of business. Maguire, Ball and Macrae (2001) identify how the language of the marketplace is being incorporated into the language of school management. The evidence from those national settings where marketisation has proceeded most rapidly is that the practical skills of external relations management have been acquired quite quickly where there is a threat to the school's future well-being. In Israel the principals of the southern Tel Aviv schools acquired considerable expertise in promotional activities, as did the headteachers of the lower ses schools in Wellington, New Zealand. The heads and principals in the schools that were privileged by market processes, however, directed most of their external relations management skills towards the principles of relationship marketing (Gronroos, 1997), with its emphasis on partnership, and word of mouth as the main recruitment strategy.

Finally, we must stress the issue that has emerged in the two previous chapters on working with people, that there is a strong need to employ culturally relevant approaches to the development of external relations that reflect the context of people both personally and within society. A key criticism of marketisation, for example, has been that it has been imposed with no consideration of the cultural setting and the cultural impact it may have. The case studies considered here show that cultural readjustment does occur, both for managers and for governments who may modify their expectations from the dogmatic to the pragmatic over time.

EXTERNAL RELATIONS MANAGEMENT – AN AGENDA FOR DEVELOPMENT?

The growth of external relations in the context of marketisation of schools and colleges has been a significant reorientation in management in the last two decades (Glatter, 1989; Lumby and Foskett, 1999). Whether in the context of highly competitive markets or in arenas of delegated responsibility and the establishment of 'self-managing schools', the need to interact with the world beyond the school gate has increased. Yet there are many important questions to be addressed in examining the present and future nature of external relations management. First, how far is the prioritisation of responsiveness a unidirectional or permanent change to educational management and how far it is simply an innovation in the system which will pass through a cycle of development and adjustment? Some national administrations (for example, Japan) may not move far along this pathway, if at all, where cultural or ideological restraints provide strong forces to resist such change. Furthermore, evidence from those countries which have adopted the most radical marketisation (for example, UK and New Zealand) is that there is some rebound in the policy implementation which sees some of the harshest effects countered by changing legislation – for example, in the shift from parental choice to parental preference systems in the UK. However, the forces of globalisation are strong and are premised very significantly on the notion of consumerism, and with this comes the increasing perception of education and training as simply a consumer good. Such a view fundamentally changes the relationship between schools and their clients, so that responsiveness, environmental scanning, the management of communication, and close attention to the development of relationships, whether transactional, collaborative or partnerships, become key elements of the management challenge. Secondly, how far and in what ways have the growth of ER management and the emphasis on entrepreneurial skills changed the nature of headship and leadership in schools? Is this a cultural stepwise change that will see the characterisation of headship and the preparation (and training) that it requires change? What will be the impact of such cultural change on the values accorded to education in society, and on the status accorded to educational activities and educators?

Finally, how far must we seek conceptualisations of external relations management and marketing that are rooted in the values and processes of education rather than borrowing concepts from the discourse of business? If we view the marketisation 'experiment' as having an implementational cycle, however, in keeping with most concepts and products (for example, Rogers, 1983), then the stage of maturity which may be close to attainment in some countries may be one in which the canons of relationship marketing are what underpins school external relations management (Stokes, 1999). If this is so, then there is an increasing convergence between the values of education and the values of external relations/marketing management with a concern for relationships and for the welfare and ongoing development of the individual. In such circumstances schools and colleges discover that they have extensive experience of developing these relationships so that 'even while claiming an innocence of marketing or more vehemently an antipathy towards it [they] are actually rather good at it' (O'Sullivan and O'Sullivan, 1995, p. 32).

8

MANAGING PARENTAL AND COMMUNITY LINKS

PARENTS, THE COMMUNITY AND EXTERNAL RELATIONS

In Chapter 7 we examined the broad range of external relationships that schools and colleges may need to manage. The extent to which these relationships are central to the leadership of the institution is dependent on a wide range of cultural, ideological and operational factors, but it is clear that few closed systems (what Sayer [1989] terms the 'monastic tradition') remain at a global scale. Here we shall explore a range of approaches to managing relationships with the local community, with a particular focus on links with parents. Parents represent a key community group with whom schools maintain a relationship, whether close or distant, and in most systems are identified as the principal external relationship that a school or college must manage. Research on school effectiveness strongly identifies that pupil achievement is directly related to the degree of parental engagement (Ho and Willms, 1996), although the processes that produce this outcome are clearly complex. How far, for example, this represents the true benefits of school–parent partnership or simply shows that it is schools serving catchments of high socio-economic status (ses), and hence generally higher parental engagement, that perform better, is not entirely clear. Nevertheless, across most national education systems there is a common commitment to the rhetoric of school–parent partnership.

It is also important to recognise the centrality of parental rights and responsibilities in the global trend towards decentralisation (see Chapter 10). The ideological commitment to parents shaping education provision, as both consumers and community representatives, is strong within decentralisation. The motivation for this may be complex and varied, of course. It may represent a commitment to the role of parents as partners, the adoption of a consumerist view, or an attempt to wrest power from professional educators. The most radical shifts in power towards parents have occurred in those systems in which parental choice dominates, for example in Australia, New Zealand, England and Wales and in some localities in the USA (for example, Kentucky and Chicago). Elsewhere the enhancement of parental roles has been less radical in an absolute sense, although still perhaps radical in the context of relatively conservative cultural settings. In Indonesia, for example, the world's largest Islamic state, the decentralising reforms of Law 2/1989 sought to enable some degree of parental participation in schools. In Latin America, similarly, reform has a strong component of such parental empowerment. Stromqvist (1986) shows how the engagement of parents in schools was a strong motivator to educational reform in Peru, and the empowerment of parents to make informed school choices and to exercise them through a modified voucher system has been a key feature of reform in Chile (Rodriguez, 1994). Similarly, recent change in Argentina (Rhoten, 2000) has enhanced parental engagement in school management in some provinces.

The trend towards promoting parental engagement with schools is strong, therefore, yet it is premised on a number of assumptions that may be mythic in character, and hence misleading in implementing new management strategies:

Myth 1 – parents are committed to engaging with schools in the pursuit of shared goals for their children.

Myth 2 – parents adopt a consumerist view in their relationship with education providers.

Myth 3 – schools have substantial expertise and experience in managing their links with parents.

Myth 4 – parental engagement is a valued element in the management of schools and colleges.

We shall examine these myths through considering a number of key questions about school–parent relationships:

• What form do school–parent relationships take?
• What factors influence the nature of school–parent relationships?
• How do these factors influence the management of parental links in different cultural settings?

SCHOOL–PARENT RELATIONSHIPS

The Organisation for Economic Cooperation and Development (OECD, 1997) has examined school–parent relationships in nine developed countries, and identified the common theme of 'partnership' within the explicit discourse of policy and management within each of the systems they examined. The nature of that partnership, though, varies significantly between countries, as reflected in the rights and responsibilities that schools, teachers, parents and pupils have that are enshrined in policy and/or legislation. Middlewood (1999, p. 114) has described the range of these relationships – 'at one possible extreme is the notion of the parent as "co-educator"; at the other is that of the parent as "consumer"'.

Both extremes may operate in a range of formats, though, and in many countries there is a clear mixture and balance between the two perspectives. The notion of 'co-educator', for example, may be one in which the balance may be strongly in favour of the school with parental involvement seen as contributing in only a small way to the central role of the school in educating the child. Alternatively it may be one in which parental expertise is seen as equivalent and complementary to that of the school (Wolfendale, 1996), with the child's experience and progress planned by teachers and parents, and each contributing those elements that they are best suited to provide. Within a 'consumer' perspective the relationship between parent and school will vary significantly according to the reality of choice. Where popular schools experience excessive demand for places it is clear that schools will be able to choose parents rather than parents choosing schools. It is clear, therefore, that the nature of parent–school relationships is highly context specific, and the management strategies that need to be adopted will depend on a clear understanding of the local environment.

CONTEXTUAL DIMENSIONS OF SCHOOL–PARENT RELATIONS

Within the OECD study a range of factors influencing the nature of school–parent relationships was identified. While emerging in the context of developed countries, these are important in understanding patterns outside this context. We shall examine each of these factors below.

The democratic rights/responsibilities of parents

In states where the engagement of parents with school is seen as a democratic responsibility as well as a right of parenthood, encouraging the participation of the community may be comparatively straightforward. In Denmark and Sweden, for example, participation by parents in school and community is widespread across a range of socio-economic groups, in contrast to many other western European countries where it is more commonly associated with middle-class parents. Promoting participation as a community responsibility has not been a successful movement in most countries, however.

Statutory responsibilities for parental consultation/ participation in relation to individual children

Consultation with parents in relation to their own children is a statutory requirement in many countries, but there have been only limited attempts to impose such consultation duties upon parents – the development of home–school contracts in England and Wales in the late 1990s is one of the few examples, and this has met with only limited success, principally in those schools where parental engagement was not a significant problem in any case. While the UN Declaration of Human Rights (Almond, 1994) gives parents the right to be consulted and to make choices in relation to their child's education, it is not clear that obligation on parents will provide benefits rather than major challenges for enforcement.

The statutory responsibilities for schools to include parents in management processes

Requiring schools to involve parents in aspects of the formal management of the school is relatively common in OECD countries, where school councils or governing bodies may reserve places for parental representatives. This pattern is common, too, in those countries which were under colonial influence in the early establishment of their education systems, for example in much of sub-Saharan Africa, and is emerging as a common theme where decentralisation trends can be identified. Deem (1994) describes how the participation of lay people in the management of schools has expanded considerably in many countries with a clearer recognition of the importance of their role and a clarification of the ways in which they can and should contribute to the school. The importance of parental voice has been promoted with legislation in, *inter alia*, the Netherlands, Spain, USA, Canada, the UK, Australia and New Zealand, which ensures that strategic planning and policy and management decisions reflect parental perspectives. Elsewhere, obligations to establish and consult with formal organisations (for example, Parental Advisory Committees in Canada, or the National Parents Council in Ireland [Middlewood, 1999]) provide a less formalised mode of engaging parents that enables wider groups to be consulted. While such requirements certainly engage parents, it is only a minority who are involved in a direct way, and there is little evidence that such processes ensure the involvement of most parents or that it is the majority voice that is heard in policy and management. Indeed, Brown (1997) is critical of the increasing voice given to those with the cultural capital to ensure their own participation and influence while those without such attributes may not only fail to engage but may be increasingly distanced from the school by the promotion of middle-class values and organisation. This reflects strongly the concern raised by Deem (1994) that participation in school management by lay individuals may be driven in part by altruistic notions of community service but may also be motivated by the desire to influence and shape policy and practice in pursuit of personal or ideological goals.

Verhoeven and Van Heddegem (1999) identify some of these generic issues of parental involvement in school management in the context of the development of Local School Councils (LSCs) and Participation Councils in schools in Flanders in Belgium following legislation in 1988 and 1991, and also draw on evidence from studies in the UK and the USA. These suggest that parental participation in school management has four important characteristics which impact upon its effectiveness and value:

1) Parents involved in such participation tend to have a perspective which is strongly influenced by the experiences that their own child or children have had in school – it is an understanding based on 'particular' rather than 'generalisable' knowledge. They also have only partial professional knowledge, in comparison to the educational professionals on such bodies, and that knowledge is often focused in specific fields such as pupil behaviour or finance which are transferable from contexts outside the school. Knowledge about educational and, specifically, learning and teaching issues is often quite limited, and participation is, therefore, constrained in both the range and depth of their contribution. This is compounded by the limited preparation available for those taking on such roles, for in few settings is there substantial training available.

2) Parents are rarely representative of the whole diversity of the parent body, and are dominated by those with significant cultural capital and with a narrow range of attitudes and values. The majority of representatives are male (61 per cent in the case of the Flanders study), middle-class and middle-aged, with at least high-school and frequently university-level education. Promoting the needs and aspirations of the whole school community may not be supported in such circumstances.

3) Relationships between parents and education professionals are strongly influenced by a range of power relations to do with social status, professional knowledge and attitudes to the view of parents as partners or customers in education. The power in most circumstances rests with the 'insiders' who can manage information flow and decision-making processes more effectively.

4) Parent participation does not always work well with the professionals within such bodies having considerably more influence in shaping policy and decision-making than do the lay members. This in part reflects the first three issues identified above, but means that '[f]rom a structural point of view, the means to participate exist but are limited. Culturally the knowledge, skills and attitudes needed for real participation are missing' (Verhoeven and Van Heddegem, 1999, p. 427).

Although there are relatively few studies of lay participation in school management outside the OECD, there is some evidence that the patterns described above are replicated. Maha (1997), for example, has examined the nature of community participation in school administration in Papua New Guinea, and the patterns that emerge match the model reported by Verhoeven and Van Heddegem. Maha's study suggests that lay members are predominantly male, middle-class and well educated (at least to high-school leaver level), and that participation by lay members is strongly skewed to matters of discipline and finance. He suggests, therefore, that while such participation has considerable potential for allowing community influence on educational policy and practice, in reality there are many structural constraints to this being achieved.

The professional status and autonomy of teachers

The relationship between schools, teachers and parents is in part a product of historical and cultural perspectives on the status and role of teachers. The OECD report suggests that the relationship between teachers and parents, for example, in Germany, France and Japan, is traditionally one in which the professional autonomy and authority of the teacher is not open to challenge by parents. Engaging parents as partners requires substantial cultural change both within schools and within the community at large, therefore. Beyond the OECD similar patterns are observed, particularly in more conservative cultural settings – we shall consider the case of Pakistan in more detail below, where the traditional view that schools should be left to manage learning and teaching is still strongly held across much of the sociocultural spectrum.

The ideologies and values of key education partners such as faith-based organisations

While education in many developed countries has developed as a strongly secular sector of society, in others the role of the church in shaping policy and values in schools is still strong. The tradition of the churches in perceiving education as enabling children to escape the challenges of their natural sociocultural setting has frequently promoted an isolationist view of school–home relations, with parental involvement discouraged. Even where the educational benefits of challenging this perspective are now recognised, for example in Ireland, there is a significant cultural challenge in changing long-standing parental attitudes to relationships with school.

The nature of family organisation and the role of each parent

Working with families requires a careful understanding of the social processes within families. While it is recognised, for example, that it is most frequently the mother who is involved in day-to-day relationships with the child and the school (OECD, 1997) the role of each parent in decision-making about school may be more complex. In Muslim communities within western European countries, for example, the role of the father may be very significant in decision-making even where there is little school–father contact. Similarly, research into school choice in England and Wales emphasises how decision-taking is a shared function of parents and children, as opposed to decision-making (that is, the accumulation of ideas and knowledge prior to taking a decision) which is very frequently the responsibility of the mother (West, 1992). In polygamous societies, for example in the Muslim communities within West African countries such as The Gambia, understanding the complex relationships within family groupings is particularly important in seeking to establish effective school–home and school–community relations.

MANAGING IN CONTEXT – SCHOOL–PARENT RELATIONS IN PRACTICE

The rest of this chapter is committed to three case studies that illustrate a range of contrasting settings for school–community and school–parent relations. The first two studies, of Uganda and Pakistan, demonstrate how such relations are managed in a community-based, collective setting (Uganda), and a strongly centralised organisational environment (Pakistan). The third considers school–parent relations from a different perspective, with an examination of the role of schools in promoting community cohesion and development in Macedonia in southern Europe.

Parents, schools and community in sub-Saharan Africa – the collective–market tension

Within the education systems of many of the less developed nations of sub-Saharan Africa, the increasing devolution of responsibility for management down to school level is built in part on the notion of the importance of connecting schools and communities. Where participation rates are comparatively low and fluctuate significantly in response to economic, social and environmental conditions, enhancing attendance at school is dependent upon the school becoming the heart of the community with substantial associated prestige and value. The importance of this 'cultural realism' view of school and community parallels the economic reality that where resources are extremely limited it must be from the local community that the school must draw any significant resources it can use. Fees charged to parents for school attendance by children are a direct element of this. Much more significant, though, are the material resources that come from the active engagement of the community in projects such as school-building, and their participation in the management and development of the school through bodies such as school councils and governing bodies.

Community involvement in the direct management of schools is strong in many of the countries of east Africa, including Uganda (Nkata and Thody, 1996), Tanzania (Babyegyega, 2000) and Zimbabwe (Bullock and Thomas, 1997). This stands in stark contrast to the position prior to independence and to some extent beyond, when community involvement was positively discouraged by the colonial governments. The shift from colonial elitism to community engagement has been a dominant feature of the school systems of the region in the last 30 years.

In Uganda the centralisation of authority with government, in strong partnership with both the Church of Uganda and the Catholic Church, 'accepted the pattern of non-community involvement [through] government-mission partnerships' (Nkata and Thody, 1996, p. 71), with the considerable dominance of the churches in that partnership. While community participation was an important element in the rhetorical aims of the system, particularly through the mission-based element with the churches providing funding for scholarships and community involvement, in reality there developed a strong schism between school and community. Government was expected to provide a sophisticated education system free of charge, yet the limited resource base led to a rapid deterioration in school quality which in turn led to significant rejection of the school system by many communities, and falling participation rates (Gonahasa, 1991). Nkata and Thody (1996, p. 71) comment that 'the state encouraged religions to provide education in order to save money, while Roman Catholics, Protestants and Islamic adherents used education to win neophytes. Community involvement was reinforced by the religious educationalists choosing to train tribal leaders and their children first, thus enhancing their authority over the community'.

From 1986 onwards, however, political change at national level has seen the promotion of the centrality of the community in policy and practice in all elements of social and economic life in Uganda through the leadership of the National Resistance Movement. At school level this has been most clearly seen through the role of parent–teacher associations (PTAs) which have become fundamental to the management of schools with a role that 'enables community influence to be strongly mediated outside of the formal governmental system' (Nkata and Thody, 1996, p. 68). Their authority comes in part from their role in promoting school–parent links, but principally through their role as fund raising organisations, where they contribute up to 70 per cent of the running costs of schools. Through this role the influence and authority of the PTAs has risen such that they are more significant in school management than the formally constituted school management committees that act as boards of governors. The role of the school management committees is to have responsibility for school policy, school financial management, staffing, discipline (staff and pupil) and for school buildings, facilities and learning and teaching resources, and they are charged with responsibility for raising additional funds through the PTA. However, the significance of the additional funding that the schools need from the PTA in effect delegates political power to the PTA.

For headteachers within schools in Uganda the management of relations with the community through the PTA is a key element in developing strategic objectives and in acquiring resources. This can provide a dilemma in the tension between the educational objectives of equity and the practical needs of generating resources, for as Bullock and Thomas (1997, p. 69) indicate, 'policy on finance depends so much on the basic task of finding resources [which] . . . makes equity a lower order priority, as those with resources are more likely to secure the benefits of the system'. This is particularly marked in the priority that is placed on the construction of school buildings, which, for most communities within the Ugandan system, is the primary educational objective. The importance of a strong 'collective' commitment through local community leaders, community and parent groups and individual parents is clear, for the role of direct labour in construction and of donation in relation to building materials is very important. Although written in the context of Zimbabwe, Bullock and Thomas (1997, p. 70) make clear this tension for headteachers: 'Community involvement in the construction of schools is suggestive of a movement towards some notion of the "collective". Moving on to families a requirement to meet some of the costs of schooling indicates an appeal to "market" principles.'

This is a key consideration in relation to the second element of school–parent relations, which is that associated with the needs of individual children and the desire to work in partnership with parents to achieve learning goals. Here there is a marked distinction between the primary and secondary education systems in Uganda. In the primary system the priority for schools is increasing participation, and headteachers and school management committees prioritise activities that will encourage parents to send their children to school and perceive it as a positive contribution to the social, cultural and economic life of their community. At secondary level, however, there is still a shortage of places in relation to demand as this has not been the principal priority of government, and hence the relationship with parents is much more a marketing-based relationship, which 'makes parents likely to adapt to school demands rather than force schools to adapt to their demands' (Nkata and Thody, 1996, p. 73). This emphasises how the balance between co-operative/collaborative and market perspectives in school–parent relations is strongly influenced not just by the ideological tenets of the education system, but also by the precise balance of power between school and community, which may in turn be no more than a reflection of where the authority that comes from the possession of resources resides.

School–parent relations in Pakistan – managing links in a centralised system

In education systems where centralisation is still the predominant strategy (see Chapter 10), the relationship that schools maintain with parents and the community is less driven by issues of resource acquisition or meeting the demands of the marketplace. More significant is the relationship that surrounds the care and development of the individual child, and the nature of that relationship will be strongly driven by cultural norms in relation to the role of parents in the school.

Simkins et al. (1998) and Memon et al. (2000) illustrate this from a study of headteachers' roles in Pakistan, which focused on a range of issues as viewed by heads of government – controlled schools and heads of non-government (that is, independent) schools. Three aspects of school–community relations are identified as significant in understanding the diversity of this element of external relations management. First, the nature of the student body is a key factor in shaping these relations, with a significant distinction between girls' and boys' schools. The Islamic cultural requirement for school segregation is an important feature of the Pakistani school system, and Simkins et al. show that the relationship with parents in girls schools, with female headteachers, is much more interactive and built on good interpersonal relationships. Secondly, the nature of the community that the school serves is of significance. In schools in Karachi serving substantially middle-class communities pressure for parental engagement is greater than in those schools serving mainly working-class communities. In particular, those schools with high status, academically or socially, identified the pressure to respond to the excess demand from parents to admit their children into the school. Thirdly, beyond pressure in relation to admissions, it is clear that involvement between parents and schools is not extensive, with most headteachers spending significantly less than 20 per cent of their time on such links. The parent–teacher associations, which are a statutory requirement for government schools, appear to be largely ineffectual. Indeed, in relation to parental involvement Memon et al. (2000, p. 54) identify that government-school heads perceive parents as interfering, and the time spent in dealing with them as a distraction from the central roles of learning and teaching, quoting a headteacher saying, 'I respect the parents' opinions and views but they demand too much from the school without providing any financial or moral support which I and my teachers don't like'. In contrast, in the marketplace of the non-governmental schools, the participation and contribution of parents is perceived as important and valuable, and as contributing to the enhancement of school performance.

Here the school is seen to be focused on meeting the needs and wants of parents, and their input is seen as enabling a continuing readjustment of activities and outcomes.

Despite government pressure for increased school–parent and school–community links, though, it is clear that in government schools in Pakistan such relationships are still in their infancy and that, other than in relation to admissions, there is still an 'arm's length' relationship. This may reflect the historical and cultural traditions of education in Pakistan in which the role of schools, originally strongly based in the Islamic traditions of the *mudrassahs* (traditional schools run by mosques or other religious organisations) (Khan, 2000), was one of taking young people from the community and educating them in a detached and protected environment. Such attitudes appear to persist strongly both in the perspectives of schools and headteachers and in the views of parents. It is only in those sectors of the community in which the principles of choice and the perception of the role of parents as consumers of education have become established, particularly in the relatively affluent middle-class communities of urban Pakistan, that the school–parent relationship is beginning to change. Khan (2000), however, emphasises that in the rural communities in which the majority of the Pakistani population live, religion and kinship, recognised in the centrality of Muslim values merged with the tribal perspectives, for example of the Pathan, produce a conservative perspective on education and the persistence of traditional views on the role of the school.

School–parent relations as a catalyst to community development – the case of Macedonia

In considering the management of relationships between schools and their communities there tends to be a focus on the outcomes in terms of the school or of the pupils within it, principally in relation to improved conditions for learning and teaching, perhaps through enhanced resources, and resultant improvements to measurable educational outputs. With a recognition of schools as a key focus for the community and a locus of community action and interest, the opportunities for wider benefits emanating beyond the school clearly emerge. The opportunity to bring together diverse groups within the community and to use education and schooling as a force for local social and economic development can be an important component of school–community policies. Peshardis (2000) considers the aims and outcomes of school–community developments in the Former Yugoslav Republic of Macedonia (FYR Macedonia).

The Macedonian school system remains strongly centralised as an inheritance from the socialist model of Yugoslavia prior to independence in 1991, with most resources simply allocated directly to schools by the national Ministry of Education. In 1996–97 the government established the Parent–School Partnership Project funded by the United States Agency for International Development (USAID) and managed by Catholic Relief Services. Its aims were to encourage the development of democratic processes within schools and communities, to facilitate the physical reconstruction of schools in the post-war period, and to foster a reduction in inter-ethnic tensions, principally between the Macedonian and Albanian communities, which represent 66 per cent and 23 per cent of the population respectively. The constitutional guarantee that education will take place in the chosen language of each ethnic group means that in many localities single schools have a number of dispersed buildings with instruction taking place in a different language in each building. This clearly creates significant management and cultural challenges within the schools, and a reduction of the complexity and tension within schools that this generates was an important target of the project.

The key component of the programme was the establishment of multi-ethnic parent councils in schools in localities which were ethnically mixed, which selected key issues for action that were priorities within their own communities. Evaluation of the Parent–School Partnership Project suggested that the most successful parent councils were those which embarked on reconstruction projects, which had a clear and tangible outcome. Where this occurred, this provided the starting point for continuing dialogue across the ethnic communities, including, for example, cross-community funding by Slavo-Macedonian families of reconstruction of schools with predominantly Albanian profiles. Peshardis (2000, p. 9) suggests that 'Primary school parent councils legitimised collaboration by de-politicising the education issue. Inter-ethnic collaboration was treated as a question of improving the quality of education and welfare of all children'.

The payoffs in traditional educational terms were also clear. Parental involvement with the school, with their children's progress and with learning and teaching was enhanced, and more than 80 per cent of parents felt that their engagement with school had been improved.

PARENTS AND SCHOOLS – BEYOND THE MYTHS

Managing relationships between schools and their communities varies substantially, for the balance between partnership, collective and market relations is contingent upon local sociocultural and economic conditions. Understanding those local conditions is a prerequisite to establishing effective managerial strategies. Furthermore, managing relations with parents is fundamentally entwined with perspectives on the nature and purpose of school. It is value driven in its aims, organisation and operation, yet seeking to understand and respond to the needs, wants, fears, hopes and values of parents and communities has not been a key priority for schools and colleges, and is hugely demanding of resources.

The evidence from our three case studies is that those 'understandings' are not yet significantly developed, and so confirms our view of the four myths of school–parent relations. First, parents are not always committed to engaging with schools, and both in less developed countries and the more affluent world there are many groups for whom school is a low priority and marginal to their lives. Secondly, the cultural distance between schools and the communities they serve also means that few parents have adopted any view that education is a 'good' and that as parents they are consumers – this is a characteristic only of the small proportion of active choosers in the strongly marketised school systems of the Anglo-Saxon world. Our third and fourth myths focus on the experience of managing the links with parents that schools have, and their enthusiasm for engaging with such relationships. While experience is growing in many countries, the professional distance between schools and parents is still a barrier that is slow to disappear, and ideas of partnership are strongly developed only rarely. Parents are still very much outsiders to the management of schools across much of the world.

Managing school–parent relations will become an increasingly central management task, though, for an important function of all schools in the twenty-first century will be to connect communities with governments and national and international worlds. A reflective development of strategy at national and school level may facilitate the rights of parents and schools to ensure that the interface between them is mutually beneficial. This issue of strategy, and its relationship to resources, is explored in the next three chapters.

Section D: Strategy and Resources

This section examines the role of strategy and planning within educational leadership and management as an approach to the effective acquisition and deployment of resources. Chapter 9 considers the nature of, and the case for, planning and strategy, while Chapters 10 and 11 examine resource allocation mechanisms at the macro-scale of the whole education system and at the level of the individual institution.

9

STRATEGY AND PLANNING

PLANNING, RATIONALITY AND THE STRATEGY PARADIGM

In the not too recent past, schools and colleges were blithely unpressured to produce plans, strategic or otherwise. National and regional administrations ordered the number of staff and students at each establishment, managed teaching resources, and left schools and colleges largely concerned with the day-to-day occupation of teaching. Something of a revolution in thinking intervened. The characteristic late twentieth-century urgent conviction of the need to improve school and college performance was balanced by a pessimistic realisation of the inertia of education. The waves of reform beat ineffectually against the rock solid wall of continuity with teaching and learning proceeding much as ever throughout the world, as explored in Chapter 2 (Jennings, 1994). A new tactic was needed, and it rested on the assumption that change was most likely to happen when decisions were in the hands of those who had to implement them, the staff in educational institutions. The consequent international trend to devolution and site-based management, which has been felt in every continent (see Chapter 10), has placed new responsibilities on educators not only to manage but also to plan the present and the future of their institution. Governments, however, are unwilling to relinquish control entirely and the obligation to produce a plan which could be scrutinised is a remaining form of control. There are requirements to produce a plan in many parts of the world including Hong Kong, Singapore, Australia and the UK (Quong, Walker and Stott, 1998). Where the state does not require a plan, then other funding organisations, such as donor bodies, may well do so. The pressure to produce a plan, however simple or sophisticated, is difficult to escape.

Some cultures may remain resistant. Ali (1996, p. 7) argues that in the Jabria school of Muslim thought, influential in the Arab world, systematic planning 'is not seen as a virtue as it is in conflict with predestination'. In a survey of South African technical colleges, less than half (42 per cent) had a formal planning document (Lumby, 2000). However, in many parts of the world, the attitude to planning ranges from undertaking it reluctantly as a political necessity to embracing it warmly. In a turbulent world, engaging in the collection of information, holding series of meetings and producing a detailed document outlining the goals and the actions to be taken to achieve them appears to impose order and is assumed to have a beneficial impact on organisational effectiveness.

The planning paradigm has permeated education systems around the globe sufficiently, though, to ensure it is a significant process in any consideration of leadership and management. Within this section of the book, therefore, we shall examine planning, strategy and resource management. Chapter 9 considers planning, its conceptualisations and practice, while the following chapters consider the management of resources at a system level (Chapter 10) and at institutional level (Chapter 11).

The ubiquitous assumption that planning is an unalloyed good is ironic given that the concept is surrounded by a remarkable degree of semantic and conceptual confusion. The words to describe it are multiple and used sometimes as synonymous and sometimes to indicate different concepts and processes. Its purpose is variously described and there is no agreement on the activities that may contribute and the sequence in which they are most effectively undertaken. The confusion in language and in concept mutually reinforce each other. Consequently, planning has become something of a leap of faith as well as a rational conviction. We believe in it without necessarily being quite clear on how it is done, perhaps attempting to achieve clarity by selecting from the range of theorists that evangelise a particular approach or process. This chapter reviews the evidence on planning in action in schools and colleges throughout the world by seeking to address a number of central questions:

- What *is* planning?
- What is the purpose of planning?
- How is planning undertaken?
- What should be the purpose and process of planning?

Within this analysis we shall also consider three of the common myths about strategy and planning in education:

Myth 1 – strategic planning is a necessary step to improve teaching and learning.
Myth 2 – strategic planning must be based on the creation of a vision to which staff are committed.
Myth 3 – a detailed plan of actions, resources and timescales, resting on the vision, can usefully guide the actions of staff.

WORDS, WORDS, WORDS

As Bell (1998) points out, the words planning and strategic are now so linked that planning which is not strategic is in some way discounted as not legitimate. The literature is unclear on how strategic planning differs from long-term planning, and throughout the world development planning, action planning, business planning and long-term planning are all used to describe plans devised by educational institutions. The planning may match some or all of the criteria suggested as characteristic of strategic planning, that is, a process which aligns values, goals, resources and actions in relation to the environment, with the purpose of arriving where the organisation wishes to be in anything from one to 10 years (Byers, 1991; Crisp, 1991; Johnson and Scholes, 1989).

The mystification of language in the literature resolves itself into a number of possible approaches to strategic planning. First, the process can be seen as essentially cultural, a way of mediating and resolving differences in values to achieve commitment and motivation. Alternatively, the process can be seen as stressing a rational sequence of decision-making which delineates choices, goals and actions. A third way is to disavow rational processes and to see planning as a fluid reactive process of constantly responding and reshaping the organisation as the environment shifts. Finally, it is possible to view planning as a blend, where meaning creation may precede and run alongside a sequence of planning and actions that are founded on logic and rationality. The dialectic or synthesis that emerges is a result of the fact that players function in different systems simultaneously, for example rational, occupational and political, and engage with the process on all three platforms (Pugh, 1993). Staff may engage in discussion on a rational level, arguing for plans from the perspective of advantages or disadvantages to learners, but at the same time there are micropolitical considerations as they are anxious to forward their personal professional values and practice and to uphold their own status and conditions. The process can therefore never be purely rational and related only to the needs of learners. Consequently, the process may reflect a number of stages where the emphasis may shift, focusing on the micropolitical more in the early stages and moving to a more rational approach in the latter stages when tensions in power and values have been at least partly resolved (Davies and Morgan, 1983).

THE PURPOSE OF PLANNING

The stated purpose of planning is usually to accomplish an enhancement of learners' experience and achievement (Bell, 1998). Evidence suggests that this aim may not be the only or the primary aim. It is clear that strategic planning is frequently a response to the requirement of funding bodies.

If money is only given if there is a plan, then a plan (of sorts) will be forthcoming. For example, the African universities most forward with strategic planning are those most heavily reliant on donor aid (Farrant and Afonso, 1997, p. 26) though the latter add the caveat that the strategic planning is 'so called' and may in fact be little more than a wish list. The World Bank Working Group on Higher Education has recommended that donors should support a planning process, and provide a model:

> Strategic Plans should:
> • Be short and readable, spelling out operational objectives;
> • Demonstrate the university's ability to plan and manage its future, and to provide a basis for government and donor investment decisions;
> • Be produced through an institutional strategic planning exercise initiated by the university and incorporating extensive internal consultation and consensus building with staff through management audits and self-studies.
>
> (Farrant and Afonso, 1997, p. 24)

The model described is just as much a wish list, as the reality of planning in many African universities is far removed from the coherent process implied. The model also ignores the fact that by tying the process to funding, the main objective of planning may be not to plan per se, but to satisfy requirements and secure resources. It may not engage staff or other stakeholders at a deeper level. There is 'deep scepticism that another bout of planning will achieve anything' (Farrant and Afonso, 1997, p. 29). The hope that institutions will engage with planning because it has value beyond satisfying requirements to access funds seems optimistic. Planning appears to be micropolitically driven, with different groupings within the institution using the process to argue for increased donations and jockeying for a larger share of the resultant spoils (Thomas, 1998).

The same dislocation between espoused purpose and actual purpose is apparent elsewhere in the world. Stott and Walker (1992) found that in their sample of 19 schools in Singapore, mission statements were too vague to be understood clearly or to have any impact on planning. They were pious general statements, very similar in nature and completely divorced from the actual priority goal of the schools, which was to achieve examination success. The mission was generally drawn up by the senior management team and staff were vague on the content, often thinking things were in the statement that were not. Consequently, the authors conclude that the first step in strategic planning, arriving at a mission, was politically driven by 'head office's expectations' (ibid., p. 55), resulting in dutiful rhetoric about development of mind and morals but with virtually no relevance to the practice of staff.

As well as achieving political approval and securing financial reward, planning may serve a third purpose, that of achieving a 'feel good' factor.

In an uncertain world, planning can provide a nostrum that appears to diminish the threat of uncertainty and change. As Quong, Walker and Stott (1998, p. 36) put it, it is 'a useful palliative'. Both at national level (Jennings, 1994) and at institutional level (Stott and Walker, 1992), even if plans are not implemented and have little impact on school activity and on teaching and learning, having a plan provides a good feeling and appears to justify the sense that there is purpose and the potential for moving on.

Contrasting with the evidence that plans serve primarily political and emotional needs, there are examples where planning appears to serve a genuine purpose of choosing direction and aligning goals. It may be that history or particular circumstances invest planning with a purpose. Jennings (1994, p. 326) argues that using vision-building to achieve a shared sense of purpose is important to black teachers in the Caribbean to escape the 'intellectual dependency on their former colonial masters'. Even where colonists have left, a residual domination may remain through donor organisations importing their own agenda and approaches. The need to rebuild a sense of identity, purpose and direction may lend a particular flavour to the process of achieving and implementing a vision.

Equally, school and college leaders may not be motivated primarily by external requirements to plan, but wish to use the process to achieve internal goals. Warnet (1994) analyses the case of a private religious school in France where the principal used the process of determining strategy to achieve the commitment and alignment of staff so that more formal controls became less necessary as all were working towards the same ends. Staessens and Vandenberghe (1994, p. 191) explore the process from the staff perspective and offer an example of a Belgian primary school where 'a vision which is more than rhetoric' informs the actions of staff on a daily basis. These examples relate primarily to the starting point of strategic planning, building a vision or mission, rather than to the process of planning for implementation. There is little international evidence of how the planning process proceeds after the initial stage. One exception is Lumby (2000) who charts planning in South African technical colleges. A minority of colleges use plans to fulfil largely bureaucratic purposes of predicting student numbers, finance, etc. The majority, however, value planning and are attempting to use it as a vehicle to assess external needs and develop the curriculum to respond. Much more research is needed to move beyond the current body of largely normative, hortatory literature and to examine what purpose planning serves in schools and colleges and how it is undertaken.

THE PROCESS OF PLANNING

Quong, Walker and Stott (1998) assert that when they ask principals what ensures the success of the school, the answer is consistent and asserts that a vision is necessary, that people must be committed to it and that there must be a written plan. This widespread belief may reflect very different understandings of what is implied by 'vision' and is despite the fact that there is little practical help in suggesting how vision can be reached. Some suggest an engagement with values is the vital first step in the strategic planning process, though it is described by different terms:

• achieving vision and/or mission (Staessens and Vandenberghe, 1994)
• purposing (Warnet, 1994, p. 219)
• recognising 'voice' (Hargreaves, 1994, p. 251).

Others suggest that rather than opening the planning sequence, essentially cultural processes dealing with values and beliefs should run parallel to or follow the stages of planning (Staessens and Vandenberghe, 1994). At whatever point this activity comes, there is a lack of clarity on its nature. Contrast Kenny, writing in an Irish context, who defines vision as relating to 'some futuristic ideal, to some notion of how things could/should be' (Kenny, 1994, p. 17) and Staessens and Vandenberghe (1994, p. 192) who describe vision in a case study Belgian school much more concretely as 'goal consensus'. Both writers agree that vision rests on values or principles which 'are by their very nature, abstract, vague and subjective' (Kenny, 1994, p. 17), 'general abstract ideas that guide thinking' (Warnet, 1994, p. 221). Stott and Walker, (1992, p. 50) describe mission in very similar terms as 'the organisation's statement of its purpose, intentions and priorities: its direction'. To complicate semantics even further, Vaill's (1984) definition of purposing also characterises a process of achieving consensus and commitment. It would seem that vision, mission and purposing are all used to indicate a process whereby values (rather vague, abstract principles) inform a process of agreeing and committing to direction. The process by which general abstract ideas translate into goal consensus is the magic metamorphosis which exists in the literature at the hortatory level, but which there is little empirical evidence from around the world to support or illustrate. Equally, if as Staessens and Vandenberghe suggest, vision creation is an ongoing socially created process, it is hard to see a distinction between vision as an aspect of planning, and cultural management, which is also an ongoing process of mediating and influencing values to decide what is important and the way things are done. Staessens and Vandenberghe (1994, p. 199) assert that 'it is almost impossible to influence vision in a direct way'. This presents principals with a conundrum: the achievement they see as crucial, achieving a vision and commitment to it, may be outside their direct control. Consequently some may utilise proxies, such as the senior management team arriving at a mission statement which everyone can recite (Stott and Walker, 1992). This is quite a long way from the definition of vision as a shared dream or picture of the future, but may give the illusion of a shared vision.

Perhaps it is helpful to demystify the process. It may be feasible to describe strategic planning as founded not on vision, but on data-gathering, the data being of two kinds. First, as Ali (1996, p. 5) reminds us, 'feelings are important and need to be treated as data'. Vision-building may be a process of collecting people's beliefs and related emotions to understand where the commonality may be, or to encourage by mutual communication some process of accommodation of differences. Viewed from this perspective, the process becomes less abstract and diffuse, and more a practical gathering of relevant data from staff and other stakeholder groups. It is also possible to see this data-gathering as both an initial stage and as ongoing. It can also encompass the fact that though many may be enrolled, there may also remain those whose beliefs and emotions cannot be contained within the accommodation and remain neutral or in conflict.

A second kind of data-gathering is also likely to both precede planning and to continue to influence changes in plans. This second kind is the collection of relevant facts and information. Numbers of potential entrants, figures describing examination success over time, numbers of trained staff required by employers, are all examples of such information. Gathering and communicating such 'facts' may appear more straightforward than dealing with values, beliefs and emotions. However, the process is likely to be micropolitical in the same way as gathering data on values. Those with more power are more influential in the process. For example, when technical institutes in Hong Kong gather information from employers about their requirements for trained personnel, principals perceive that the figures are inflated because of the employer's wish to appear more significant or more successful than is in fact the case (Lumby, 2000a). The same kind of impulse may cause the internal inflation of figures, for example in stating required resources for a particular department or course. The collection and interpretation of data of both kinds may be strongly influenced by micropolitics.

Although often overlaid by impressive rational-seeming documents presenting clear statements of values or mission, or figures, the data-gathering process on which the statements are founded remains unstable, with persistent shifts in accommodation and understanding. The process is one of constant adjudication and power-broking. This is, of course, for those schools and colleges that attempt the process. Many do not try to gather and communicate beliefs and emotions or may settle for proxy activity. Many also simply do not have the capacity to gather external data in any meaningful way. Staff may have insufficient time (Warnet, 1994) or insufficient resources, or be inexperienced in the collection of relevant information (Lumby, 2000). Engaging with planning for its own value requires strong leadership.

ACHIEVING INVOLVEMENT AND COMMITMENT

There is much literature suggesting that change happens when staff are involved in planning. Jennings (1994) criticises the implementation of curriculum reform in the Caribbean because of insufficient involvement of staff. Wong, Sharpe and McCormick (1998) suggest that staff in schools in Hong Kong are more likely to be committed to the plan if they are involved in devising it. However, there is also evidence that there is no clear relationship between having a plan and achieving what is described in it. Quong, Walker and Stott (1998, p. 34) deny 'a linear relationship between intent and outcome'. The theme of a dislocation between stated goals and their achievement is more widely spread throughout generic literature. Various schools of strategic planning emphasise that the least likely outcome of a plan is that it is straightforwardly implemented. Quong, Walker and Stott (1998) list 10 different schools of thought, several of which do not envisage a direct relationship between plans and outcomes. Logical incrementalism, for example, suggests that plans evolve by building a small step upon another small step in an evolutionary process as opportunities arise (Quinn, 1980). How, then, can the ubiquitous exhortation in the literature to involve staff in order to ensure implementation be related to the fact that the plans appear to be only loosely linked to what actually happens in the institution? Perhaps the edifice of belief in strategic planning is built on a false foundation. It is not commitment to the plan which matters but commitment to the job, to teaching, to students, to the community, what Warnet (1994, p. 227) calls a 'moral commitment'. The major purpose of planning may be not to arrive at a course of action, but to reconfirm a vocation. Planning may be interpreted as a ritual which affirms the worth of teaching and training in the light of the near universal sense of threat experienced by staff, as discussed in Chapters 5 and 6. The written plans are a mere vehicle, hence their description in a number of ways as chameleon-like. They are rolling plans (Wallace, 1992), broad (Wilkinson and Pedler, 1994) and likened to the improvisation of jazz (Bell, 1998). The whole process may be iterative, 'zig zag' in the Arab world (Ali, 1996, p. 12). In such a spirit, modelling itself on the planning process, this chapter returns to the starting point, the purpose of planning.

THE PURPOSE OF PLANNING – ALTERNATIVE PERSPECTIVES

The purpose of planning can be viewed quite differently from that outlined in mainstream texts. The latter suggest that planning results in both inspiration and a course of action that is implemented. The evidence reviewed suggests that frequently neither result. Staff often do not engage with planning. They are not always invited to consultation and do not habitually attend consultative meetings when invited. Both teachers and managers forced to plan by external requirements may consider the process as potentially a diversion from their core activity of teaching and learning (Thomas, 1998). In much of the world, plans are not the rational clear statements advocated but rather general, if not vague, statements of mission and goals.

It may be that plans can serve a variety of purposes. First, the statement of values and goals may be vague for a variety of reasons. Initially, to achieve the illusion of agreement statements may need to lack specificity. Once detail is included, disagreement follows. There is a positive relationship between generality of statement and seeming unanimity of support. Thus the requirements of the first aim of planning, to achieve alignment, may be in conflict with requirements of the second, a clear plan of action. The second purpose served by vagueness is that it lessens the purchase of those who may wish to challenge. It is much easier to assess whether goals have been achieved when they are clear. Vague plans weaken the chance of spotting discrepancy between intention and outcome. Plans, therefore, may be a means of controlling particularly the external environment by manipulating the platform through which a response is made. Regional and national administration must look to what was intended. A suitably vague plan can divert and weaken the basis of criticism. A third purpose is that plans can conceal reality, hiding unpalatable facts beneath a blanket of acceptable rhetoric. Most education professionals would find it unacceptable to aver publicly that their goal was primarily to achieve examination success, or to attract high-fee paying parents/students. The rhetoric of plans, particularly missions, can obscure intentions which do not align with accepted professional values (Stott and Walker, 1999). To summarise, one purpose of planning may be to provide camouflage, presenting an apparently unified front behind acceptable goals of sufficient vagueness to deflect challenge. Much evidence suggests these micropolitical purposes (Quong, Walker and Stott, 1998; Stott and Walker, 1999; Thomas, 1998).

However, there is also some evidence that suggests that the strategic planning process can achieve the overt, advocated purpose of guiding choices and decisions in order to improve teaching and learning. An example of where the process seems genuinely to inform activity, and specifically teaching and learning activity, is provided by Staessens and Vandenberghe (1994). The teachers in a case study Belgian school were able to articulate a small number of specific goals which impacted directly on their practice. They wished to provide good education which involved keeping up to date with developments in their profession through reading literature, giving each pupil individual attention and working hard. However, these goals were 'not the result of rational analysis and planning but [are] the result of the daily activities that shape the way the teachers perceive their task and their school' (ibid., p. 192). Interpreting this case example, it seems that goals are agreed not by planning but by something which the authors call vision-building but which could as easily be described as cultural evolution. Indeed, the process described seems to match exactly Schein's definition of culture:

> A pattern of shared basic assumptions that the group learned as it solved its problems of external adaptation and internal integration, that has worked well enough to be considered valid, and, therefore, to be taught to new members as the correct way to perceive, think and feel in relation to those problems.
>
> (Schein, 1997, p. 12)

In just such a way the staff of the school talked to each other on a daily basis and through this communication evolved a 'pattern of shared basic assumptions' of what good education was and how it was enacted. The overall picture which emerges is that 'planning' as it is understood in the literature, actually describes two separate processes. One is cultural management, or cultural influencing, where the basic assumptions and values are negotiated on an ongoing process. The second is a more overt production of usually a written document delineating mission and goals, the purposes of which may be to satisfy bureaucratic requirements, to provide camouflage and, sometimes, to map out actions over time. There is little international evidence that plans substantially influence the core activity of teaching and learning. The normative link between the cultural process and the bureaucratic process is not convincingly supported by international empirical evidence.

'A HOPELESS QUEST?'

In some parts of the world, planning takes place at regional or national level. Schools and colleges are not called upon to make choices about what they teach or how, or what resources to use. Even where institutions have devolved responsibility, some have questioned whether schools and colleges can plan strategically at all. They are unable to make the sort of decisions about their organisation that businesses can. They cannot dramatically change what they do. They are constrained by legislation and community expectations. One might argue that choices are peripheral, not strategic. As one principal put it 'Let us try a bit of this, let us not do that. Actually, in a big sense there is nothing particular, just lots of little tiny moves' (Lumby, 1999, p. 77). As choices are relatively minor, any plan is unlikely to have a major effect on the institution. Given that change happens rapidly and that written plans are out of date often the moment they are achieved, it might seem right to take Quong, Walker and Stott (1998, p. 39) at their word and 'abandon strategic planning as a hopeless quest in an uncertain world'. Certainly it would seem appropriate to abandon the hype, the mystification, the overstated claims and to recognise that 'planning' comprises two processes which, rather than being closely related, work in dialectic. First, all institutions evolve culture, the shared assumptions, the basic parameters of what is seen as permissible and appropriate. Managers may influence this process. Whether it is called managing culture or building vision is irrelevant. The future element of vision-building stressed in the literature, the dream or picture of years to come, is absent in the empirical data. 'Vision' appears to conform to the understanding of what culture is. One element of planning is therefore managing culture. The second process is taking and recording bureaucratic decisions about what is to be taught and with what resources. It is necessary. Without it, institutions would move forward in a more disorganised fashion. It is informed by the culture of the institution, but not tightly linked. The planning process can therefore provide a vehicle for managing culture and for managing operations. It is not the semi-mystical dream-building suggested by some literature, and staff in educational organisations know it is not. It serves a variety of cultural, political, emotional and practical purposes, thus demonstrating the mythical nature of some of the frequently presumed characteristics of planning that we identified at the start of this chapter. The real trick for school and college leaders is to discern the purpose that planning and strategy need to serve in the individual case, and to use them effectively to that end.

10

MANAGING RESOURCES FOR EDUCATION

PLANNING AND STRATEGY – THE RESOURCE ISSUE

The growth of a paradigm of planning and strategy that we have considered in Chapter 9 is premised on a view that values shape the use of resources both at a system level and at the level of individual schools and colleges. This chapter and the next consider these resource management issues, while emphasising the global contrasts in the levels of resourcing available to education.

Whatever the resource reality, the call from within most educational systems is for more resources to be made available from the national economy, but resource allocation to education is a political issue, often with a high public profile. Governments seek both political benefit and the enhancement of educational outcomes from resource improvements whose political value is much greater than their real financial value. The provision and management of resources to education, therefore, is inevitably a focus of political conflict at national, regional and school levels. To contribute to this debate we need to consider a number of central questions:

- What are the key resources that educational leaders must manage?
- What patterns of resource allocation can be identified at a global scale?
- What alternative models of resource management are there?
- What are the positive and negative implications of each model for school and college leaders, teachers and students?

In considering these questions we shall identify three important myths that are frequently regarded as self-evident truisms in educational resourcing:

Myth 1 – increasing resource allocation automatically raises levels of pupil achievement.

Myth 2 – resource levels for education are directly related to national levels of economic development.

Myth 3 – decentralisation of resource management is now the international 'norm'.

Resources are the means by which the processes of education can be operationalised. Three key groups of resources are normally recognised – financial resources; physical resources, including buildings, plant and learning support resources (what Caldwell and Spinks [1992] call 'materiel'); and human resources, including teaching, managerial and support staff. Caldwell and Spinks (1992) extend this list to five groups, though, by adding knowledge and power as key resources. These represent less tangible elements in the resource mix, and are themselves in part a function of the other three components, yet they may be the most significant in influencing the effectiveness of resource acquisition and resource usage within any single institution. In particular, the inclusion of power and knowledge recognises the strong political dimension of resource management and implicates individual values, attitudes and cultural capital as important in resource decisions.

The acquisition and use of resources is traditionally described with reference to a resource cycle, which identifies four key stages that are strongly linked and interdependent:

1) Resource acquisition. These are the processes by which organisations obtain the resources they need or want, and may include direct funding by local or national government, income generation from fees, fund raising activities or commercial enterprises.
2) Resource allocation. This involves the allocation of resources to the functions of the institution, and may be driven by centralised directive or local school-based planning and decision-making.
3) Resource application. This involves the use of the allocated resources in the specific functions of the school or college.
4) Evaluation. This is the process of review to determine what the impact of resource allocation and use has been. While an important element of internal review within institutions, evaluation is frequently driven by demands for external accountability.

The processes by which the resources are allocated and applied can be highly variable in their efficiency and effectiveness, however, leading to significant contrasts even where resource inputs are similar. In particular, the baseline conditions to which resources are applied in schools and colleges are never identical between two institutions. Every school is distinctive in its socio-economic characteristics and in the power, knowledge and expertise of its managers and other staff, and as Coleman and Anderson (2000, p. ix) indicate 'it would appear that even in countries where education is relatively starved of funds, the way in which a school or college is managed impacts on the quality of education that the student receives'.

This raises the important issues of effectiveness, efficiency and value for money in the application of resources within education. Effectiveness is the degree to which the intended outcomes of the organisation have been met. Intended outcomes (see Chapter 3) might be determined at national, regional or school level, and are themselves strongly value laden, and will vary in precise detail from school to school and country to country. The effectiveness of education and training as judged in a western developed economy may be quite different from effectiveness in a rural school in east Africa. Inherent within a consideration of effectiveness is the concept of equity, too, for in allocating resources within an education or training system a common explicit aim is that individual pupils should either receive equal allocations of resource or allocations of resource related to their individual needs. Equity is an important social concept that is almost universally applied at national level in education policies and is an important indicator by which the achievements of the education system are judged.

Efficiency, on the other hand, is the relationship between inputs and outputs, and Levačić (2000, p. 13), defines an efficient use of resources as 'one which produces a given quantity or value of output at least cost'. Value for money is achieved when schools are both effective and efficient in their outputs, in that they both achieve the system's intended outcomes and do so with an efficient use of resources.

RESOURCING EDUCATION – GLOBAL PATTERNS AND CONTRASTS

Global contrasts in resource provision for education are stark in absolute terms. Harber and Davies (1997) suggest that the 35 countries of the Organisation for Economic Cooperation and Development have an average commitment of resources to education per capita that is 40 times that in sub-Saharan Africa, 30 times that in east Asia, 20 times that in South Asia, 10 times that in the Arab states of the Middle East, and seven times that of Latin America. Such contrasts do not simply represent the differences in level of economic development, however, for there are significant variations in the proportion of national wealth that is applied to education and training, representing different prioritisation of education within national development programmes.

While levels of resourcing in the developed world may be relatively high, for the majority of the world's pupils, and particularly those in rural areas, learning is an almost resource-free experience. The UNESCO report on world education in 1998, which surveyed provision in 14 less developed countries, indicates this graphically:

> In the majority of countries surveyed the average classroom is not much more than a designated meeting place for a teacher and a group of pupils: in 10 out of the 14 countries one third or more of the pupils

are gathered into classrooms without a useable chalkboard. In virtually all countries there are no teaching aids such as wall charts, and
almost no pupil will ever see a world map . . . In eight out of the 14
countries, more than 90 per cent of the pupils attend schools which
do not have electricity; and one third or more of the pupils attend
schools which do not have water at all.

(UNESCO, 1998, pp. 54–5)

It would be naive, however, to believe that resource provision can simply
be read off from average indicators of development within countries.
Within less developed countries the resource provision within the most
favoured schools attended by children from the highest socio-economic
groups will often exceed that of many schools within more developed
countries. The contrasts, for example, between schools in the predominantly black township of Soweto and those in the more affluent suburb
of Sandton, in Johannesburg in South Africa, are signally greater than
between the Johannesburg suburban schools and schools in the UK or
France – and the suburban schools may have better levels of IT provision,
better pupil–teacher ratios and better buildings than many less favoured
schools in inner-city Europe or North America.

Contrasts in wealth between the countries of the developed and developing world though are compounded by significant demographic differences. Population structures in, for example, western Europe mean that
the proportion of the population of school age is declining while the proportion of the population in the economically active sectors of society is
relatively large. In less developed countries the school-age population is
a much greater proportion of the total (up to 50 per cent), and is increasing at a significant rate so that 'the size of the educational task facing them
is greater than for the richer countries' (Colclough 1993, p. 6).

The contrast in resource levels means that the focus of management priority varies significantly. In many less developed countries the priority is
resource acquisition at a basic level, for finance, buildings, learning
resources and, perhaps most significantly, teachers are in very limited
supply. In more developed countries, higher resourcing levels exist so the
priorities are more in the field of planning resource usage and operating
systems of accountability.

At a simple level the link between levels of resourcing and levels of
what Levačić (2000) terms learning outputs (direct short-term measurable
achievements by schools and colleges) and learning outcomes (longer-term
achievements for society and the economy) is straightforward. Levels of
pupil achievement, participation rates and economic well-being are
greater where resource allocation to education is greater. However, at a
more-refined level of analysis the linkage becomes much more difficult to
demonstrate, for learning outputs and outcomes are the product of a
complex range of factors. First, it is possible that enhanced resource inputs

into education are the product of economic development and growth and not the cause of it. Resource inputs into education are generally greater in wealthier economies, yet the marginal economic benefit of increased investment to such economies may be much smaller than for poorer countries. Secondly, there is little research evidence of the relationship between specific resource inputs and particular outputs and outcomes. Hanushek (1997) emphasises that there is no consistent relationship between resource input and pupil achievement in that at the micro scale other factors may be much more influential than resource levels in determining those outputs – for example, pupil motivation, socio-economic conditions and teacher expertise. Despite this concern about the micro scale, however, at the macro scale Laine, Greenwald and Hedges (1997), drawing on evidence from studies in the USA, suggest that there is a consistent direct positive relationship between expenditure per pupil, teacher ability and experience, and pupil achievements, and a strong inverse relationship between school size, class size and learning outputs. However, it must be stressed that clear research evidence of such relationships is markedly absent from most educational systems and that generalisation is neither possible nor valid.

RESOURCE MANAGEMENT MODELS – CENTRALISATION, DECENTRALISATION AND THE ROLE OF THE MARKET

Resource provision and management models range across a spectrum from centralised to decentralised systems. Centralised systems are those in which the resources are held and managed at some distance from the point of activity, demonstrated in its 'purest' form where resource decisions and processes are undertaken by national government departments with no resource responsibility held at regional, local or school level. Decentralised systems are those in which responsibility for allocating and managing the use of resources is delegated to much closer to the point of service – local government, individual schools or even individual teachers may hold responsibility for planning and operationalising some form of resource management. In practice, a full range of possibilities exists within this spectrum. Some functions may be retained centrally, while others may be delegated. Large or small proportions of the total resource may be delegated. Delegation may occur to different levels of the system, or some functions may be undertaken at different levels. Where decentralised systems occur with delegation to regional or local level, or to the individual school or principal, there may still appear to be a strongly centralised system at school level if only limited responsibility has been delegated that far down the system.

It is important, too, to recognise that decentralisation of resource allocation may be accompanied by increasing centralisation of other components of the education system. In England and Wales and in Australia, for example, delegation of financial responsibility to schools has been accompanied by increasing centralisation of curriculum definition and control. By standardising the learning outputs that schools must provide it becomes easier for government to judge the efficiency and effectiveness of individual schools.

Decentralisation of resource systems in education may be identified as one of the global metatrends of the last two decades, although its form and extent presents a complex and varied pattern. As Bullock and Thomas (1997, p. 1) suggest, 'Policies of decentralisation are being adopted in a great many countries, North and South. Despite a common language for describing these policies, however, even a cursory examination makes it apparent that their nature and purpose can differ substantially'. Indeed many countries have not pursued decentralisation and retain a strongly centralised resource system, and we shall examine some of these models in the case studies presented later in this chapter. The push towards decentralisation is seen as a response to two broad political and economic aims:

1) The pursuit of more effective and efficient use of resources, to gain an increase in the outputs and outcomes without a concomitant increase in resource allocation. This belief is premised on the view that those closest to the point of service will have a better understanding of the ways resources can be used to meet specific needs, and recognises that needs vary substantially from locality to locality and school to school.
2) The empowerment of teachers and managers to enable them to be responsive to local and individual need. With empowerment, though, comes the requirement for accountability, and decentralisation often brings with it a range of accountability systems, including inspection, auditing and formal quality assurance systems.

An important component of decentralisation where it occurs is the move toward local management or self-management. This concept was developed initially by Caldwell and Spinks (1998), who define self-management more recently in the following terms: 'The self managing school is a school in a system of education to which there has been decentralised a significant amount of authority and responsibility to make decisions about the allocation of resources within a centrally determined framework of goals, policies, standards and accountabilities' (Caldwell & Spinks, 1998, pp. 4–5). We shall examine each of these models below.

Centralised resource management

Centralisation in the management of resources remains a dominant characteristic of many countries both in the developed and developing world. This shows the importance of recognising that the system that evolves in any country is as much a product of the sociocultural and political environment as of the economic circumstances. We shall consider here the examples of Germany and Bangladesh, which represent contrasting examples of centralisation.

Education in Germany is the responsibility of the regional governments in each of the states (Länder), and is managed through the Ministry of Culture in each state (Haenisch and Schuldt, 1994). Historically the system has been strongly centralised with resources and curriculum controlled from the state capital. The primary concern within the Länder has been with the nature of curriculum rather than resource allocation mechanisms. The states have made significant progress in the last decade towards delegating responsibility for the planning of learning and teaching to individual schools and teachers, with an emphasis on the professional accountability of schools rather than financial or political accountability to the state. Centrally defined curricula still drive the system, but they are couched as frameworks and structures within which teachers can exercise considerable autonomy. Decentralisation of responsibility for learning and teaching, though, has not been accompanied by decentralisation of resource management. The states still hold direct control for teachers' salaries and deployment, for buildings and physical resources, and the small elements of the budget devolved to schools are strictly controlled in terms of what they may be used for – the state governments, for example, provide limited lists of prescribed textbooks that schools must use. Germany provides a strong example of centralisation, therefore, even though responsibility and accountability for learning and teaching is strongly devolved.

In Bangladesh, the central control of government is even stronger than in Germany, for, although a structure of district education departments is in place, the education system is largely managed directly from central government in Dhaka (Hossain, 1994). The system is hierarchical and bureaucratic with a chain of communication downward to schools and back up to central government. Curriculum, assessment and resources are all centrally planned and directed. Central government provides staff salaries directly to teachers via banks within the regions. Textbooks are purchased centrally and distributed by government via district education offices. Services that can only be provided at school level, such as in-service training, buildings maintenance and utility bills, are paid directly to suppliers by government in response to requisitions from schools transmitted (often very slowly) through district education offices. Schools do receive small, decentralised funds, for consumables, which are managed by the headteacher in conjunction with the school management committee, comprising local community members. Autonomy for decision-making in relation to resources is strongly constrained, therefore, but the system of financial operation involves significant numbers of staff undertaking routine bureaucratic procedures in regional and national government offices.

Decentralisation of resource management

The delegation of resource management that has occurred in many countries retains responsibility and accountability at regional or local level rather than within individual schools. This has the advantage of ensuring some responsiveness to local environmental conditions while protecting the system from a range of significant risks. We can identify a number of these areas of risk within delegated systems.

First, there is concern about the capacity of headteachers and district officials to take on and manage the responsibility for financial and resource management. This is a significant professional training and development issue, for the supply of headteachers and senior managers with appropriate training and personal skills is a real concern in many countries. Headteachers may be the only staff trained beyond minimal levels, and that training will be principally in teaching and learning rather than in management. Decentralisation, therefore, has as a prerequisite a commitment to professional development and training.

Secondly, there may be concerns, real or unfounded, of the risks of the misappropriation of resources and of the potential for fraud. Where there is significant geographical and power–distance between central resource providers and the point of resource usage, with a significant bureaucratic system mediating those distances there is potential for 'resource leakage'.

Thirdly, in many of the least developed countries the key resource questions relate to large-scale issues of the provision of school buildings and teachers. These are issues that are often hard to address at the local or even regional level, for the size of resource investment required is too substantial. In Bangladesh (Hossain, 1994), staff absence rates of 50 per cent, for example, reflect the low income and status of teachers, but with a limited supply of qualified teachers there is little that can be done at local level to address the problem.

Fourthly, delegation of funding to school level is dependent upon a management information system, however rudimentary, to provide key data to enable calculations of delegated funding, and neither the data nor the systems may be available. Pupil participation, for example, may be highly variable. Average daily attendance in Bangladesh, for example, is less than 50 per cent (Hossain, 1994) of enrolled pupils, and enrolment may be less than 70 per cent of the local school age population. In such circumstances obtaining a reliable figure for pupil enrolment as a basis for formula funding, for example, will be problematical. Furthermore, the management of delegated systems requires a management system at school and regional level that is complex. Such systems can work in developed countries where access to computer systems and the availability of administrative staff with high levels of personal education and skills training allows the systems to operate effectively. It is clear that the establishment of both delegated resource systems and sophisticated monitoring systems has only been possible in developed countries as a result of innovation in computer technology.

Despite these constraints, however, some form of decentralisation is found in many countries. In Chile (Rodriguez, 1994), a formerly strongly centralised system in which curriculum and resources were controlled at national level was replaced in 1980 by a system in which responsibility for staffing and buildings was delegated to local government, to the municipalities. Curriculum control is still held by the national Ministry of Education, but there is considerable scope for municipalities and individual schools to be responsive to local needs and circumstances within the national curriculum framework. Financial control, too, is still held by the ministry, although a market system has been established which links the flow of funding to individual schools to pupil recruitment. A voucher system enables parents to choose the school that they wish, and so funding is linked to perceptions of quality of each school operationalised through parental choice. Additional funding is available to schools from government through development funding targeted at schools on the basis of school performance in national tests and socio-economic indicators within the school 'catchments'. Chile, therefore, combines some of the market-driven characteristics of some of the most decentralised systems (see below) with delegation to local and regional bodies and the retention of some resource allocation functions at national level.

Indonesia provides an example of a national setting in which strategies of decentralisation have appeared quite recently. As recently as 1989 national government reorganised the management of schools along strongly centralised lines through Law 2/1989 with decision-making and control retained at distance from the region and the school. Government provided funding to district education authorities on a per school basis, with equal allocations irrespective of school size or the socio-economic characteristics of the catchment. In 1998, for example, this sum was 950,000 rupees, or approximately $US100 per school. The administrative and funding model was complex with the Department of National Education holding responsibility for funding secondary schools, and the Ministry of Home Affairs funding primary and pre-school education. Islamic authorities retained responsibility for the significant number of Islamic faith-based schools. Furthermore, funding passed through several tiers of national and local government (national, regional, district and sub-district levels) before reaching schools, imposing a bureaucratic and inefficient system.

From 2001 a policy of decentralisation has been introduced (Indonesian Ministry of National Education, 2001). This policy retains a series of checks and balances in the allocation and distribution of funding by involving a number of government ministries, including the Ministry of Home Affairs, the Ministry of National Education and the Ministry of Finance, with overall allocations agreed by a Central Committee

(Indonesian Directorate of Primary and Secondary Education 1999). National scale funding is a combination of government finance through taxation and allocation, and contributions from international development aid, such as the Asian Development Bank and the World Bank. The latter funding is channelled through specific projects, for example for the development of teacher training or the provision of textbooks.

Funding is directed to the local education authorities for distribution. Following the establishment of a decentralised budgetary system through Law 22/1999 and Law 25/1999 the local education authority retains responsibility for the payment of teachers' salaries, the building and maintenance of school buildings, and curriculum development, but a formula is used to allocate funding to schools for resources and extracurricular activities based on:

- a fixed sum per school, but varying between urban and rural schools. Allocation to schools is through funding with three levels of unit costs – those for Djakarta, the capital; those for schools outside the capital; those for each school sector, with a distinction between primary, junior secondary and senior secondary schools
- a sum that is proportional to the number of pupils (but not their age or, for example, any profile of special needs within the school)
- a sum related to the socio-economic and geographical environment of the school, so that rural schools and schools in poorer localities receive enhanced financial support.

This formula provides some connection between local needs, individual school needs and the flow of funding, but does not empower the headteachers of schools with control over staffing levels and rewards. Families with children in senior secondary schools also contribute to school funding by paying fees, and in primary schools fees are invited on a voluntary basis. Part of the revenue this generates is paid by the school to central government for redistribution, while a further part is paid to contribute to resource provision and for extracurricular activities within the school. In this way schools have an additional flow of funding for their direct usage.

The Indonesian model of decentralisation ensures that the key locus of decision-making and choice is delegated to local authorities, with a lesser delegation directly to schools. Enhanced delegation to schools may emerge as a result of the professional development programme for headteachers and school managers that the restructuring process in 2001 has included. However, as in many less developed countries, the impact of global and national financial systems has had a substantial effect on school funding. In Indonesia funding of education rose steadily throughout the 1980s and 1990s so that it constituted some 8 per cent of GNP in the mid-1990s. However, regional economic recession and internal political instability prompted a significant decline to 2.8 per cent by 1999 and to 0.8 per cent by 2001 following the economic fall of Asian markets. While delegation and a reduction in bureaucracy may assist in ensuring increased efficiency in the use of resources, the impact of such reductions in funding in a state with an annual population growth rate of 2.5 per cent will ensure that resource provision for education will remain a significant operational and political issue.

Resource management in the marketplace

Strong delegation of resource management responsibilities is a phenomenon most clearly observed in the English-speaking world. It represents the most substantial commitment to 'self-management' by delegating a high proportion of resources to the school or college, whose senior management has responsibilities for utilising that resource in the most effective way. Such models, however, are not delegation without constraint, for they have a number of important characteristics.

First, resource delegation is normally accompanied by increasing centralisation of control for the curriculum. By defining more closely what the curriculum must be and how it should be structured government provides a strong benchmark against which judgements of effectiveness can be made. In essence the product of education is more tightly defined and schools are seen to be the providers of that service.

Secondly, delegation brings with it strong systems of accountability. Political and financial accountability normally occurs through audit (both financial and in terms of learning outputs and outcomes) and inspection, while accountability to the community is achieved through the imposition of parental choice and quasi-markets.

Thirdly, delegation is dependent on the creation of appropriate bureaucratic systems to enable the processes of delegation and accountability to operate. This has an impact on management within the school in terms of both internal processes and external focus. It imposes upon school managers the requirement to develop a more managerial culture within their school through the use of strategic planning, target setting and a focus upon measurable outputs. At the same time it requires headteachers and principals to develop enhanced responsiveness to the external environment, for it is to external stakeholders that the school or college must be continuously accountable.

Although varying in detailed form such models of operation are to be found in England and Wales, Australia, New Zealand and some parts of the USA. In each of these examples responsibility for the curriculum is retained at national level (UK) or at state level (Australia and the USA), although in New Zealand schools have rather more freedom to establish their own curricula within frameworks developed at government level, and there is some evidence of the easing of curriculum frameworks in the UK in the context of Curriculum 2000.

Decentralisation in the USA has a complex pattern of operation as each state has independent authority over its educational systems and structures, and Caldwell (2000) suggests that in the majority of states there is still only limited delegation below school district level. Steffy and English (1996) emphasise the different models generated with reference to Kentucky and Chicago, illustrating clearly how a complex raft of historical and politico-cultural issues have shaped the outcome of change, not least the role of key individual politicians in driving through or resisting reform. This context is emphasised by Steffy and English (1996, p. 73) who assert that 'the Kentucky Education Reform Act (KERA) is first and foremost a political reform'.

Hess (1999) has reviewed the impact of local management in the Chicago public school district which was introduced in 1988. This represents one of the most radical models of delegation of resources to schools in the USA. The impacts of the reform have been substantial in terms of changing the emphasis in the managerial roles of school boards and managers. The responsibility for managing delegated budgets in relation to school-defined strategic objectives appears overall to have had some measurable impact on learning achievements and in value added. However, there is a variable pattern from school to school and Hess suggests that insufficient account has been taken of the baseline contrasts in the profiles of the pupil communities in different schools.

This conclusion mirrors the concerns raised about the impact of delegated funding that have been expressed in relation to England and Wales (Asthana and Gibson, 2000) and New Zealand (Thrupp, 1999). While measurable improvements in pupil achievement can be identified in each national setting, the strongest influence upon the outcomes for individual schools seems to be the socio-economic profile of the natural catchment of the school. If this is the case, then the risk in market-driven models of financial and resource delegation is that those schools in lower ses localities will see a relative decline in pupil achievement without the direct intervention on equity grounds that more centralised systems can provide.

RESOURCING EDUCATION – CHALLENGING THE MYTHS

The resourcing of education is linked to global patterns of wealth and the underpinning economic principles of public finance. Contrasts in resource levels may explain differences in levels of pupil achievement, and this understanding means that increasing resource input into education is a key priority for all national administrations. Alongside the desire to increase resource inputs, though, is the pursuit of effective models of resource allocation at national level, and it is here that the cultural and political dimensions of educational policy and management may be most strongly observed. Our analysis suggests, too, that in facing this political debate we must recognise that a number of myths or oversimplifications, identified at the start of the chapter, characterise common understandings of resource management.

First, despite the general link between resource inputs and educational outputs it is a myth that increasing resource allocation will automatically produce enhanced pupil achievement. While there is a direct intuitive link between inputs and outputs, systems of education are so complex that only excellent management will ensure the link is effected. Secondly, it is a myth that resource levels in education are related in any simple way to national levels of economic development. Resourcing decisions result from a complex cultural, ideological and political process, important within which is the degree to which education is valued within the culture. Thirdly, the perspective that decentralisation of resource management to school level is either predominant in any global view or is even a primary aim of most national systems is not valid.

While delegation of resources is perceived to bring possibilities to schools that may be seen as advantageous in some economic, political and cultural settings, it can also bring responsibilities and distractions that are not always welcome. In some socio-economic settings, delegation is inappropriate and unhelpful, not least because of the inevitable consequences of the subdivision of small quantities of resource. In Chapter 11 we shall explore how resources at institutional level are managed.

11

MANAGING RESOURCES AT THE INSTITUTIONAL LEVEL

INSTITUTIONAL RESOURCE MANAGEMENT

In Chapter 10 we considered the general issues of resource management within educational systems, and a range of broad system level approaches. Here we shall focus on the institutional level to examine the evolution of school-based management, and the range of models for the management of resources that can be identified within the varied contexts that characterise 'self-management'. This analysis is founded in a number of essential questions for school leaders:

- What are the perceived benefits of self management?
- How far can institutional level resource management be demonstrated to generate economic and educational benefits?
- What are the priorities for leaders in optimising self-management outcomes?
- What strategies are used in the institutional management of the resource cycle and what issues do they create?

SELF-MANAGEMENT – MAKING THE CASE

It is clear from the earlier analysis that the extent to which self-management has been established is quite variable, and the form of school-based management is highly contextual. The precise operation of, for example, local management of school (LMS) in England and Wales, school-based management in the USA and the School Management Initiative (SMI) in Hong Kong is very different, even though all are approaches to self-management. What they have in common, though, is delegation to the institution of some degree of responsibility for making choices about how to use resources provided by local or national government, and even to enhance those resources through entrepreneurial activities. Caldwell and Spinks (1998, pp. 4–5) emphasise the constraints and accountabilities that frame such devolvement, though, in their definition of the self-managing school as 'a school in a system of education to which there has been decentralised a significant amount of authority and responsibility to make decisions about the allocation of resources within a centrally determined framework of goals, policies, standards and accountabilities'.

The arguments promoting self-management are rooted in a commitment to efficiency, empowerment, and the engagement of institutions with their communities. Osbourne and Gaebler (1993), writing in the context of public services in general, suggest that the advantages of decentralisation accrue to the system as a whole, to the individual institution, to staff at all levels and, as a consequence, to those using the service. This is the result of:

- the greater flexibility and responsiveness of small 'units' close to the point of delivery of the service, where the impact of actions is highly visible and the micro-scale identification of needs in local communities does not get hidden by the macro-scale picture of national or regional needs
- greater levels of innovation in decentralised organisations, because of the possibility of direct reward, either in the perceived quality of the service or in terms of formal rewards
- the generation of higher morale, greater commitment and, hence, increased productivity from individuals and groups empowered to take responsibility for their own actions and impacts.

Caldwell (2000) has reviewed the research evidence on the impact of devolved school management internationally. Research through the early years of the 1990s examined self-management in the initial stages of its evolution. Both what Caldwell terms 'first generation' and 'second generation' research failed to demonstrate any significant linkage between self-management and enhanced pupil outcomes. The first-generation research was that undertaken within the USA in systems where the level of financial delegation was limited (for example, Summers and Johnson, 1996), whereas second-generation research considered environments where significant delegation was occurring (for example, Bullock and Thomas, 1997; Levačić, 1995). In both cases, while there was some evidence of improved efficiency in reducing unit costs, it was clear that financial delegation was having little impact upon learning and teaching – as Bullock and Thomas (1997, p. 219) suggest, 'we must [recognise] . . . that structural changes in governance, management and finance may leave largely untouched the daily interaction of pupils and teachers'.

Caldwell, however, identifies a third generation of research emerging in the late 1990s which provides a more positive picture of the link between resource delegation and enhanced learning outcomes. This research has two thrusts – the analysis of data on financial performance by schools (for example, Bradley, Johnes and Millington, 1999), and the use of large datasets relating to pupil performance that has accumulated from national/state level testing of pupils over a number of years (for example, the Cooperative Research Project [1998] focused on schools in Victoria, Australia), which has enabled sophisticated statistical analysis to be applied to the evidence.

OPTIMISING SELF-MANAGEMENT AND RESTRUCTURING LEADERSHIP

This data on financial performance confirms that enhanced efficiency in resource use is emerging from delegation. In particular, operating in the marketplace means that schools seek to reduce costs and/or enhance value for money within all elements of their operations, both in terms of internal systems and external purchasing. The analysis also suggests that delegation of resources may enhance learner outcomes (see Chapter 3), and promote the conditions under which that enhancement may be achieved. Caldwell (2000) summarises the strategic and operational management factors that seem to be important to promote enhanced learning outcomes as follows:

1) Schools must recognise that the primary aim of decentralisation is the enhancement of learning and make this explicit in the objectives of all elements of resource management.
2) Clear links must be made within all strategic and operational planning processes between self-management and learning and teaching.
3) Staff selection processes need to operate with a clear priority of enhancing the learning objectives of the school.
4) The effective use of resources for professional development to enhance staff skills must be linked to learning objectives.
5) The creation of high-performing teams 'underpinned by a culture that values quality, effectiveness, equity and efficiency' (Caldwell, 2000, p. 37) needs to be a priority.
6) 'Backward mapping' must be used, in which planning starts from the objectives for learning and teaching and then identifies the resource allocation and management strategies necessary to achieve those goals.
7) Monitoring of all these processes must be undertaken by senior staff to ensure that resources are allocated to respond to underachievement or failure in reaching the learning goals.

This all suggests that it is in the strategic planning process and the staff appointment and professional development arenas where the benefits of delegated resource management can be most clearly effected. Indeed, as long ago as 1990 Malen, Ogawa and Kranz identified the implementation of clear planning models as a characteristic of schools successfully adopting school-based management in the USA. Where models of decentralisation do not include responsibility for staffing resources or for substantial strategic planning at the school level, therefore, it may be the case that the economic benefits will accrue to the system but without real educational benefits. However, it must be recognised that there is not yet a strong enough evidence base in relation to a wide range of models of decentralisation for us to be confident about which factors may be most effective at promoting enhanced learning even where the level of delegation is not so substantially at school level as in the cases of England and Wales and Victoria, Australia. Furthermore, we have also shown in Chapter 9 that the presence of a planning process does not in itself guarantee effective links between planning and outcomes.

Managing within an institution where responsibility for all elements of the resource and budget cycles has been devolved places on principals a requirement to apply a wider range of leadership and management skills than might be expected before decentralisation. Clarke and Newman (1992) have described the characteristics of this 'new managerialism', and suggest that three important elements are:

- a shift from a perspective based on a public service ethos towards a more business-focused ethos
- an increasing emphasis on responding to the external environment
- a rise in the emphasis on entrepreneurial skills.

Each of these characteristics of educational leaders represents a spectrum of possible positions and skills rather than a simple polarity of positions. The situation of any individual leader will depend upon a wide range of factors including personal inclination, the nature of devolved responsibility they must hold, the culture of the school and the community, and the specific range of issues that the institution's operating environment has generated. Nevertheless, Anderson (2000, pp. 41–2) identifies that

> since the early 1990s, the innovative management of change and external relations has become a vital activity for effective headteachers, principals and other managers and, for some of these people, the experiences have brought to light hitherto undiscovered or, possibly, frustrated abilities and skills of innovation and entrepreneurialism. Thus both a new term has been introduced into educational language – the entrepreneurial leader – and a new attribute associated with effective educational leaders.

The emergence of the entrepreneurial leader and the entrepreneurial school (Campbell and Crowther, 1991) is not only an identifiable element of self-management, but may be regarded as an essential requirement for success in such environments (Caldwell and Spinks, 1992). Entrepreneurship requires skills of creativity, innovation and risk-taking, not just in terms of the resource cycle but also in terms of curriculum, learning and teaching. Boisot (1995), for example, emphasises the importance of 'intrapreneurship', which is the promotion of initiative and individual innovation within the organisation, and Caldwell and Spinks (1998) identify this as a significant element within self-managing schools.

MANAGING THE RESOURCE CYCLE AT THE INSTITUTIONAL LEVEL

To examine the nature of school-based resource management and the emergence of the skills of planning and entrepreneurship we shall consider management in each of the phases of the resource cycle (see Chapter 10). At the level of individual schools the focus on different elements of the resource cycle is clear in contrasts between different countries. In many less developed countries, for example, the emphasis on income generation is of considerable importance, whereas elsewhere there may be more emphasis on resource allocation and implementation.

Obtaining resources

With a low level of central resource allocation for the majority of school managers at a global scale the task of acquiring even minimal levels of resources to support learning and teaching is a priority task. While increasing funding from formal public expenditure systems is a desirable goal, the realities of, for example, population growth that is faster than economic growth, and the burdens of international debt, are major constraints. The World Bank (1995) recognises that, in such contexts, seeking to diversify the sources of funding for education is desirable, and that much of this may fall to individual schools and headteachers to operationalise.

This issue is well illustrated in the case of Uganda where delegation of some resources from central government to schools has been established since 1986. Nkata and Thody (1996) show, however, that this provides only a very low level of centralised funding from government, so that it is the responsibility of the school principal and the parent–teacher association (PTA) to generate income from pupil fees and from fund-raising. Funding for learning materials and for capital works are derived from the same source of fees and from voluntary contributions. Income is strongly influenced, therefore, by the socio-economic characteristics of the locality the school serves, and also by the political and cultural traditions. Nkata and Thody show how the traditions of prioritising boys' education and of valuing European rather than African traditions has constrained headteachers from enhancing equity and Africanism within the curriculum. Parents will simply not support the school financially if it seeks to develop strategies outside the cultural norms. Overall Nkata and Thody (1996, p. 8) suggest that between 65 per cent and 90 per cent of income comes from fees and voluntary contributions, with 'teachers being almost entirely dependent on PTA funding for their salaries'. The explicit government policy of encouraging schools to charge fees to seek to redress some of the underfunding issues may be seen as economic pragmatism through an emphasis on the centrality of family and community values, and 'appealing to local self-interest or altruism' (Bullock and Thomas, 1997, p. 69) which are perceived as strong within Uganda. However, the negative impact is that parents who cannot afford the fees simply withdraw their children from school, and schools unable to attract sufficient funding may be forced to recruit unqualified teachers. Nkata and Thody (1996) suggest that in some localities, for example, as many as 70 per cent of teachers may be unqualified. For the headteacher in such circumstances the management challenge has both marketing and political dimensions, for he/she must both manage the relationship with the PTA and with the local community, promoting the importance of school attendance and the reform of the curriculum while seeking to encourage access and participation.

The importance of obtaining resources in schools in less advanced economies is well illustrated too by the prominence of school businesses within the funding systems of schools in China. Fouts and Chan (1997) show how the central funding mechanisms in China direct much of the finance towards a relatively small number of schools so that most schools need to seek additional income. This 'creation of income' (*chuangshou*) is a government-imposed requirement for state schools and has been promoted since 1981. Ng (2001, p. 380) reports that *chuangshou* 'has rapidly become an indispensable source of income, with over 90 percent of schools and universities engaging in it'.

Ng (2001) provides a case study of the 'creation of income' amongst schools in the Haizhu district of the city of Guanzhou in south-east China. The schools in the study generate an average of 22 per cent of their income for themselves through a range of school enterprise activities. The majority of this income arises from the following activities:

1) Fees from school selection. Pupils are allocated to secondary schools on the basis of prior academic performance, but parents may choose to send their children to an alternative school providing they pay significantly higher (sometimes premium) fees. The high value accorded to education amongst Chinese parents means that many seek to place their children in higher status schools and the funding of school fees to do this is a family priority. In some of the more popular schools in Ng's study up to 25 per cent of pupils pay fees as out-of-catchment students.
2) School-run factories. The idea of 'work-study', with students spending part of their day working in a school-run factory or enterprise, has a

long history in China, and is based on a cultural commitment to community engagement and vocational training as well as income generation. Most schools generate some income in this way, although rapid
economic growth in China in the last decade has rendered most of these
enterprises uneconomic, and many are declining or closing.

3) Premises rental. This is most frequently in the form of leasing space to
   shops where schools abut main roads, but also includes use of space
   for factory work and warehouse accommodation.

4) Other activities. This covers a wide range of activities, including adult
   education classes, provision of restaurant services, typing and photo-
   copying services.

The importance of 'creation of income' to the schools is clear, both in
terms of the direct benefits of having additional income at their disposal,
but also in terms of a range of management and wider educational impacts.
Ng (2001, p. 386) comments that 'except for a few prestigious keypoint
schools, the buildings, facilities and equipment provided by the government for schools in Guangzhou are generally rudimentary'. Hence the
opportunity for enhancing facilities, providing new buildings and purchasing learning support materials such as computers can be very important. In addition, funding is used to enhance teacher salaries through the
payment of bonuses, which can be as much as 70 per cent of salary in
schools with significant funds from the 'creation of income' and averages
30 per cent across all schools, and to support staff development
programmes.

Ng identifies some of the wider but less tangible benefits as those deriv-
ing from the enhancement of teacher morale and the development of
increased autonomy for the schools. These two ideas are strongly linked,
for enhanced morale derives not just from improvements to salaries and
facilities but also from the opportunity to exercise discretion and authority in relation to the development of the school. This is seen in part as an
important factor in reducing the drift of teachers from the profession and
maintaining stability in staffing in the schools.

The identifiable benefits of *chuangshou*, however, are balanced in part
by some of the negative dimensions of the programme, and Ng (2001, p.
389) identifies concerns in relation to equity and efficiency, and the 'cor-
rosive effects on teaching and corruption'. The combined impact of location, the socio-economic characteristics of the school catchment, school
history, and the level of entrepreneurial skills of school managers and
teachers means that there are large differences in the levels of additional
income that schools can generate. This disparity is exacerbated by the
system of matched funding in which income created by the school is
matched by the local education authorities. The schools which are successful, too, tend to be those with pupils from more affluent backgrounds,
so that the pupils who benefit least from the system are those from the
lowest socio-economic groups.

The 'creation of income' programme brings with it a number of inherent risks, however, and negative impacts on teaching and learning relate to two issues. First, the detrimental effects on the school environment of the use of school premises for non-educational activities, generating noise, pollution and the bustle of commercial activity can be distracting to pupils. Secondly, the importance of income generation distracts senior management, and Ng observes that 'some administrators admitted that they had spent more effort on school-run businesses than on school management' (Ng, 2001, p. 390).

A final area of concern relates to the opportunities for corruption within the *chuangshou* system. The possibilities for directing funding to inappropriate uses (for example, the use of income from student fees to pay teacher bonuses is not allowed) may be widespread, while more significant illegal activities relating to fraud, deception and individual profiteering have certainly been recorded in Guangzhou. While regarded by Ng as an insignificant factor within the whole 'creation of income' economy, the necessity for school managers to establish effective controls and accountability systems for their income adds yet another non-educational element to their role as administrators.

In most countries of the developed world levels of state funding, whether directed through simple allocation models or whether based on per capita formulae, provide much higher levels of income and resourcing, such that the pressure to generate additional income from other activities is less than in many less developed countries. While Anderson (2000) recognises that schools engage in a wide range of entrepreneurial activities, including fund-raising activities, sponsorship, the seeking of benefactors and bidding to government, business or charity organisations, the contribution to school budgets is, except in rare cases, less than 5 per cent of total income. The challenge in relation to income generation here is much more significant where funding is based on *per pupil* financial models, and where the recruitment of pupils through marketing activities becomes a priority for school management. Lauder and Hughes (1999) show how schools studied within the Smithfield Project in New Zealand included several for whom pupil recruitment, and hence funding, was a major challenge in a context of declining rolls following the establishment of parental choice systems. Here substantial management effort was directed to promotion, relations with parents and image development. This stands in stark contrast to those schools with buoyant recruitment for whom little marketing activity was necessary. Lauder and Hughes (1999, p. 109), for example, quote the principal of one of the successful schools (Sheppard High) who indicates, 'Last year we turned away about 150 . . . I do not spend a single cent on publicity. I have the plainest, simplest prospectus . . . I don't have to market the school . . . Marketing is a non-issue.'

The development of marketing cultures and strategies in schools and colleges has been considered in more detail in Chapter 7.

Allocating and managing resources

An important component in the management of resources is the necessity to implement formal mechanisms for allocating resources to activities and then managing their usage. The commitment to a technical-rational view of management that has characterised reform in many OECD countries has placed a premium on rational planning processes, as we have seen in Chapter 9. Such planning is based on models that incorporate the identification of goals, the design of strategies to achieve those goals, the allocation of resources to the strategies and activities, and an evaluation of achievements against those goals. The place of resource allocation within such models is central, yet of the three broad approaches to resource allocation that are found in practice (Simkins, 1998; Davies 1994) only one is *sensu stricto* a rational planning approach:

1) Incrementalism. This approach allocates resources to activities on the basis of figures from previous years. While simple to operate, though, it takes no account of changing priorities or of the necessity for responsiveness.
2) Political approaches. Such approaches allocate resources on the basis of micro-political decisions within the school, with the influence, power and status of individuals or groups playing a stronger role than an objective measurement of need. As Greenwood (1980, p. 29) indicate: '(A group's) share of scarce resources depends upon the skill of its advocates in the use of essentially political tactics, such as knowing how much to bid for . . . how to read the political climate, how to generate and utilise public support'.
3) Allocation linked to formal planning and goal setting. This approach requires groups within the organisation to bid for resources in support of the achievement of identified, measurable goals.

In practice most resource allocation systems incorporate some combination of these approaches, for even the strongest commitment to goal-setting will see some groups more adept at reading the political setting or influencing decision-making, and the overall resource levels available will be driven by any incremental growth or reduction at institutional level. This conflict between rational planning and the realities of resource allocation in practice is a common characteristic of resource management

Wong, Sharpe and McCormick (1998) have examined the rational planning model, based significantly on Caldwell and Spink's ideas, that underpins the SMI that has been progressively introduced in Hong Kong since 1991. Amongst the criticisms levelled at rational planning models is their lack of flexibility and responsiveness. In particular, sequential, rational planning systems may only work well in comparatively stable environments, and not in the turbulent environments in which schools operating in quasi-markets may find themselves. Wong, Sharpe and McCormick examine the adoption and operation of the SMI model in the context of these issues, and have identified a number of characteristics of how the model operates in Hong Kong:

1) Despite the fact that 'the school management cycle recommended by SMI displays some characteristics of a sequential, rational, "hard system" model' (Wong, Sharpe and McCormick, 1998, p. 69) both senior management and teachers adopt a flexible approach to implementing plans to enable them to be responsive. Thus, although 'the school plan is prepared at the start of the term to guide initial actions . . . teachers may use their professional judgement whether to follow or amend the specifics of the plan during the academic year as the environment changes' (ibid., p. 74).
2) The support of senior management in recognising the professional knowledge of teachers is an important element in promoting a positive view of the planning system/model.
3) The availability of adequate resources to operationalise the plan is an essential element in promoting confidence in the outcomes of planning.
4) When teachers are allowed to participate in the planning process they tend to develop a strong sense of ownership of the intended outcomes.

Overall, Wong, Sharpe and McCormick (1998, p. 79) conclude that 'providing there is sufficient support from the Principal and that sufficient resources are made available for the task, systematic planning using a flexible approach and involving teachers in the planning process is likely to lead to better planning outcomes'.

This raises the issue of the level of resourcing as a determining factor in the establishment of formal school-based planning as a key component of decentralised systems. Despite the movement towards school-based management, in systems where the level of financial resources is very limited the potential for being responsive to the external environment may be small. Furthermore, where a limited supply of suitably trained teaching staff is a significant resource issue, the potential for planning at management levels below that of the headteacher may be difficult to implement. Hence the implementation of sophisticated planning models within the school may be premature in resource-poor education systems. Nsaliwa and Ratsoy (1998) have examined the process of decentralisation in Malawi that was initiated in 1989–90 and show that little responsibility for any element of resource management has passed from the Ministry of Education even down to regional education offices, let alone to headteachers. Rather, here decentralisation is perceived to be 'a general trend [that is] not one of major shift in authority to the schools but rather a gradual and perhaps continuing growth of influence by the schools' (Nsaliwa and Ratsoy, 1998, p. 69). Planning within schools in Malawi is limited to choosing and paying for school supplies, and there is no evidence that this process is operated outside incremental and political mechanisms within the schools.

Evaluation – linking resource management to learning outcomes

If the purpose of schools and colleges is the development of pupil learning, then a key consideration in resource management at school level is whether there has been an enhancement to learning for the full range of pupils in the school. School effectiveness at the level of individual schools has been a growing concern for most OECD countries, although we have shown in Chapter 3 how there is very limited evidence of links between strategy, planning, resource management and pupil-learning outcomes. Raw indicators such as expenditure per pupil or pupil–teacher ratios will continue to be the tools for measuring resource management and enhancement for such schools, and the technology of assessing outputs and value added is only now emerging within the wealthiest economies. We have examined some of the evidence for these links earlier in this chapter, but the arguments about the choice of approaches to measuring learning outcomes still continues. As Levačić (2000, p. 21) indicates:

> Owing to the difficulties of valuing a highly diverse and intangible range of learning outcomes, and the lack of precise knowledge about the education process itself, the concepts of effectiveness and efficiency are not easy to operationalise for educational organisations ... Knowledge from research on school and teacher effectiveness needs to be combined with consideration of resource use and costs.

Identifying the processes involved in such linkages is a major research challenge in educational leadership and management.

EXPLORING THE MYTHS

The management of resources at institutional level is one of the emerging challenges for school leaders, and a key issue for those developing policy at all levels. We have shown in the analysis here that the degree of autonomy and responsibility varies between national systems, and the challenge of resource management is highly context specific so that the priorities differ from system to system and school to school. Broadly speaking, though, the challenge in most developing countries is to acquire even minimal levels of resources, whether finance, buildings or staffing. In some cases the recognition of this issue has led national governments to promote innovation and enterprise at school level, while in others it has simply emerged as an operational necessity. In more developed countries the minimum levels of funding are higher, so that two broad groups of priorities can be identified – pupil recruitment to ensure that the school's share of public funding resources is as large as possible, and the establishment of planning and implementation systems to enable increased effectiveness to be achieved in the context of locally defined priorities as well as national agendas. There is much research still to be undertaken, though, to explore the links between resource management and learning outcomes, and this will be one of the priorities if decentralisation is to be shown to be an effective strategy for education as well as a politically appropriate approach to the management of public sector education. In enhancing the knowledge and skills of leaders in relation to resource management we must recognise, though, that there exist a number of myths that need to be challenged in any system analysis and review. In particular, leaders must question:

- the assumption that local management will enhance pupil achievement, for the resource-outcomes link is dependent on the effectiveness of management approaches and strategies
- the value of rational resource planning models in the dynamic context of school and college operational environments
- the balance of gains and losses to the institution from adopting the management approaches that autonomy demands.

In considering institutional management of resources it is clear that the appeal to reason and rationality that a paradigm of strategy and outcomes-based planning is hard to connect with the reality of leading a school or college. While planning offers is a helpful framework for analysis and decision-making, its limitations mean that the development of responsiveness, creativity and an entrepreneurial perspective may be just as important in pursuing success for the institution, however defined. The paradigm of planning will not disappear in the foreseeable future, but understanding its values and limitations will enhance its utility to school and college leaders.

Section E: Learning futures

Management and leadership have both contemporary and future dimensions. Managing the 'here and now' is a major challenge, but a key element of the task is to move the institution on, to align it with what society will demand of education and training in the future. The direction of the future, and the capacity and desire to change it varies considerably across the world, of course, and within this book we have identified a number of metatrends shaping future patterns of education. In Section E we focus on two developments that have attracted significant attention at a global scale to consider the variation in their impact and potential. In Chapter 12 we consider the widening participation movement in all its forms, while in Chapter 13 we examine the emergence of the notion of the learning organisation.

12

WIDENING PARTICIPATION

THE CONCEPT OF WIDENING PARTICIPATION

Widening participation is an international movement that is one of the meta concepts driving change in the organisation, leadership and management of education. For schools it encompasses the extension of 'compulsory education', issues of pupil inclusion and notions of entitlement. For post-compulsory education it involves reaching out to groups not traditionally engaged with education and/or training, and promoting the idea of lifelong learning. Like each of the 'grandes idées' that we have identified it is not a discrete concept. Its influence reaches into many if not all aspects of leadership and management, and its presence provides a backdrop to issues such as the growth of 'learner outcomes' approaches (Chapter 3), the rise of quality matters (Chapter 4) and the emergence of self-management (Chapter 10). Within this chapter we shall seek to address a number of questions that impact on leaders and their roles in schools and colleges:

- What *is* widening participation, and what are its central aims?
- How do the challenges of widening participation differ internationally?
- How does widening participation emerge in policy and management in less developed countries/developed countries?
- What is the relationship between widening participation and lifelong learning, and what are the management implications?

Widening participation represents but one of a number of overlapping concepts. These include increasing the engagement of societies with learning, diversifying perspectives on what constitutes learning and what its purpose for the individual and society may be, and embedding in communities a continuing engagement with learning. These ideas present a complex challenge of identifying the needs and incentives for learning for non-participating groups, balancing those against the wider needs of society and then restructuring education, training and learning systems to facilitate this expansion. Linked to this is the concept of lifelong learning. Lifelong learning is the process of engaging individuals, communities and organisations in recognising the importance of learning to cultural, social and economic development at all stages of people's lives. Its priority is the expansion of learning for individuals beyond the compulsory education of childhood, not just into the sort of post-compulsory education that young people gain prior to entering the labour market, but also into training and retraining, and enhancing skills throughout working lives and through personal development through to old age. The ultimate objective of both widening participation and lifelong learning is a transition to a learning society in which education and training, both formal and informal, are a high-profile and high-status activity for all, with a community commitment to the value of learning in contributing to social and individual growth.

The pressures towards widening participation are both economic and social/humanitarian. The links between education and training levels in society, economic output and economic competitiveness at the macro scale, and the link at the individual level between educational attainment and potential earnings are strong presumptions in government policy in many countries. As a result, the pursuit of economic development and of competitiveness in the global economy are a key political aim of most countries, built on an explicit policy of enhancing the performance of the education and training system. This 'human capital' view of society is clearly an important driver towards widening participation, despite the fact that, as we have demonstrated in earlier chapters, the presumed causality between educational and economic performance may be a myth. Valid or not, though, it is a key policy-driver, which is then reinforced by a humanitarian view of the importance of education in the personal development of the individual and of their communities.

THE LANDSCAPE OF WIDENING PARTICIPATION

We may suggest that the widening participation process has a number of identifiable stages that can be seen in mapping its global patterns. First, in many countries, and particularly less developed countries, it exists in the form of increasing participation rates, initially in elementary schooling and then in secondary schooling, with an aim of universal participation in formal education to a clearly established school-leaving age. Secondly, where formal school education becomes more or less universal, the expansion of early post-compulsory education becomes the dominant priority, with a pressure to increase the normal length of young people's participation. Thirdly, where high levels of participation in further, higher and tertiary education begin to be achieved the priority shifts towards embedding learning activities across the wider community, with a focus on raising aspirations and achievements for citizens at all ages, in all life stages and at all levels of prior attainment. This is the phase that the most developed economies have reached, and which is driving the lifelong learning agenda in most OECD countries, where 'one government after another has placed lifelong learning at the core of policy, and this priority has been repeatedly endorsed by the main intergovernmental actors' Field (2000, p. 249).

These three stages are neither discrete in form nor discontinuous in their existence, but all make demands on policy-makers and education leaders in consistent ways. First, all demand significant resource input. Secondly, they demand increased quality/standards and efficiency within the system, not least because politicians need to minimise the costs of the expansion they are promoting.

Thirdly, they push the education/training system in each country to become larger and inevitably more complex, with the links between the elements of the system more difficult to establish and sustain. Managing such complexity and entropy is challenging for those within the education/training system. For those at the front line, leading institutions, the enhanced complexity and pressure to raise standards is the price of the widening participation agenda. Managing external relations, recruiting more pupils, raising attainment for each pupil so that they are enabled to participate in later phases of education are now new elements of the management role. As Hargreaves (1997, p. 9) indicates:

> School systems continue to be perceived as performing inadequately. Teachers, it is said, need to do better, students are allegedly neither acquiring enough knowledge in school nor 'learning how to learn' and developing the motivation and flexibility for learning in lifelong education linked to changing job requirements. Politicians everywhere thus demand greater effectiveness from the education service – and greater efficiency, too, as the costs of lifelong education inexorably mount.

Fourthly, all changes and development in education and training systems require linked, and sometimes, prior, cultural changes, so managing education development independently of other aspects of society is not possible, and the connectivities within the community need establishing, maintaining and managing. The demands of human resource management have in this way been enhanced by the widening participation agenda.

Finally, all this is unlikely to be achieved without direct political intervention and direction, so we might expect to see increasingly directive government engagement with the system with clear establishment of goals and targets. Accountability has been a dominant theme of the 1990s and the early twenty-first century.

INCREASING PARTICIPATION – THE CHALLENGE FOR LESS DEVELOPED ECONOMIES

Globally, the expansion of participation in primary and secondary education has been a steady trend in the second half of the twentieth century. By 1970 a very high proportion of the world's primary-age children was being enrolled in school (gross enrolment ratio [GER] of 90 per cent). In the last quarter of the century rapid expansion of secondary and tertiary education, together with the continuing rise of primary enrolment saw primary GER rise to 102 per cent, secondary GER increase from 36 per cent to 60 per cent, and tertiary GER rise from 9 per cent to 17.5 per cent (UNESCO, 1998). However, the global pattern masks many stark regional contrasts. While in the world's developing countries GER is 100 per cent for both primary and secondary education and over 50 per cent for tertiary education, in the world's least developed countries GER is 71 per cent (primary), 19 per cent (secondary) and 3 per cent (tertiary), with the lowest ratios in the least developed countries of Africa. Expanding participation in primary and secondary education is, therefore, for many countries the principal policy and management challenge to government, to school boards and to headteachers.

Managing the economic and social role of schooling and promoting the recognition of personal and community gain from education in the context of severe financial constraint and of rural and urban poverty is a major challenge, and far beyond simple legislation. It is fundamentally entwined with the total social and economic development process, and is highly sensitive to predominant economic conditions. In Tanzania, for example, enrolment in primary schools fell from 98 per cent to 56 per cent throughout the 1980s in response to challenging economic circumstances and a recognition that the majority of primary children still left school illiterate (Ishumi, 1994). This emphasises an important issue, in that taking children into school does not guarantee the quality of education they receive, and increasing enrolment must be accompanied by substantial developments in teacher training and supply, curriculum reform, quality assurance and resource provision.

The reform of the education system in Namibia in south-west Africa during the 1990s illustrates a range of policy and implementational responses to the challenge of increasing participation (Auala, 1998). Following independence from South Africa in 1990 the government inherited a disparate education system, with 11 ethnically based education authorities and very low gross enrolment ratios (primary GERs of 100 per cent for whites, but 30 per cent for other ethnic groups). The new Namibian Ministry of Education and Culture's policy document *Toward Education for All: A Development Brief for Education, Culture and Training* (1993) identified the key policy objectives as:

- the expansion of access to education and training
- improvement in the quality of education
- equitable distribution of resources
- democracy
- enhanced school effectiveness
- the development of a culture of lifelong learning.

To achieve these broad goals a number of specific areas of action were established, and Auala (1998) identifies four of these as of particular significance – language policy, curriculum and examination reform, teacher education, and resource distribution. Language policy involved the recognition of the equality of all national languages, and their use as a medium for instruction to the age of 9, but the adoption of English as the language of instruction beyond that age. Curriculum and examination reform was a key development in recognition of the fact that 'at independence, the curriculum was largely irrelevant to the changing needs of Namibian society' (Auala, 1998, p. 59). Fundamental reform of the primary and secondary curriculum was undertaken by the National Institute for Educational Development and fully implemented by the end of 1995.

Teacher training policy recognised the need to increase the number of teachers being trained, but also to change the dominant approaches to learning and teaching in Namibian schools from traditional teacher-centred styles to active learning and pupil-centred approaches. Alongside initial teacher training a programme of in-service training for existing teachers has been implemented to promote the same approaches.

Underpinning the development programme has been a substantial enhancement of resource commitment to education, with the education budget being increased by 75 per cent from 1990–91 to 1993–94. Much of this investment has been in the promotion of curriculum reform and teacher education, but targeting in rural areas and in those regions with particularly low enrolment and/or with specific economic and social challenges has emphasised school construction programmes.

Auala suggests that reform in Namibia has led to positive change in many educational indicators. The total number of schools has increased by 16 per cent, and pupil enrolment increased by 21 per cent between 1989 and 1993. Education is compulsory up to the age of 16, and enrolment ratios are increasing in all age groups. The number of teachers has increased by 20 per cent. Despite the enhancements, however, the implementation of change is a long-term process, and Auala identifies a number of areas where much progress remains to be made. In particular, the problems of teacher supply and teacher quality remain significant, and the progress towards the adoption of new approaches to learning and the new curriculum is slow. For principals in schools the reforms have made significant demands in managing change and restructuring, yet the daily challenges of providing teachers, classrooms and lessons remain a major concern. Fundamentally the key problem is financial resources, for until the building of sufficient schools and the training of enough qualified teachers can be achieved, the statutory target of universal education to age 16 is still some way from achievement.

Structural change is, too, only one element in the development of universal primary and secondary education, for cultural change in communities and their view of education and its relevance is a more important development. Babyegyega (2000) has shown how engaging the community in educational development has been adopted as a key strategy in Tanzania through the Community Education Fund Project. School boards and headteachers are required to mobilise parents and community leaders in developing a school plan, which will achieve enhanced enrolment and an emphasis on a relevant and understood curriculum for the community. We have examined this management challenge in detail in Chapter 7.

WIDENING PARTICIPATION IN THE DEVELOPED WORLD

The second form of widening participation is that which characterises those countries where education at primary and secondary levels is almost universal, and where the enhancement of educational and training achievement across the population is being pursued through:

- the expansion of post-compulsory education – the tertiary sector of further and higher education
- the provision of second chance opportunities for those, often older individuals, who did not achieve many formal credentials in passing through the education system first time round
- the processes of inclusion, of ensuring that those from disadvantaged or underachieving sectors of the community are able to engage with the formal education and training system.

These are all forms of widening participation that demand specific actions, but Fryer (2000) has identified a number of key management challenges that all three raise. First, they demand a fundamental review of the structural and social barriers to participation, from language constraints to child care provision, from the nature of learning and teaching approaches to the relevance of programmes to the individual and to the labour market. Without such attention to process and system management widening participation may be confined to those sectors of society that have traditionally taken up opportunities in post-compulsory education. In the UK expansion of further and higher education during the 1990s, which had the express intention of increasing participation from underrepresented groups, served simply to increase participation from those from middle - class professional families (Trow, 1998). Secondly, and strongly associated with the first idea, widening participation requires organisations to be led by the needs of the communities and stakeholders they serve. Robinson

(2001), for example, suggests that the successful expansion of the Australian vocational education and training system, mostly in Technical and Further Education (TAFE) Colleges is in large part because of the

> [transformation] of Australian VET from being largely driven by the supply side (that is by training authorities and TAFE colleges themselves) to being a more demand driven (industry led) system. This has been a controversial . . . change in order to make the skills gained in VET more relevant to the workplace.
>
> (Robinson, 2001, p. 14)

Thirdly, increasing participation in post-compulsory education is fundamentally dependent on raising levels of attainment and aspiration in schools. Our consideration of the management of learner outcomes and resources (Chapters 3 and 9) has explored the specific challenge this has presented to schools and their leaders.

Fourthly, the complexity of such developments requires partnership between all sectors of the community and the public and private sector to ensure the diversity of needs is met by an appropriate diversity of provision. Chapman and Aspin (1997, p. 137) emphasise the importance of widening participation lying not just with the formal education systems but, rather, on 'the vital importance of the role played by various kinds of partnership in learning, rather than concentrating chiefly on the role of government as a monopoly provider of formal education and training'. Tight (1998) shows how the widening of participation in Sweden amongst these target groups has been achieved largely through complex partnership arrangements and strong commitment to the centrality of identifying individual needs within the system. Partnerships, of course, demand effective leadership both to establish and maintain them, and our consideration of managing external relations has shown how schools and colleges have adopted strategies to meet these needs.

The external relations challenge is underlined by the recognition that widening participation for education managers is in many respects simply a marketing issue, for it requires the meeting of the needs and wants of those currently not participating in learning such that they will engage with an appropriate educational or training experience. There are, however, two quite distinct components to this process, and Foskett and Hemsley-Brown (2001) distinguish between *facilitating choice* and *increasing demand*.

Facilitating choice involves enabling those who already wish to participate in learning but are unable to do so because of the circumstances in which they find themselves. This may be the result of economic, social, or cultural factors or because of structural characteristics of the existing system – for example, the real or opportunity costs of a programme, the lack of available child care, or their inability to attend courses during the day time. Attempting to address such issues is a common strategy, and may include such processes as simplifying application or admissions systems, providing open, distance or 'off-site' learning pathways, providing child-care facilities or subsidising programme costs.

Increasing demand involves persuading those who had not considered participating in learning to do so. This is a much larger challenge than facilitating choice, for it involves addressing key cultural perspectives on the nature and value of education and training. Those choosing not to participate in learning may be doing so because of earlier personal experiences of compulsory education or because of negative perspectives on what learning is for and like. Fryer (2000, p. 3), for example, suggests that many choosing not to participate in learning as adults or in their late 'teens have experienced failure, rejection or exclusion in earlier educational experiences, and that such people 'do not volunteer to be humiliated a second time'. Increasing demand, therefore, requires a clear understanding of how the perceptions, attitudes and beliefs of young people and adults can be modified by changing the experiences they and their families have within the learning system and the messages they receive from society about the value and personal relevance of engaging in learning. Foskett and Hemsley-Brown (2001, p. 220) suggest that 'expanding participation of adults and organisations in learning . . . requires more than simply "selling" learning to them'.

These processes can be illustrated by the establishment of the system of waanangas in New Zealand (Cherrington, 1999) to provide tertiary education amongst Maori communities. Waanangas are post-secondary educational institutions, funded by government, which draw on the cultural backgrounds of the Maori to provide education and training at tertiary level to raise achievement and participation. According to Cherrington (1999, p. 93): 'The Maori . . . represent a high percentage of . . . those who have been failed by mainstream education; those who want a second chance in gaining an education; those who are long term unemployed; and those who represent the lower socio-economic groups in New Zealand society.' Working in the context of close Maori communities the waanangas have developed curricula that both match the quality and structural expectations of national quality agencies and provide a Maori cultural learning environment. The waanangas are communities rather than campuses, and have as a strong strand within them high levels of direct contact between learners and teachers. The management of the waanangas is based in close linkages between the Maori community leaders and the waananga leaders, and this serves to raise the status and profile of the educational processes they provide and to ensure integration with Maori traditions. In this way, local cultural needs, national government objectives and global economic imperatives are being met through partnerships between communities and government.

WIDENING PARTICIPATION AND LIFELONG LEARNING – THE HOLY GRAIL?

The rise of the concept of lifelong learning as the mature stage of the widening participation movement has been a phenomenon of the second half of the 1990s. Its growth can be illustrated in the context of the European Union, where it emerged from a European Commission White Paper (*Growth, Competitiveness and Employment*) in 1994. The vision of the European Commission was that lifelong learning and continuing training are essential to combat global economic competition but also play a significant role in developing ideas of social inclusion. This vision was reinforced from beyond the EU by the OECD's report on *Lifelong Learning for All* (1996), and then underwent a rapid process of emergence in EU policy and diffusion into policy perspectives from most of the individual countries within the EU. The European Commission's White Paper *Teaching and Learning: Towards the Learning Society* (1996) shaped national policies such that lifelong learning had been adopted in education and training policy very quickly in the UK and Germany (1997), Finland, the Netherlands, Norway and Ireland (by 1998).

Despite the rhetoric of policy, however, there is as yet little strong evidence of fundamental cultural and operational shifts in the OECD countries towards embedding lifelong learning. Field (2000, p. 251) comments that '[while] policy endorsement of lifelong learning is virtually universal . . . a favourable policy climate has paradoxically failed to generate much that is new or innovative in terms of specific policy measures'. Field goes on to argue that there are only two areas where policy developments have translated into operational changes – the strongly vocational areas where the focus has been on skills development, and the development of policy to, de facto, extend the numbers continuing in education and training beyond the minimum school-leaving age. In the Netherlands, for example, much of the funding for lifelong learning has been used for lowering the age of primary school admission, for addressing exclusion amongst secondary age pupils and for enhancing in-service training for teachers. Three important aspects of this emerging pattern are of significance for educational management.

First, the lack of expansion in adult learning is not surprising when it is clear that few countries have had substantial traditions of operating in this field. A UNESCO report in 1997 confirms that 'almost everywhere in the world, adult education is a widely neglected and feeble part of the educational scene' (Giere and Piet, 1997, p. 4), and governments have neither the experience nor the resource base, therefore, to close the gap between rhetoric and reality.

Secondly, the areas of expansion that are identifiable are where there is a clear and evidenced payoff for participants. Foskett and Hemsley-Brown (2001, p. 200) suggest that '[for most people] learning is seen as the route to economic and social benefits, leading to an enhanced lifestyle. Its value is not intrinsic but extrinsic, and lies in the payoff to the individual'. For both individuals and organisations the areas of success in promoting lifelong learning are those with clear immediate payoffs.

Thirdly, as a result of the lack of public sector expertise and the emphasis on 'just-in-time' and 'cost-benefit' views of such learning, much of the growth in the sector has been not in public sector education and training but in the private sector. The rise of 'corporate universities' (for example, the Motorola University) and of independent training providers poses a major challenge to public sector providers. Not only are public sector providers often unable to respond to changing demand on the short timescale that business can achieve, but they also have limited entrepreneurial skills or finance for investment. Furthermore, their diverse social and political aims make focused development such as that possible within business more difficult to achieve. The expansion of the private sector in promoting the lifelong learning agenda raises challenging long-term issues for education managers in the public sector, though, for it raises the spectre of more private–public partnership as one of the strategies for management throughout the education/training system.

These issues in the establishment and development of lifelong learning are clearly illustrated by the case of Japan, where the concept of lifelong learning has been strong within the culture, and the business and educational system throughout its rise to economic success in the second half of the twentieth century (Fuwa, 2001). Three critical factors have played an important role in embedding the concept so firmly. First, the high level of educational attainment and credentialisation within the population has both raised the profile of learning within society and emphasised its significance for personal advancement. Over 40 per cent of young people attend university, and the social and family pressure towards school achievement embeds learning within society at an early age. Ouston (1998, p. 17) comments that:

> Parents are very aware of the increasingly competitive structure of post-compulsory education and of the need for their children to do well in examinations in order to enter good upper secondary schools and universities. Many parents . . . send their children to juku where children are taught the school curriculum in small, streamed classes. Kudomi (1994) estimates that over 60% of lower secondary school students in Tokyo attend juku, and the majority attend at least three nights a week.

Secondly, there is a long tradition of adult education within Japan, with almost 18,000 adult education centres in 1996 (Fuwa, 2001), and high rates of participation in programmes at these centres. Most provide liberal education and leisure programmes, and have much higher participation amongst middle-class individuals and women.

Thirdly, training within business and industry has been an important element in Japanese economic success. The company vocational systems (*kigyounai kyouika*) engage most employees in learning and provide incentives and rewards for engagement and success in relevant programmes, and within companies promotion is strongly credential driven.

Against this background lifelong learning emerged as a formal concept in Japan only in 1981, as a key objective within the report of the National Central Advisory Committee for Education. In 1990 the government established the National Advisory Committee for Lifelong Learning (NACLL), whose purpose was to promote lifelong learning through:

- the encouragement of voluntary engagement with learning amongst all age groups
- the promotion of recurrent training and education for adults
- the extension of opportunities to learn about contemporary issues
- the encouragement of learning within the family.

Fuwa (2001) emphasises that lifelong learning as a concept may be more embedded in Japanese culture than in most other developed countries, but identifies several key management challenges to developing the idea further. First, formalised learning amongst adults is rooted in utilitarian values and is driven strongly by the commitment to learning of the business sector. However, for those working outside large corporations there are still major constraints both practically and attitudinally towards engaging with formal learning. Secondly, voluntary engagement with learning outside the workplace is mostly focused on recreational and hobby learning. Thirdly, the Japanese commitment to learning in the family is strongly linked to the promotion of examination success for their children rather than the embedding of a genuine project of widening learning. These constraints mirror many of the issues facing widening participation and lifelong learning development in many other developed countries, and suggest that it is the cultural characteristics of a highly credential-driven competitive labour market and a commitment to economic growth in large Japanese corporations based on training and the incentivisation of learning that makes Japan appear more advanced in pursuing the lifelong learning agenda. The role of government and public sector organisations in promoting lifelong learning based on implicit libertarian values may be seen, perhaps, as less likely to be successful than a utilitarian, incentivised approach in the business and commercial sector.

It is clear that promoting lifelong learning is a challenge to countries in the developed world. To those in the developing world it is a somewhat more remote aspiration. Oduaran (2000) has considered the concept of lifelong learning in the context of education and training systems in Africa. Linking the rise of lifelong learning to the processes of globalisation, he suggests that African economic development is as dependent on engaging with education and learning as development in developed economies.

However, since in most of the continent the establishment of sound primary and secondary systems is still the major challenge, Oduaran (2000, p. 268) sees the opportunity for developing an education system which in its first principles promotes lifelong learning in 'a context of African-ness', rather than having to bolt-on the concept to an existing system. This he believes reflects the Singaporean model of development, where political will, financial investment in training at all levels within the community, and the tying together of social and economic development has built on the cultural roots of the communities within Singapore. However, Oduaran recognises that the major constraint is a financial one, for amongst African nations average expenditure on education is 2 per cent of gross domestic product (GDP) compared to a global mean of 5 per cent.

LOOKING TO THE FUTURE

Increasing participation in education and training systems is a global aspiration for governments and for those involved in managing the system itself. There is a clear commitment for education as a tool for economic and social development. The specific targets and priorities are driven by local cultural, social and economic circumstances, ranging from the need to draw children into primary and secondary education to the pressure towards promoting lifelong learning as a central cultural tenet. Evidence from across the range of settings suggests that there is an almost universal recognition that the impact of globalisation increases the need to expand both the quality and quantity of education and training (that is, of 'learning') within societies. However, it is equally clear that while financial investment is an important requirement in driving such developments, their acceptability and success is also dependent on a cultural project, an engagement between formal education systems, communities, business and industry, families and individuals to raise the profile of the priority accorded to learning. The evidence so far is that widening participation is an emerging reality at a global scale, but it is also clear that there are a number of significant myths surrounding understandings of widening participation. The first myth is that widening participation has a single, universally accepted meaning. We have shown that its meaning and focus is dependent on the precise state and status of each specific education and training system, and that understanding the context is essential before an understanding of widening participation priorities can be achieved. The second is that even where widening participation is identifiable as a policy aim its progress is being driven by a cultural revolution, based in a social project of lifelong learning. Our evidence suggests that, rather, its growth is a reflection of economic choices by individuals and by governments seeking to enhance the economic benefits to society.

The third myth is that lifelong learning is a concept that has universal recognition and value. Our analysis suggests that lifelong learning remains a substantial myth in any global picture, which still shows that the majority of the world's children will not be educated beyond primary level, and even then that education will be fitful and limited.

Despite the myths, however, we would suggest that widening participation will continue to be a policy and leadership challenge for the foreseeable future. At all levels of educational management, from national policy-setting to individual principal and school the strength of commitment to education as a tool for social and economic development will ensure that seeking to increase the scale of educational provision within societies and communities will remain a priority.

13

ACHIEVING A LEARNING ORGANISATION

FINDING A RESPONSE

Our second 'Learning futures' focus is the concept of the learning organisation and the leadership and management issues linked to its emergence and diffusion. Previous chapters have reflected a worldwide anxiety to increase the range of children and adults receiving or remaining longer in education, and to ensure the education they receive is appropriate to the twenty-first century. They have also explored some of the main approaches which have been adopted to reform the leadership and management processes that underpin teaching and learning. However, success has been limited. The strategy of many governments, to impose wholesale curriculum and organisational reform, has not resulted in the anticipated changes, often being met with incomprehension, anxiety, exhaustion or resistance. At the beginning of the new century, it may be that something different, something more, is needed. In a postmodernist world, the need for a qualitatively different response has long been recognised in business and industry. The concept of a learning organisation has seemed to hold out a possible answer. In education, parallel calls for the learning school, the learning community, the learning society have burgeoned. Fullan (1995, p. 230) asserts somewhat bleakly that 'the school is currently not a learning organisation. And teaching is not a learning profession'. However the concept has clearly captured the imagination of many and remains a powerful inspiration to explore the relationship of schools and colleges to learning. The importance invested in the idea of the learning organisation varies throughout the world, with particularly the USA, Canada, Australia, New Zealand and, to some extent, South Africa, focused on exploring the relevance and usefulness of the concept to education (Leithwood, Lawrence and Sharratt, 1998; Tuohy, 1994). Sometimes the engagement of educational institutions is no more that a rhetorical aspiration, the use of a fine-sounding phrase, but there are examples of more rigorous efforts to define, research and use the concept to achieve the great leap forward which is so desired and so elusive. This chapter will consider the following questions:

- Why do schools and colleges wish to become learning organisations?
- How can a learning organisation be defined or understood?
- What practice appears likely to achieve a learning organisation?
- Why is there a varied degree of interest in different parts of the world?

PRESSURES FOR CHANGE

There is an extensive generic literature reflecting general agreement in business and industry on the conditions which demand the creation of learning organisations. Drawing on lessons from major global corporations, Marquardt (1995, p. 218) lists the requirements for businesses to survive. They must:

- learn more effectively from their mistakes;
- shorten the time required to implement strategic changes;
- anticipate and adapt more readily to environmental impacts;
- make greater organizational use of employees at all levels of the organization;
- expedite the transfer of knowledge from one part of the organization to another;
- become more proficient at learning from competitors and collaborators;
- stimulate continuous improvement in all areas of the organization;
- accelerate the development of product and process innovation.

Marquardt argues that the consequence of these demands is the need to become a learning organisation, and that 'the business of business is learning' (ibid., p. 217). All the imperatives listed above apply equally to the survival of educational institutions, and how much more is the business of schools and colleges learning, for they must learn not only for the benefit of all those within the institution, but as a model of lifelong learning for the community. However, holding the general aspiration to become a learning organisation is one thing; knowing how to achieve it is another. Despite assumptions that learning would come easily to those involved in education, evidence suggests the contrary, that learning of students and staff at an individual level, and learning at organisational level, requires development in a number of ways.

STAFF LEARNING

Teachers are a conservative group of people. A widely used psychometric test, which has been validated across a number of cultures, shows teachers clustered at the midpoint of a spectrum of psychological attitudes to adopting innovative or adaptive approaches (Kirton, 1976). The innate conservatism may be entrenched further by the culture of teaching. Day-to-day practice may include a variety of demands which are antithetical to deep learning. Huberman (1992) characterises the development of teachers as essentially an ad hoc, hit and miss process of trying things out, retaining what works, finding methods that help to survive the demands of large or difficult classes or an over full curriculum. There is little systematic development. Nor is there necessarily any sharing of practice. Southworth (1996) argues that primary school teachers do not discuss pedagogy, partly because they wish to avoid any conversation that could be construed as critical, and partly because the daily press robs them of time. Critical self-assessment may be squeezed out by lack of time and discouraged by the perceived need to appear in control. Consequently, although teachers may believe themselves committed to ongoing learning and articulate such a commitment, they are perhaps particularly subject to the dichotomy noted by Argyris and Schön (1981) between saying one thing and doing another. Cardno (1995) notes the gulf between espoused theory and theory-in-use in New Zealand schools. Principals in two case study schools saw themselves as effective leaders using appraisal to identify the learning needs of staff. In fact they avoided raising issues in order to preserve relationships. Open discussion of learning needs was viewed as deeply threatening to the equilibrium of the relationships. Staff are unused to reflecting on the relationship between their stated beliefs and values and the degree to which their practice reflects them. Where learning does take place, it may be of a circumscribed nature. Leithwood, Lawrence and Sharratt (1998), writing of schools in the USA, report a prevalence of learning which is exploitative rather than exploratory, that is learning which does not challenge existing premises, but only seeks to find answers to meeting immediate problems within the existing framework. The nature of staff learning, therefore, may be trammelled.

ORGANISATIONAL LEARNING

Staff may not be very effective learners individually. Equally they may not be very successful when learning together within teams or as an organisation. Roth and Niemi (1996) argue that organisations develop systems that work and then freeze those systems in rules and operating procedures, rewarding those who conform. The result is inertia which presents a considerable barrier to change. Critiques of educational organisations certainly echo this, suggesting that schools are frozen back in the 1960s (Stoll and Fink, 1996) or, in some ways, even further back in the nineteenth century (Bowring-Carr and West-Burnham, 1997). There is a need for the organisation to unlearn before it can move on to learn. When staff work together they may not find this easy to achieve. Firstly, Roth and Niemi (1996) paint a grim picture of teamwork, suggesting that where teams are made up of those with expertise in a range of areas, in order to offer the synergy of a range of skills and experience, the effect is the opposite of the whole being greater than the parts. The thinking that emerges is often 'considerably below the individual managers' capacities' (ibid., p. 208). When this general phenomenon of teamwork is set beside a professional culture where 'the norms of mutual and uncritical support of individuals and subject departments take precedence over enhancing teaching and learning' (Silins and Mulford, in press), the freezing of the organisation potentially becomes of an Arctic depth.

THE NEED TO CHANGE

The implications of the above discussion on the learning of educators at individual and organisational level suggest that current prescriptions for improving the quality of learning of the educational community do not work or do not work sufficiently well. The often proposed means to successfully manage change, that is, staff development, teamwork and collegiality, do not appear to be powerful enough to overcome embedded structures, processes and culture. Indeed, they seem to constitute structural factors which maintain, on the one hand, equilibrium but, on the other, stasis. After three years of working to improve standards, Clarke (1999, p. 6) reflected that what his team found most troubling in the schools they worked with was 'the persistence of learning barriers . . . [which] . . . profoundly influence day-to-day life . . . The only thing worse than having these defences is living with the denial of their existence'. The challenge to those involved with education is to recognise the inadequacy of current learning at every level and to address this by finding new ways to achieve improvement.

ACHIEVING THE LEARNING ORGANISATION

There is no dearth of proposed routes to achieving the learning organisation. Research has resulted in a plethora of recommended approaches. The suggestions tend to take the form of lists of necessary actions or conditions. Unfortunately, the former tend to be rather vague and aspirational. Fullan (1994, p. 29) presents the recipe provided by the National Education Commission on Time and Learning:

1. Reinvent schools around learning not time.
2. Fix the design flaw: use time in new and better ways.
3. Establish an academic day.
4. Keep schools open longer to meet the needs of children and communities.

5. Give teachers the time they need.
6. Invest in technology.
7. Develop local action plans to transform schools.
8. Share the responsibility: finger pointing and evasion must end.

Fullan (1995, p. 233) admits that this list implies 'a wholesale change in the culture and organization of schooling the likes of which we have not yet seen'. As with most descriptions of Utopia, recommended actions are predicated upon changes in values, beliefs and attitudes. Consequently the argument becomes circular. In order to achieve the state which is a changed culture, a changed culture must underpin the actions taken to get there; chicken and egg, which comes first?

Leithwood, Lawrence and Sharratt (1998), drawing on three independent studies in the USA involving 14 schools and 111 teachers, conclude that leadership, structure, policy and resources at school and district level are the variables most highly ranked in directly and indirectly influencing organisational learning, though the order of ranking varied amongst schools. They use the evidence to suggest that transformational leadership is key. Their characterisation of transformational learning suggests that a leader who promotes organisational learning:

- identifies and articulates a vision
- fosters the acceptance of group goals
- conveys high performance expectations
- provides appropriate models
- provides individualised support
- provides intellectual stimulation
- builds a productive school culture
- helps structure the school to enhance participation in school decisions (adapted from Leithwood, Lawrence and Sharratt, 1998, pp. 264–7).

In a similar search for factors which lead to a learning organisation, Silins and Mulford (2002) use data from two Australian states. They identify four dimensions that together define organisational learning in high schools:

- trusting and collaborative climate
- taking initiatives and risks
- shared and monitored mission
- professional development.

In discussing these factors they conclude that leadership is critical:

Leadership characteristics of a school are important factors in promoting systems and structures that enable the school to operate as a learning organisation. School leaders need to be highly skilled in transformational leadership practices which work, directly and indirectly through others, towards bringing about: consensus in the organisation's mission; structures for shared decision making; continual learning through reflective practice; high standards of professionalism; and, a supportive and appreciative climate that promotes a culture of trust and collaboration.

(Silins and Mulford, in press)

The findings of both research projects are very similar. However, the factors they suggest support the achievement of a learning organisation have a ring of 'mom and apple pie'. Most would approve a leader's efforts to achieve a shared vision, trust others, be appreciative of others' efforts, etc. The problem is that such processes, as discussed in this volume, are highly problematic. Although a simplistic manual of 'how to do it' is clearly not feasible or desirable, the descriptions in literature of a learning organisation, including those above by Leithwood, Lawrence and Sharratt and Silins and Mulford, provide aspiration and perhaps inspiration but little clue on what might be done differently to achieve the desired result. For example, Silins and Mulford suggest that trusting colleagues and encouraging them to take risks are two factors which in combination with a shared mission and professional development, define a learning organisation. There is much evidence that shared mission is something of a chimera (see Chapter 9). Increased measures to ensure accountability, such as publication of league tables and summative inspection regimes, render both risk-taking and trust very difficult to maintain. Given the absence of explicit ideas on how such aspirations are to be achieved, the prescriptions for the learning organisation largely fall back on a model of the heroic or charismatic leader who is able to surmount problems to achieve the rather general and very difficult outcomes such as trust and high-performance expectations. An exception to the ubiquitous level of generalisation is Falinski (1992) reported by Prawat (1996). Falinski, as principal of an American primary school, had a specific aim to 'build a constructivist school' (Prawat, 1996, p. 101). In other words, her aim was to centre development on changing the nature of learning for her pupils. Falinski details her engagement with one mathematics teacher who considered herself and was considered by others a very competent teacher. The principal observed her teaching and as well as noting positives, also suggested that 'the active engagement of students in their own learning' was missing (Prawat, 1996, p. 101). The reaction of the mathematics teacher was initially one of shock and hostility. The account details how commitment to a constructivist mode of learning was achieved with this teacher and with others. Some teachers left. The process was not comfortable, moving as it did outside the existing culture of uncritical support. In this case, a cascading process was a key tool. The mathematics teacher, once committed, worked with other teachers to spread understanding and commitment. By this means commitment to a new way of learning for children and for teachers grew. The school learned its way forward.

Despite the generalisation and perhaps idealism of current literature on the learning organisation, the concept remains a powerful aid for imagining a future. The way forward may be to move the intensity of the research focus from leadership and to transfer it to a rigorous investigation of workplace learning. Following in Argyris's footsteps (Argyris and Schön, 1981), it may be that by understanding more fully how barriers to learning are created and maintained, how people can be helped to unlearn before learning, what collective learning means in practice, all specifically in an educational environment, leaders will be in a position to help move schools and colleges from their current position to more learning-centred practice.

ANALYSING LEARNING IN THE LEARNING ORGANISATION

Models of individual learning exist, though they are varying and contested. Some theorists, such as Honey (1991) define learning as not only acquiring knowledge, insights and skills but also translating them into changed behaviour. Some add the idea of personal competence, in that action requires the appropriate knowledge, understanding and skills, but also, for example, courage or persistence (Gunter, 1996). A further extension is the notion that learning is contingent not only on the person in question, but on the prevailing power distribution, in that the learner must be allowed to translate new knowledge, understanding and skills into changed behaviour. Therefore power may need to be invested in them from another source, in order to allow them to make change and thereby to truly learn (Borzsony and Hunter, 1996). The most ubiquitous model of learning connected to the concept of the learning organisation, is that of single- and double-loop learning. Single-loop learning is characterised as scanning the environment to detect anything which may be moving the organisation off course, and making adjustments in response to come back onto course. The basic goals and processes are not questioned. Double-loop learning questions the goals themselves and the methods of operating. Some suggest a further level, triple-loop learning, where the underlying values are also reviewed (Gunter, 1996; Morgan 1986). While single-loop learning may be effective at keeping things on course, if it is the wrong course, you need not to stay on course but to move from it. Double-loop learning is needed in such a case but is difficult to achieve, largely because challenging accepted ways of doing things or being innovative is often uncomfortable and may upset those in power or upset existing power structures, both of which are perceived as risky activity for progressing a career or even sometimes keeping a job.

Theories of individual learning may be a useful starting point to begin thinking about the learning which underpins the learning organisation, but as Leithwood, Lawrence and Sharratt (1998) point out, they are limited in their relevance. Individual learning is not organisational leaning. The relationship between the two is subject to developing theory, which is as yet uncertain and exploratory. Tuohy (1994) distinguishes two approaches to the learning of groups. Perhaps the more common approach is where members develop their own meaning and by discussion try to move forward to forge some common knowledge or understanding. In the second model, group members arrive at meaning through dialogue with others, rather than remoulding prior beliefs. This attempt to characterise a different approach to community learning is not entirely convincing, in that no individual is going to come to dialogue as a *tabula rasa*. Prior values, beliefs and opinions are bound to exist. However, the alternative models reflect a desire to discover a model which provides a framework of learning that moves beyond current understanding of learning in groups, where organisational learning is merely the sum of the individual learning of group members. Leithwood, Lawrence and Sharratt (1998, p. 246) engage with a similar attempt to find a theoretical model of collective learning. They explore the idea of 'mutual adaptation' that is not only adjusting one's own contribution to the team to take account of new goals and the nature of the team itself, but also negotiating with others to mutually accommodate multiple adjustments. Such theory is still somewhat opaque, and concerns the learning of teams or small groups. Theory about learning of the whole organisation is equally underdeveloped. Literature on workplace learning offers a range of theories of how people learn, individually, socially and in a situated way (Boud and Garrick, 1999; Lave and Wenger, 1991). However, theories about learning in a variety of different workplaces cannot be unproblematically transferred to the learning of teachers in the workplace of a school or college. The context in which learning takes place and the nature of the working role may be critical. If learning is contingent on the nature of workplace, then the professional context of teaching, the isolation of the working role in the classroom/workshop, and the fact that many teachers spend most of their time with children rather than other adults, may mean that the organisational learning of educators requires specific theoretical models. Existing literature is sparse (Hodkinson and Issitt, 1995; Maynard, 1995). Much more research is needed to understand the barriers which exist to organisational learning in education and to develop theoretical models which will provide a positive guide to how it can be achieved, not just in the cultures which currently are engaged with this concept, but in the range of cultures which exist in schools and colleges in different parts of the world.

SHAPING LEARNING

If the nature of organisational learning is one key, then the locus of control of teaching and learning may be another. Chapter 12 discussed the different ways in which the desire to widen participation is being interpreted and implemented throughout the world. However, if when a wider range of learners arrives at schools and colleges they meet only the curriculum which was designed previously for a narrower range of learners, their needs are unlikely to be met. Evolving a curriculum to engage particularly disaffected learners and to help them achieve is a central concern in many parts of the world. It requires a deep understanding of the perspective of such students and their learning preferences. However, there may be a wide gulf in the life experience, world view and expectations of staff and learners. The implication of this gulf is that, rather than the traditional control of learning by government and staff, teaching and learning may need to be shaped by a wider constituency. It may need to involve not only staff, but parents, employers and, critically, students. This is, of course, a very challenging objective, given the barriers and difficulties that exist, for example in working with parents, as explored in Chapter 8.

In South Africa, reform of governance has guaranteed places on the governing body not only for parents but also for elected representatives of learners in secondary schools (Department of Education, South Africa, 1996a). Borzsony and Hunter (1996) provide an example of a Scottish university which involves a number of players in the decision-making process, valuing each for its contribution. The young, rather than being dismissed as having too little knowledge or maturity, are valued for their expertise. 'Young partners know more than anyone about being young at the end of the twentieth century' (ibid., p. 23). Additionally their knowledge in some areas, for example new technology, may actually be greater than that of subject specialist staff. The benefits discerned of involving a wider group in shaping the curriculum are speedier decision-making, more effective implementation of decisions and improved learning for students. The assumption underpinning such an inclusive approach to the control of the curriculum is that learning is necessary for all, not just those formally designated pupils or students. Teachers or lecturers need to learn from students and from employers and parents. Learning flows not from the top of the hierarchy down, but in multiple directions, based on the empowering principle that all have something to offer in shaping teaching and learning. A commitment to listen to employers, parents and students may exist rhetorically in many schools and colleges. The concept of the learning organisation demands that rhetoric be turned into reality, but such change is not appropriate in all cultures.

CULTURAL MATCH

The principle of involving all, of demanding self-questioning even of those at the highest level of authority, has implications for the power structure and culture of an organisation. Consequently, as Lloyd, (1996, p. 6) points out, 'learning organisations cannot operate effectively within power-driven cultures'. There is a required commitment to sharing. Consequently, in common with other management techniques such as total quality management, unless the underlying culture of the organisation is sufficiently in tune with the values implied, the concept may be introduced with enthusiasm but will ultimately fail. It may be that in cultures which have a high power–distance factor, with an expectation of authority and decision-making by senior managers in the institution, and tight control of learners by staff, the learning organisation is not an approach which is likely to be appropriate or successful. This may go some way towards explaining why the concept appears of greater interest in low power–distance countries like America and New Zealand, or in countries where the power–distance is subject to massive adjustment as in South Africa, and of less interest to some Asian countries with high power–distance cultures. Dimmock (2000, p. 266) argues that in Chinese society 'as a consequence of conflict avoidance and of the requirement for harmonic relationships, decisions and policies are seldom challenged or approached creatively by the group'. He characterises such cultures as 'replicative systems'. Any culture which places avoiding conflict above improvement is unlikely to find the concept and theories of a learning organisation helpful. It would be easy to stereotype all Asian cultures as replicative and western cultures as innovative. However, this chapter has argued that avoiding conflict is embedded in education throughout the world, but may be more intensely felt in some cultures than others. As Senge (1993) points out, strategies to avoid conflict or to avoid the open appearance of conflict are just as prevalent in the West. People may well support their seniors whatever their own view. The underlying incentive for conflict avoidance may be the collective good in Asian cultures or individual self-interest in western cultures. Perhaps both self-interest and commitment to the community exist all over the world. What is certain is that if theories of the learning organisation are to be of value to a school or college, some realistic hope of openness and of sharing power amongst the hierarchy of staff and between staff and students and between the institution and the community must exist. The achievement of a learning organisation demands that the nature of learning itself, whether in the classroom, workshop or working environment, be transmuted into a process which is less based on the hierarchy of those who know, the staff, and those who do not, the learners, but more a journey to consider and encompass the ambiguity and constant procreativity of knowledge.

LOOKING TO THE FUTURE

Marquardt (1995, p. 224) is certain that there will never be a manual of '50 Ways to Create a Learning Organization', but in some sense that is what we already have; a series of lists of things to do which will lead to becoming a learning organisation. The problem is in the level of generality and idealism in the lists. At the moment there are only a handful of empirical studies on schools and colleges becoming learning organisations, and they generally provide aspirational and rather broad guidance, which do not add a great deal to our sum of knowledge on how to achieve a learning organisation (Leithwood, Lawrence and Sharratt, 1998). We have little in the way of theories of collective learning amongst teachers on which to draw. Moreover a learning organisation may be an uncomfortable place, where embedded structure and practice no longer provide a safe haven of stability (Morgan, 1986; Southworth, 1996). Despite these multiple disincentives, the concept remains both a compelling vision in many parts of the world and, for some, a practical prospect. One Australian college has focused on learning systems and seen: 'the technically-focused, discipline-centred School of Agriculture at Hawkesbury Agricultural College transform itself (over 15 years or so) into the systems-oriented, learner-centred School of Agriculture and Rural Development' (Kay and Bawden, 1996, p. 19). The emphasis in the college is now on experiential, project-based, collaborative learning, a long way from the transmission of technical knowledge that existed previously. The timescale of 15 years is a salutary reminder of how long such a profound change in culture and practice may take.

Fullan (1995, p. 234) calls the learning organisation a 'felicitous phrase, distant dream'. So it may be. But dreams are the lever for the future and the developing theory of the learning organisation may ultimately underpin the achievement of distant dreams.

Section F: Leadership

The changes and processes explored earlier in the volume can all be traced to their source in the leadership of those who work in schools, colleges, regional and national administration. This final section focuses on the key process of leadership, how it is understood and enacted.

14

LEADERSHIP

ALL CHANGE?

The macro changes sweeping the world that have been explored in this volume translate into micro change within the work of leaders in schools and colleges. The leadership role now often involves dealing with a range of issues previously managed by local bureaucracies, and responding more strongly to the wants, needs and demands of stakeholders. The role of chief executive, previously alien to education, has become commonplace. Research from Israel, America, New Zealand, Australia, Hong Kong, and Thailand bears witness to an increase in pressure, complexity, turbulence, workload, and consequent anxiety for educational leaders (Goldring, 1992; Hallinger, Taraseina and Miller, 1994; Parkray and Hall, 1992; Smyth, 1996). The extent of the changes has led some to argue that a certain homogeneity in the role of principal is resulting. If there are universalities, they may lie in the harmonisation of tasks and practice or they may run deeper. Consider the experience of three principals working on three different continents. The first works in a rural primary school in Kwazulu Natal in South Africa:

> There are a lack of funds . . . to repair the old buildings of the school . . . therefore during rainy days my teachers and pupils suffer very much as the corrugated iron has big holes and rust. I have written many letters to the inspectors but the funds are helping better schools near big main roads. As I have worked here at school for 22 years as principal, riots and faction fights in the area have depressed me, as the whole of the good work that I did in my first year has gone. Hooligans, thieves, robbers have stolen doors, tables, chairs, desks and burnt valuable schoolbooks. They have killed a female teacher near the school.
>
> (Lumby, forthcoming, a)

The second is an American high school principal:

> I wondered if I could do it . . . if a woman could do it . . . if I had
> the guts to do it. Knowing I would be the one to walk into a volatile
> situation and maybe in some cases put my life on the line as opposed
> to somebody else's. Those things you have to think about before you
> become a principal, because when you become a principal, you don't
> have time to think about it then.
>
> (Parkray and Hall, 1992, p. 1)

The third is a headteacher working in a school in a township in Hong Kong.
He notes the disaffection of his students, and their vulnerability in the face
of the breakdown of social order. His reflections are not optimistic:

> Problem families tend to spawn problem students. Under such cir-
> cumstances, the school has become a sort of surrogate parent to many
> teenagers; the parents simply pass their children to us and expect us
> to take full care of them . . . I still feel that there is so little a school
> can do on its own to solve such an immense social problem.
>
> (Cheung, 2000, pp. 230–1)

Despite the odds, all three persist in efforts to support learners, not just
in academic terms but as young people in need of care. They work, of
course, in very different environments. The level of resource, training, cultural and historical backgrounds could not be more different. And yet they
share some of the same experiences. The threats of violence and crime,
the underresourcing of their school, the pressure of time, are day-to-day
realities. All carry the responsibility for educating poor children whose
parents may be absent or have relinquished a parenting role. They all
recognise that what they can achieve in the school is limited and fragile.
If they could speak to each other, there would be much to explain about
the differences in their work but also, perhaps, at the heart, recognition
of similarity in their experience. All have invested themselves in their
role. Leadership for them is not just a technical issue of managing curriculum and resources. Their leadership is most profoundly a moral commitment to their students in the face of the likelihood of frequent failure.
In these tough schools, and in more advantaged schools, leadership is the
electricity which powers action and it can derive from one or many in an
organisation. It may be enacted very differently, but it is the use of underlying professional and moral commitment to drive forward which is a possible universal core to educational leadership.

THE PERENNIAL QUESTIONS

In tension with this sense of a possible underlying universal similarity of
role, there is growing recognition that the context in which educational

leaders work may exert a profound influence on the understanding and enactment of leadership in schools and colleges, and that the history and nature of each individual may equally exert a strong shaping force. The vision of a world rapidly becoming more uniform crumbles in the face of intensely felt differences between countries and within countries. For example, the supposed worldwide sweep of technology is hardly evident for leaders in primary schools in sub-Saharan Africa who struggle with inadequate, dilapidated buildings bursting at the seams with malnourished children (Henveld, 1994). If the supposed global changes are taken only to apply to wealthy nations, then the United Arab Emirates, where self-management is not seen as appropriate and principals have little power to take decisions, seems equally untouched by some 'global' changes (Shaw, Badri and Hukul, 1995). Differences within countries are also apparent. Goldring distinguishes the different cultures and practice of four categories of school within Israel (Goldring, 1992). Within the United Arab Emirates, Shaw, Badri and Hukul, (1995) note that any discussion of the management of schools needs to take account of the great difference between urban and rural schools, the latter catering for Bedouin children with very specific traditional values. Equally in China, there is a gulf between the nature of urban coastal and rural inland schools (Cheung, 2000).

This chapter will review what research evidence tells us in answer to some of the perennial questions which arise in relation to educational leadership:

- What do we know about the practice of leadership?
- Does leadership in schools and colleges lie primarily with the principal?
- Are ubiquitous western concepts such as transactional, transformational and instructional leadership universally applicable?
- Do leaders make a difference to learners?

RESEARCHING THE PRACTICE OF LEADERSHIP

What researchers conclude about the nature of leadership is the result of the questions they ask. To this extent, the methodology is the message. There are a number of possible approaches. First, one may gather data on what those in a leadership position believe, do or achieve and extrapolate that this equals leadership. Alternatively, a hypothesis of what leadership is can be posited and the activities of those in leadership positions assessed using the hypothesised qualities/activities as criteria. A third method may be iterative between the first two.

Much research is based on a profoundly positivist approach. The method may be to gather data on what leaders (largely principals) think they do and/or others think they do, and apply statistical tests to arrive at a valid list of activities. The list can then be applied to leaders in other settings to see if they do the same things with the same priorities. Hallinger, Taraseina and Miller, (1994) using the Principals' Instructional Management Rating Scale (PIMRS) in Thailand, and Sara (1981) applying the Leader Behaviour Description Questionnaire (LBDQ) to four developing countries are two such examples. The resulting data can be neatly manipulated against spectra or matrices of behaviour. However, there are problems. Such a method may help us understand what the sample of leaders do, but not whether it is management or leadership (Gronn, 2000). Nor will it necessarily tell us if the actions are effective. What has been shown to correlate statistically with student achievement in one context may not correlate in another. Nor does this approach help us learn if a principal does not exhibit the defined leadership behaviours, whether others in the school or college are undertaking that role. If leaders do not exhibit the expected behaviours extrapolated from the data, there is a tendency to apply a deficit model, blaming lack of training or the local/national administrative system or placing the behaviours on a point of evolution, working towards 'leadership'. Finally, and most problematically, the descriptions of leadership behaviour tend to be premised on western paradigms.

Much literature and training which adopts an 'international' perspective in fact applies western paradigms and thinking (Dimmock, 2000; Jansen, 1995). For example, Hallinger, Taraseina and Miller (1994) in the PIMRS assume that encouraging staff input into formulating goals is an appropriate action to measure in relation to leadership. In some cultures, such involvement would not be seen as appropriate or relevant. In the United Arab Emirates (UAE), a command system is accepted by culture and tradition and schools have, in any case, little power to take decisions. Should one interpret this as meaning that principals in UAE schools do not exhibit leadership or that the western model of leadership is not universal?

The understanding that largely North American theories cannot be applied elsewhere and that different cultures may require different leadership is not new. The seminal work of Hofstede (1997) provides one generic model for relating culture to management and leadership. However, the long-standing acceptance of profound cultural differences does not seem to impede researchers on leadership founding their work on key western concepts which may be inappropriate in many cultures, and this will be explored in more detail later in the chapter.

Ribbins (1999, p. 87) argues that, in contrast to the positivist approach, recognising that 'there are as many realities as there are individuals', leadership may be understood by an interpretive approach, which allows for the possibility of exploring the unique dynamic and complex 'moving picture' which constitutes the leadership practice of an individual. Thus he suggests a need to consider context, culture and case. As he acknowledges, there are both strengths and weaknesses with his preferred approach, which draws on ethnographic and biographical techniques. Such accounts may offer rich understanding of an individual case, but do not easily facilitate the sharing of practice across institutions and other boundaries. They do not provide convincing connections between cause and effect. However, such weaknesses may not be as significant as they appear. For practitioners, knowledge of international metatrends or of comparative studies is of academic interest, carrying little weight compared to the critical and absorbing need to understand their own school or college, in the context of their own neighborhood, region, culture and country. Learning about practice in other schools or other countries can only stimulate the search for unique individual answers. It cannot provide all-purpose prescription, though this is what positivist surveys may appear to offer. Consequently, the search for universal truths in leadership may be something of a distraction, either presenting an appearance of something which does not actually exist, or worse still, enticing practitioners from developing their own way.

Such a view is somewhat polarised, with positivist approaches blurring distinctions and interpretive approaches powerfully illuminating individual cases, but not necessarily those of others. Both may offer a degree of support to those seeking to understand the practice of educational leadership, by offering a touchstone for comparison and thereby stimulating reflection on existing and potential practice. Where problems may arise is in the adoption of a normative approach to leadership, using data from surveys or ethnographic materials to suggest a monolithic understanding of leadership.

SYSTEMIC OR DISPERSED LEADERSHIP

Leadership roles in the school or college may be represented formally by an organisation chart indicating roles and responsibilities. In most such diagrams, the ultimate responsibility lies with the principal, though this is not always the case. In China, the Communist Party Secretary shares responsibility with the principal (Bush and Qiang, 2000). However, whatever the formal statement, leadership may be undertaken by a number of different people, or may even be absent and yet the organisation continues effectively. Gronn (2000) points out that in many ways teachers know perfectly well what to do and can continue in the absence of instruction or inspiration very well. Handy (1993, p. 96) puts it trenchantly: 'Surely any intelligent, well intentioned group of individuals can tackle any problem without the need for a leader?' The significant term is 'a leader'. Though a leader may not be required, and leadership itself not always necessary for all tasks, an element of leadership prevents stagnation, securing motivation and improvement. Leadership may not be enacted by a single person, or even by a group in any long-term sense. Both Kouzes (1999) and Ogawa and Bossert (1997) argue for leadership as a systemic process which flows throughout an organisation. The leadership role is taken up and relinquished in a seamless flow as appropriate to the prevailing conditions. Morgan (1986) develops this idea and suggests that the total function of leadership may be fulfilled by the composite or synergised activity of a number of people, rather as the complete image of a hologram is created by partial images projected from a number of different sources. Contributing to the process is open to all organisation members. Alternatively, leadership may be dispersed, that is, a number of people see themselves or are seen by others as providing leadership as part of their permanent role.

The models of systemic and dispersed leadership are supported by the fact that much literature queries the extent to which leadership, rather than administration, is seen as relevant to the principal. The role of principal is largely administrative in many countries including Norway ('Being a principal in Norwegian compulsory schools has historically been linked to housekeeping and maintaining order' [Moller, 2000, p. 220]) and in China ('Chinese Principals are expected to spend a considerable amount of time dealing with supervision and various administrative problems' [Washington, 1991, p. 4]). Dealing with the need to raise funds or secure basic services and facilities may take up the majority of a principal's time, not only in countries with developing economies in Africa (Van der Westhuizen and Legotlo, 1996), but even in those where there is an expectation that leadership tasks will take priority, such as Australia (Beeson and Mathews, 1992). It is not only in poor countries where principals find 'their mission statement buried beneath a pile of problems' (Van der Westhuizen and Legotlo, 1996, p. 74). Where leadership is seen as a legitimate activity, the amount of time spent on leading may relate to a range of factors. For example, in a study of government and non-government schools in Karachi, the percentage of time each principal spent on leading teachers varied from none to 25 per cent. The analysis identified a range of factors which increased or decreased the time spent, including the degree of freedom invested in the headteacher by the government or in the case of private schools, the school board, the nature of the governing body, the principal's interpretation of role, and the amount of time needed for other activities such as external relations (Simkins et al., 1998).

Given the range of perceptions and models, Smyth (1996) suggests the need for a different metaphor for how educational organisations are run. The mechanistic model, based, he suggests, on Newtonian physics, with a leader out in front inspiring and controlling, is defunct. An alternative is the metaphor of a family. This may be a persuasive substitute. First, the family is recognised as a functioning unit universally, but at the same time, there are many variations on what 'family' may mean to an individual. The family fortunes may be dependent on a strong controlling father, or may reflect the dispersed leadership of a commune. It would not seem appropriate to most to suggest one approach to assuring that a family flourishes. Nor is it appropriate to advocate implicitly or explicitly one approach or image of leadership of educational institutions.

The diversity in the perceived relevance of leadership, in the range of people who are assumed to be in a position to lead or are expected to lead, is matched by a diversity of models of leadership. As Hallinger and Heck point out, the concept has metamorphosed considerably, shedding a variety of conceptualisations on the way, though usually in relation to the principal's role rather than a wider view of those who may offer leadership: 'The conceptualisation of principal leadership has evolved considerably over the past 25 years . . . Predominant notions of the principal's role have evolved from manager, to street-level bureaucrat, to change agent, to instructional manager, to instructional leader, to transformational leader (Hallinger and Heck, 1996, pp. 738–44).

This chapter has argued that what we know about leadership is largely the result of the questions we have asked and how we have chosen to try to answer them. In international terms the answers have been gathered largely on the assumption that it is the principal who is chiefly concerned with the leadership role. It remains to review how the leadership role has been characterised.

TRANSACTIONAL AND TRANSFORMATIONAL MANAGEMENT

Definitions of the nature of leadership have been overtaken by attempts to characterise different kinds of leadership, the chief of which are transactional, transformational and instructional or educative leadership. Definitions of transformational leadership abound (Bass and Aviolo, 1994; Caldwell and Spinks, 1992; Goldring 1992; Heck, 1993). The common elements appear to be the leader's focus on vision and involving all and inspiring all to achieve it, in Kotter's (1999, p. 77) succinct definition 'establishing direction, aligning, motivating and inspiring people'. The literature is both descriptive, in demonstrating that there has been a shift to this approach amongst principals, and prescriptive, containing an implied or explicit judgement that transformational management is the appropriate leadership approach. In Israel, 'Principals are expected to move from transactional to transformational leadership' (Goldring, 1992, p. 50). Much of the school effectiveness research which seeks to identify the characteristics of effective schools, explicitly promotes a model of leadership which, in its emphasis on empowerment of staff, is recognisably transformational (Reynolds and Teddlie, 2000). Transformational leadership is contrasted with transactional leadership 'a simple exchange of one thing for another' (Beare, Caldwell and Millikan, 1997, p. 28), for example, offering staff security and a pleasant working environment in exchange for keeping students, parents and regional administrators happy. The latter shades into definitions and discussions of management, the ongoing maintenance of effective relationships and systems. Many millions of words have been expended on trying to untangle the substantive nature and the semantics of the differences between administration, management, and both transactional and transformational leadership. Despite acknowledgment of the critical nature of context, the latter dominates as the preferred approach to leadership in western literature.

There are however problems with applying this dominant model in every context. As Gronn (2000, p. 4) suggests it reflects a 'heroic, neo-charismatic' style of leadership which is at odds both with the collectivist culture in many countries and with other emerging theories about the dispersed or systemic nature of leadership. Literature on transformational leadership tends to focus on the principal rather than all those who may contribute to a leadership function. Secondly, as Beare, Caldwell and Millikan (1997) suggest, it underestimates the necessity, even perhaps the centrality, of transactional activity. Schools and colleges function largely on a day-to-day basis where ongoing management is the foundation of activity, rather than vision-inspired long-term change. Finally, there has been a long-standing acknowledgement that leadership is created by the significance accorded to activity by people, in the light of their own need (Duke, 1996). Therefore, a principal whose role is largely administrative, whose activities are limited to the transactional, whose main focus may be not long-term fundamental change, but creating stability and continuity, or even acquiring very basic facilities such as water, may nevertheless be leading in a way which is perceived to be meeting the needs of the institution, the community and the nation.

INSTRUCTIONAL LEADERSHIP

The second key characterization is instructional leadership. Leithwood, Steinbach and Begley (1992, p. 285) assert that 'instructional leadership has become [such] a widely preferred image of the principal's role'. They are joined in this judgement by Goldring and Pasternak (1994) who suggest that research indicates that effective schools have principals who are instructional leaders. Hallinger, Taraseina and Miller (1994, p. 322) place this belief firmly in an international context, linking school improvement with 'strong *instructional leadership*' (emphasis added). Instructional leadership emphasises that the focus of the leader(s) within a school or college must be above all on improving teaching and learning. However, Goldring and Pasternak also sound a warning note that the definition of instructional leadership is unclear and that a connection between whatever is defined as instructional, or sometimes educative, leadership and student performance has not always been found to exist.

The opportunity to implement instructional leadership is not universal. For example, in China, principals have 'limited involvement in curriculum matters' (Washington, 1991, p. 4). In Japan, the principal's role 'is largely symbolic and ritualistic' (Willis and Bartell, 1990, p. 121). In Thailand, principals view themselves primarily as administrators (Hallinger, Taraseina and Miller, 1994). In America principals are not necessarily qualified teachers and so may have limited experience of instruction. In Canada, instructional leadership is the ideal for the white community, but not necessarily for indigenous minority ethnic peoples (Begley, 1994). Where instructional leadership is seen as appropriate at school level, it may not be connected with the principal's role, but as in Australia (Begley, 1994) and China (Bush and Qiang, 2000) seen as the responsibility of groups of teachers. A case study of an Australian secondary school (Dimmock and Wildy, 1995) concludes that the curriculum linkage between departments is more significant in achieving improved student performance than instructional leadership on the part of the principal or senior managers. A review of literature suggests that no convincing international connection between effective instructional leadership on the part of the principal or senior managers and student performance has been established. Rather than leadership for effective student performance centring on the transformational or the instructional leadership approaches, Goldring and Pasternak (1994) suggest that the leadership functions which achieve improved student performance may be embedded in a number of people and roles within an educational organisation. Equally, if the intended outcome of leadership is the achievement with others of long-term improvement, it is clear that no monolithic description or prescription can apply across cultures.

Perhaps an underlying problem is that much of the research and discussion of transformational management is underpinned by unstated assumed western paradigms which colour the analysis with value judgments assumed to be universal but which are in fact very culturally specific. Three of the principal examples are discussed below.

'Children come first'

Anderson (1996, p. 947) describes 'the kids come first mantra', a belief that the central concern of schools and colleges should be the individual learner and, linked to this, a conviction that the aim of education is to develop the potential of each individual. Leaders are seen therefore to have a primary role in focusing all on the development of individual learners. In many cultures children are not viewed in this way. They may be seen as primarily contributing to the economy of the family and the nation. Their individual rights are secondary to those of adults. Individualism is not an aim (Bush and Qiang, 2000; Dimmock, 2000). Nationally, educational aims may well be not to assure the best life chances to each individual citizen, but to allow each child to play a part in maintaining social and cultural stability and achieving economic growth. For example, Ryan, Chen and Merry (1998) describe a rural primary school in Shaanxi province in China where the principal aim is to equip learners with a basic education before they go on to work in the fields. In relation to Thai schools, Gipson (2000) contrasts the Buddhist notion of gamma which encourages 'docility and compliance' with western constructions of individualism and non-conformity. The result in educational terms is that there is 'no Thai synonym for student-centred education' (ibid., p. 319). Smyth (1996) says schools come unstuck when they are for anything other than placing children first. Such a view assumes a universal agreement with the premise that does not, in fact, exist.

Autonomy, empowerment and professionalism

The western view of professionalism is that educators are highly trained and skilled and as such should be given maximum freedom to take decisions that are, in their judgement, in the best interests of the learners for whom they have responsibility. The tradition in Norwegian schools illustrates this: 'There has been a strong norm of non-interference in the teacher's classroom activities, and individual autonomy is part of the tradition in schools ... Trust in teachers' work has for long been a tacit dimension in principals' approach to leadership' (Moller, 2000, pp. 211–12). Consequently, much of the debate on leadership of site-based management has centred on whether professionals in the institution have lost or gained autonomy. There has also been a conviction that for improvement and change to take place, professional teachers must be involved in goal-setting and planning (Fullan, 1999). Participative leadership has come to be seen as the universal aim, based on the premise that individuals have the right to be heard, their views taken into account and the agreed best way forward chosen. This view ignores the tradition in some cultures of the dominance of hierarchical authority and/or the need to maintain harmony. Dimmock (2000) describes case examples of Asian principals behaving as suggested by their line manager, even though they do not personally support the choices made. Writing of management in Saudi Arabia, Bjerke and Al-Meer (1993, p. 35) tersely assert 'Saudi managers do not advocate participative management'. Klein (1994) compares the great respect for elders entrenched in the culture of Zulus in South Africa with that in Thailand. In both cases, empowerment and autonomy would not be the normative aim. Rather respecting and obeying elders would override any individual judgement. This is not to suggest that such systems are entirely autocratic. Zulu tribal chiefs may well facilitate considerable discussion within the community before reaching a decision. In China, teachers work together through *jiaoyanzu*, group discussion, to improve their practice and suggest ways forward (Bush and Qiang , 2000). However, both forms of participation are within the framework of a system of hierarchy and respect for hierarchy that is different in nature from the mere imposition of a bureaucratic authority. Teachers may genuinely revere the wisdom accorded to age or religious position as well as the authority invested by bureaucratic position, and see harmonious collectivism as the key, not exercise of their individual views or rights.

A second assumption underlying western interpretations of leadership is that leaders will adopt a relationship of equality with other professionals, 'first amongst equals'. In fact the opposite may be true in some cultures. As Bjerke and Al-Meer (1993, p. 31) point out, in the Arab world: 'Subordinates expect superiors to act autocratically. Everyone expects superiors to enjoy privileges, and status symbols are very important.' Thus the conspicuous demonstration of wealth may be seen as an essential element of leadership in large parts of the world, though this is not reflected in the research on leadership as it runs counter to the value judgements of the West, that modesty and equality are the goals.

Gender equality

The aim of equality for men and women is assumed in much of the literature on leadership. There is no doubt that in many education systems, women do not have the same opportunities as men. Where they do hold the majority of posts, as in Saudi Arabia (Bjerke and Al-Meer, 1993), it may be because teaching is seen by men as an unattractive option. It is argued that women are universally ascribed a lower status than men and that the sexism of society inevitably translates into sexism within educational organisations. During the 1980s and early 1990s, resistance to sexism was largely enacted through a focus on training and employment strategies, with an aim in many countries to increase the number of women in senior posts. In the latter half of the 1990s and into the twenty-first century, resistance has been enacted in a different form, with much writing on leadership stressing the appropriateness of feminine qualities for educational leadership (Coleman, 1996). If, as is argued in many countries, women are not suited to the management role (Coleman, Qiang and Li, 1998; Klein, 1994), then a campaign is afoot to metamorphose the management role, and to show that it is indeed appropriate for women or men who exhibit a feminine style. However, the assumption that a new feminine or androgynous style is needed to manage schools and colleges in the twenty-first century, which appears assumed as a universal by some (Caldwell, 1997), is no such thing. It is possible to distinguish countries where there is a national policy to promote equality (though this may be in opposition to long-standing sexist culture and practice), and those countries which do not at the policy level espouse equality. A benevolent father figure may be the image which is most persuasive for effective leadership in some cultures, or there may be a profound commitment to different roles for men and women, each drawing on different sources of power. Such 'bilateralism' (Razali, 1998, p. 25) cannot be analysed (or judged) by reference to western thinking (Bjerke and Al-Meer, 1993; Dimmock and Walker, 1998; Ribbins, 1999).

This selection of some of the chief assumptions which underpin much writing on leadership highlights that the literature largely does not recognise how different the goals of leadership may be, and the different value judgements in play concerning appropriate roles and relationships.

DOES LEADERSHIP MAKE A DIFFERENCE?

Many may see principals as holding the power to lead change, but there is evidence that they may have less power than is thought (Hesselbein, 1999) and that they exercise their power cautiously and conservatively (Moller, 2000). It is also clear that internal and external factors may prevent the achievement of change, however powered by vision and agreement. Henveld (1999, p. 4) outlines the efforts of principals in Zimbabwe to use existing resources to bring about 'desired changes at the school level'. He concludes grimly that 'to date, conditions in Zimbabwe have prevented this plan from being implemented'. Similarly, in the Marshall Islands, lack of resources and training were seen by teachers to be more significant barriers to achieving effectiveness than the leadership provided by principals. Chapman and Adams (1998) suggest principals in much of Asia are trammelled by environmental rather than educational factors. If external factors can negate internal leadership, then perhaps leadership has to be seen as more dispersed than within the organisation. Leadership may be necessary at regional and national levels, though just as a talented leader within a school or college may be thwarted by factors beyond her or his control, so governments may be constrained by conditions which circumvent their efforts to improve educational provision. Leadership may make a difference. When it does not, the causes may lie with the leadership of individuals and/or with complex other national or global factors.

Despite the fact that leadership cannot always make a difference, there is evidence that it often does (Hallinger and Heck, 1996; Leithwood, Steinbach and Begley, 1992). Most of the evidence relates to the effect of principal's actions and attitudes. The effect is generally indirect, through creating a climate or improving aspects of teacher attitude or performance rather than through a direct effect on student achievement. Writing of secondary schools in Singapore, Heck believes: 'Principals do not affect individual students directly as teachers do through classroom instruction, but [that] activities of the principal directed at school-level performance have trickle down effects on teachers and students (Heck, 1993, p. 153). As well as the contrary views that leadership does not affect student performance and that it does, there is considerable discussion suggesting that we simply do not know, that the complexity of interaction within a school or college defeats the limitations of research methodology. Basing their analysis on 40 studies that explored the relationship between principal leadership and school outcomes or effectiveness conducted during the time period between 1980 and 1995, Hallinger and Heck note:

> Our analysis suggests that the complexity of the relationship between principal leadership and student outcomes overmatched the conceptual and methodological tools being used by researchers. Beyond the simple question of whether principals make a difference, researchers have since sought to further understand how the context in which the principal works influences the expectations and requirements for leadership and the subsequent responses of principals.
>
> (Hallinger and Heck, 1996, p. 745)

They conclude that although some progress has been made in understanding leadership and its effect on schools, the diverse philosophies, contexts and methodological treatments of leadership research mean that there is no universal language or paradigm in which comparisons or conclusions can be made. Therefore, there are not yet satisfactory tools for measuring leadership and its effect.

CULTURAL LEADERSHIP

Writing in summary of a study of leadership in four developing countries in Asia and Africa, Sara (1981, p. 30) concludes that there is a universal theory of leadership and that: 'Regardless of cultural context and situation, an individual is considered a leader if he engages in behaviours that facilitate establishment of goals and achievement of such goals and behaviours that promote individual welfare and group maintenance and cohesiveness.'

In complete contradiction, basing his view on forty studies of leadership, Heck (1996, p. 726) states boldly: 'We assert that there is no universal paradigm for theory for examining organisational behaviour that is valid in all contexts.' The weight of current opinion concurs. 'Commentators cannot agree upon a set of behaviour that amounts to leadership' (Gronn, 2000, p. 6). If, as Gronn suggests, even within work based on western paradigms, there is no agreed concept of leadership, then in the wider context of leadership in many different countries and cultures, there can be no universal pattern. Context matters. Culture matters. Of course the idea of contingency theory, where effective leadership is shaped in response to the environment is not new. Nor is there any shortage of discussion on leadership as an engagement with culture, defined by Dimmock (2000, p. 43) as 'the enduring sets of beliefs, values and ideologies underpinning structures, processes and practices'. Such approaches may prove fruitful, because although there may be no universal pattern of behaviour called leadership, researchers and practitioners need some common language in order to communicate and learn from each other. Therefore, although the quest to find agreed definitions may be rather outdated and uninteresting to practitioners, possible ways of approaching the study of those in leadership positions may be helpful. Fullan (1996) presents a useful framework, suggesting four broad areas or issues for the future:

- issues of purpose
- issues of culture
- issues of process and performance
- issues of people.

Taking these four issues as a framework, it is possible to provide some conclusions on the nature of leadership.

1) Purpose. Leadership is in relation to what outcomes are expected by the institution and by society. The value judgements of individualistic western societies are not universal.
2) Culture. Beare, Caldwell and Millikan (1997, p. 31) refer to leaders as 'entrepreneurs of values' suggesting, not just the mediation, but implicit in the business metaphor the promotion or 'selling' of values to others. Anderson (1996) links culture, politics and struggle, offering a different gloss to cultural leadership. If leadership is whatever people need it to be, one function of leadership may be to engage with the complexity of culture to maintain or to challenge.
3) Process and performance. Bearing in mind the purpose of the educational organisation, what processes and aspects of performance will lead to their achievement? As Shaw, Badri and Hukul (1995) argue strongly, there is no substitute for research undertaken into the specifics of a culture or country involving those who have knowledge of the environment, to provide local relevant information and ideas to balance the current prevalence of the 'hard-won wisdom of decades of experience in the West', but which 'may easily encounter incomprehension and rejection' (ibid., p. 13).
4) People. How will leadership be undertaken? It may be in dispersed or systemic form, rather than resting primarily with the principal or senior management. What will people expect from leaders in terms of their orientation to others in the organisation?

Gronn (2000, p. 6) has referred to 'the romance of leadership'. The concept certainly exerts a fascination and many believe that it is critical to the effectiveness of educational organisations. Rather than the current mass of research establishing standards that people cannot meet or feel to be a poor match to their own situation, those who work in education can feel liberated by the lack of universal theory. At the most fundamental level, leadership is the individual's moral energy. Beyond this each is free to mould leadership practice with the people whom they encounter in their working lives in relation to the local pressing realities.

REFERENCES

Adler, N. (1997) *Organizational Behaviour*, 3rd edition, Cincinnati, OH: South Western.

Aedo-Richmond, R. and Richmond, M. (1999) Recent change in post-Pinochet Chile, in Moon, B. and Murphy, P. (eds) *Curriculum in Context*, London: Paul Chapman Publishing.

Agudo, J. (1995) The education market in Zaragoza, paper presented to the European Conference on Educational Research, Bath, UK.

Akinnusi, D. M. (1991) Personnel Management in Africa, in Brewster, C. and Tyson, S. (eds) *International Comparisons in Human Resource Management*, London: Pitman.

Ali, A. (1996) Organizational development in the Arab world, *Journal of Management Development*, vol. 15, no. 5, pp. 4–21.

Almond, P. (1994) Parental rights and obligations, in Halstead, M. (ed.) *Parental Choice and Education: Principles, Policy and Practice*, London: Kogan Page.

Ambler, J. (1994) Who benefits from educational choice? Some evidence from Europe, *Journal of Policy Analysis and Management*, vol. 13, no. 3, pp. 454–76.

Anderson, G. (1996) The cultural politics of schools: implications for leadership, in Leithwood, K., Chapman, J., Corson, D., Hallinger, P. and Hart, A. *International Handbook of Educational Leadership and Administration*, vol. 1, London: Kluwer Academic.

Anderson, L. (2000) The move towards entrepreneurialism, in Coleman, M. and Anderson, L. (eds) *Managing Finance and Resources in Education*, London: Paul Chapman Publishing.

Ansoff, H. I. and McDonnell, E. J. (1990) *Implanting Strategic Management*, 2nd edition, New York: Prentice Hall.

Argyris, C. and Schön, D. (1981) *Organizational Learning*, Reading, MA: Addison-Wesley.

Armitage, A., Bryant, R., Dunnill, R., Hammersley, M., Hayes, D., Hudson, A. and Lawes, S. (1999) *Teaching and Training in Post-Compulsory*

Education, Buckingham: Open University Press.

Asmal, K. (2001) Address by the Minister of Education, Professor Kader Asmal, MP in support of World Teachers' Day (5 October 2001) to National Assembly, Cape Town, Wednesday, 3 October, accessed online 20 February 2002 http://education.pwv.gov.za/Media/Speeches_2001/October01/teachersday.htm.

Asthana, S. and Gibson, A. (2000) 'What's in a number?' Commentary on Gorard and Fitz's 'Investigating the determinants of segregation between schools', *Research Papers in Education* vol. 15. no. 2, pp. 133–53.

Auala, R. (1998) Secondary education reform in Namibia, *International Studies in Educational Administration*, vol. 26, no. 1, pp. 57–62.

Avalos, B. (1998) School-based teacher development: the experience of teacher professional groups in secondary schools in Chile, *Teaching and Teacher Education*, vol. 14, no. 3, pp. 257–71.

Babyegyega, E. (2000) Education reforms in Tanzania: from nationalisation to decentralisation of schools, *International Studies in Educational Administration*, vol. 28, no. 1, pp. 2–10.

Bagley, C., Woods, P. and Glatter, R. (1996) Scanning the market: school strategies for discovering parental preferences, in Preedy, M., Glatter, R. and Levačić, R. (eds) *Educational Management: Strategy, Quality and Resources*, Buckingham: Open University Press.

Bahar, A., Peterson, S. and Taylor, W. (1996) Managing training and development in Bahrain: the influence of culture, *Journal of Managerial Psychology*, vol. 11, no. 5, pp. 26–32.

Barber, M. (1996) Creating a framework for success in urban areas, in Barber, M. and Dann, R. (eds) *Raising Educational Standards in the Inner Cities*, London: Cassell.

Bartlett, W. (1992) *Quasi-markets and Educational Reforms: A Case Study*, Bristol: University of Bristol.

Bass, B. M. and Aviolo, B. J. (1994) *Improving Organizational Effectiveness Through Transformationary Leadership*, London: Sage.

Beare, H., Caldwell, B. and Millikan, R. (1989) *Creating an Excellent School: Some New Management Techniques*, London: Routledge.

Beare, H., Caldwell, B. and Millikan, R. (1997) Dimensions of leadership, in Crawford, M., Kydd, L. and Riches, C. (eds) *Leadership and Teams in Educational Management*, Buckingham: Open University Press.

Beattie, N. (1990) The wider context: are curricula manageable? in Brighouse, T. and Moon, B. (eds) *Managing the National Curriculum: Some Critical Perspectives*, London: Longman in association with BEMAS.

Beeson, G. and Mathews, R. (1992) Beginning principals in Australia, in Parkray, F. and Hall, G. (eds) *Becoming a Principal: The Challenges of Beginning Leadership*, Boston, MA: Allyn and Bacon.

Begley, P. (1994) Contemporary images of school leadership in Ontario, the Northwest Territories, and Western Australia, *Alberta Journal of*

Educational Research, vol. 40, no. 3. pp. 319–36.

Bell, L. (1998) From symphony to jazz: the concept of strategy in education, *School Leadership and Management*, vol. 18, no. 4, pp. 449–60.

Bergen, B. (1988) Only a schoolmaster: gender, class and the effort to professionalize elementary teaching in England 1870–1910, in Ozga, J. (ed.) *Schoolwork: Approaches to the Labour Process of Teaching*, Buckingham: Open University Press.

Bjerke, B. and Al-Meer, A. (1993) Culture's Consequences: Management in Saudi Arabia, *Leadership and Organization Development Journal*, vol. 14, no. 1, pp. 30–5.

Blunt, P. and Popoola, O. (1985) Personnel Management in the Nigerian Public sector, in Fashoyin, T. (ed.) *Collective Bargaining in the Public Sector in Nigeria*, Lagos: Macmillan Nigeria.

Boisot, M. (1995) Preparing for turbulence; the changing relationship between strategy and management development in the learning organisation, in Garrett, B. (ed.) *Developing Strategic Thought: Rediscovering the Art of Direction-Giving*, London: McGraw-Hill.

Borzsony, P. and Hunter, K. (1996) Becoming a learning organisation through partnership, *The Learning Organization*, vol. 3, no. 1, pp. 22–30.

Bottery, M. (1999) Global forces, national mediations and the management of educational institutions, *Educational Management and Administration*, vol. 27, no. 3, pp. 299–312.

Boud, D. and Garrick, J. (eds) (1999) *Understanding Learning at Work*, London: Routledge.

Bowe, R., Ball, S. with Gold, A. (1992) *Reforming Education and Changing Schools: Case Studies in Policy Sociology*, London: Routledge.

Bowring-Carr, C. and West-Burnham, J. (1997) *Effective Learning in Schools*, London: Pitman.

Brace, M. (2001) A nation divided, *Geographical Magazine*, vol. 73, no. 11, pp. 14–19.

Bradley, S., Johnes, G. and Millington, J. (1999) School choice, competition and the efficiency of secondary schools in England, unpublished paper, Centre for Research in the Economics of Education, University of Lancaster.

Bray, M. (2000) *Double-Shift Schooling: Design and Operation for Cost-Effectiveness*, 2nd edition, London: Commonwealth Secretariat.

Brown, P. (1997) Education and the ideology of parentocracy, in Halsey, A., Lauder, H., Brown, P. and Wells, A. (eds) *Education: Culture, Economy, Society*, Oxford: Oxford University Press.

Brown, P. and Lauder, H. (1997) 'Education, globalization and economic development', in Halsey, A. H., Lauder, H., Brown, P. and Wells, A. S. (eds) *Education, Economy and Society*, Oxford: Oxford University Press.

Bullock, A. and Thomas, H. (1997) *Schools at the Centre: A Study of Decentralisation*, London: Routledge.

Bush, T. and Qiang, H. (2000) Leadership and culture in Chinese education, *Asia Pacific Journal of Education*, vol. 20, no. 2, pp. 58–67.

Byers, L. (1991) *Strategic Management*, 3rd edition, New York: HarperCollins.

Caldwell, B. (1997) Global trends and expectations for the further reform of schools, in Davies, B. and Ellison, L. (eds) *School Leadership in the 21st Century*, London: Routledge.

Caldwell, B. (2000) Local management and learning outcomes: mapping the links in three generations of international research, in Coleman, M. and Anderson, L. (eds) *Managing Finance and Resources in Education*, London: Paul Chapman Publishing.

Caldwell, B. and Spinks, J. (1992) *Leading the Self-Managing School*, London: Falmer Press.

Caldwell, B. and Spinks, J. (1998) *Beyond the Self-Managing School*, London: Falmer Press.

Campbell, D. and Crowther, P. (1991) What is an entrepreneurial school? in Crowther, F. and Caldwell, B. (eds) *The Entrepreneurial School*, Sydney: Ashton Scholastic.

Cardno, C. (1995) Diversity, dilemmas and defensiveness: leadership challenges in staff appraisal contexts, *School Organisation*, vol. 21, no. 2, pp. 117–31.

Cardno, C. (1998) Working together – managing strategy collaboratively, in Middlewood, D. and Lumby, J. (eds) *Strategic Management in Schools and Colleges*, London: Paul Chapman Publishing.

Carless, D. (1997) Managing systemic curriculum change: a critical analysis of Hong Kong's target-oriented curriculum initiative, *International Review of Education*, vol. 43, no. 4, pp. 349–66.

Carlson, R. (1975) Environmental constraints and organisational consequences: the public school and its clients, in Baldridge, J. and Deal, T. (eds) *Managing Change in Educational Organisations*, Berkeley, CA: McCutchan.

Chan, Y. and Watkins, D. (1994) Classroom environment and approaches to learning: an investigation of the actual and preferred perceptions of Hong Kong secondary school students, *Instructional Science*, vol. 22, pp. 233–46.

Chang, J. H.-Y. (2000) Education in Singapore: a study of state values as cultural capital, *Education Research and Perspectives*, vol. 27, no. 2, pp. 24–42.

Chapman, D. and Adams, D. (1998) The management and administration of education across Asia: changing challenges, *International Journal of Educational Research*, vol. 29, pp. 603–26.

Chapman, J. D. and Aspin, D. N. (1997) *The School, The Community and Lifelong Learning*, London: Cassell.

Cherrington, K. (1999) Te Waananga O Aetearoa – He Puate Hou: A New Dawn in Tertiary Education, *International Studies in Educational Administration*, vol. 27, no. 1, pp. 92–101.

Cheung, R. (2000) Securing a better future: a Hong Kong school principal's perception of leadership in times of change, in Dimmock, C. and Walker, A. (eds) *Future School Administration*, Hong Kong: Chinese University Press.

Chitty, C. (1997) The school effectiveness movement: origins, shortcomings and future possibilities, *Curriculum Journal*, vol. 8, no. 1, pp. 45–62.

Clarke, J. and Newman, J. (1992) Managing to survive: dilemmas of changing organisational forms in the public sector, paper presented at the Sociology Association Conference, Nottingham.

Clarke, P. (1999) The future of learning schools, *Management in Education*, vol. 3, no. 2, pp. 4–6.

Colclough, C. (1993) Primary schooling for all: how can it be achieved in Africa? Paper presented to the International Symposium on the Economics of Education, Manchester, May.

Coleman, M. (1996) The management style of female headteachers, *Educational Management and Administration*, vol. 24, no. 2, pp. 163–74.

Coleman, M. and Anderson, L. (eds) (2000) *Managing Finance and Resources in Education*, London: Paul Chapman Publishing.

Coleman, M., Qiang, H. and Li, Y. (1998) Women in educational management in China: experience in Shaanxi Province, *Compare*, vol. 28, no. 2, pp. 141–54.

Commonwealth Secretariat and World Bank (1992) *Priorities for Improving Teacher Management and Support in Sub-Saharan Africa*, London: Commonwealth Secretariat.

Coombe, C. (1997) Unleashing the power of Africa's teachers, *International Journal of Educational Development*, vol. 17, no. 1, pp. 113–17.

Cooperative Research Project (1998) *Assessing the Outcomes: A Report of the Cooperative Research Project on 'Leading Victoria's Schools of the Future'*, Melbourne: Department of Education, Employment and Training.

Cortazzi, M. (1998) Curricula across cultures: contexts and connections, in Moyles, J. and Hargreaves, L. (eds) *The Primary Curriculum: Learning from International Perspectives*, London: Routledge.

Creemers, B. (1992) School effectiveness, effective instruction and school improvement in the Netherlands, in Reynolds, D. and Cuttance, C. (eds) *School Effectiveness: Research, Policy and Practice*, London: Routledge.

Crisp, P. (1991) *Strategic Planning and Management*, Blagdon: Staff College.

Crocombe, R. and Tuainekore Crocombe, M. (1994) *Post Secondary Education in the South Pacific*, London: Commonwealth Secretariat.

Davies, J. and Morgan, A. (1983) Management of higher education in a period of contraction and uncertainty, in Body-Barrett, O., Bush, T., Goodey, J., McNay, J. and Preedy, M. (eds) *Approaches to Post School*

Management, London: Harper and Row.

Davies, L. and Gunawardena, C. (1992) *Women and Men in International Management: An International Inquiry*, IIEP Research report no. 95, Paris: International Institute for Educational Planning.

Davies, P. (1994) Do it again – with conviction, *College Management Today*, vol. 2, no. 7, pp. 6–7.

De Voogd, G. (1998) Primary schooling: a US perspective, in Moyles, J. and Hargreaves, L. (eds) *The Primary Curriculum: Learning from International Perspectives*, London: Routledge.

Deem, R. (1994) Free marketeers or good citizens? Educational policy and lay participation in the administration of schools, *British Journal of Educational Studies*, vol. 42, no. 1, pp. 23–37.

Department for Education and Employment (DfEE) (1999) *National College for School Leadership – a Prospectus*, London: HMSO.

Department for Education and Employment (DfEE) (1999a) *Teachers Meeting the Challenge of Change: Technical Consultation Document on Pay and Performance Management*, London: DfEE.

Department for Education and Skills (DfES) (2000) *National Standards for Headteachers*, London: DfES.

Department of Education, South Africa (1996) *Education White Paper 2. The Organisation, Governance and Funding of Schools*, Pretoria: Department of Education, accessed online 26 February 2002 http://www.polity.org.za/govdocs/white_papers/educwp2feb.html#SEC 3.

Department of Education, South Africa (1996a) *Changing Management to Manage Change. Report of the Task Team on Education Management Development*, Pretoria: Department of Education.

Dimbleby, R. and Cooke, C. (2000) Curriculum and learning, in Smithers, A. and Robinson, P. (eds) *Further Education Re-formed*, London: Falmer Press.

Dimmock, C. (1998) Restructuring Hong Kong's Schools: the applicability of western theories, policies and practices to an Asian culture, *Educational Management and Administration*, vol. 26, no. 4, pp. 363–78.

Dimmock, C. (2000) *Designing the Learning-Centred School: A Cross-Cultural Perspective*, London: Falmer Press.

Dimmock, C. and Walker, A. (1998) Comparative educational administrations: developing a cross-cultural conceptual framework, *Educational Administration Quarterly*, vol. 34, no. 4, pp. 558–95.

Dimmock, C. and Wildy, H. (1995) Conceptualising curriculum management in an effective secondary school: a western Australian case study, *Curriculum Journal*, vol. 6, no. 5, pp. 297–323.

Duke, D. (1996) Perception, prescription and the future of school leadership, in Leithwood, K., Chapman, J., Corson, D., Hallinger, P. and Hart, A. (eds) *International Handbook of Educational Leadership and Administration*, vol. 2, London: Kluwer Academic.

Duraisamy, P., James, E., Lane, J. and Jee-Peng, T. (1998) Is there a quantity–quality trade off as pupil–teacher ratios increase? Evidence from Tamil Nadu, India, *International Journal of Educational Development*, vol. 18, no. 5, pp. 367–83.

Dyer, C. (2000) *Operation Blackboard: Policy Implementation in Indian Elementary Education*, Oxford: Symposium.

Edmonds, R. R. (1979) Effective schools for the urban poor, *Educational Leadership*, vol. 37, no. 1, pp. 20–4.

Eraut, M. (1994) *Developing Professional Knowledge and Competence*, London: Falmer Press.

European Commission (1994) *Growth, Competitiveness, Employment*, Luxembourg: European Commission.

European Commission (1996) *Teaching and Learning: Towards the Learning Society*, Luxembourg: European Commision.

Falinski, J. (1992) Becoming a constructivist school: a principal's perspective, Paper presented at the annual meeting of the American Educational Research Association, San Francisco.

Farrant, J. and Afonso, L. (1997) Strategic planning in African universities, *Higher Education Policy*, vol. 10, no. 1, pp. 23–30.

Fergus, H. (1993) The development of curriculum and materials, in Bacchus, K. and Brock, C. (eds) *The Challenge of Scale: Educational Development in the Small States of the Commonwealth*, London: Commonwealth Secretariat.

Field, J. (2000) Governing the ungovernable: why lifelong learning policies promise so much yet deliver so little, *Educational Management and Administration*, vol. 28, no. 3, pp. 249–61.

Fisher, C. and Yuan, A. (1998) What motivates employees? A comparison of US and Chinese responses, *International Journal of Human Resource Management*, vol. 9, no. 3, pp. 516–28.

Fitz-Gibbon, C. (1994) Performance indicators, value added and quality assurance, in Ribbens, P. and Burridge, E. (eds) *Improving Education: Promoting Quality in Schools*, London: Cassell.

Foreman, K. (1997) Managing individual performance, in Middlewood, D. and Bush, T. (eds) *Managing People in Education*, London: Paul Chapman Publishing.

Foskett, N. H. (1992) An introduction to the management of external relations in schools, in Foskett, N. H. (ed.) *Managing External Relations in Schools*, London: Routledge.

Foskett, N. H. (1999) Strategy, external relations and marketing, in Lumby, J. and Foskett, N. H. (eds) *Managing External Relations in Schools and Colleges*, London: Paul Chapman Publishing.

Foskett, N. H. and Hemsley-Brown, J. V. (2001) *Choosing Futures: Young People's Decision-Making in Education, Training and Careers Markets*, London: RoutledgeFalmer.

Fouts, J. T. and Chan J. (1997) The development of work-study and school enterprises in China's schools, *Curriculum Studies*, vol. 29, pp. 34–46.

Friedman, M. and Friedman, R. (1980) *Free to Choose*, London: Secker and Warburg.

Fryer, R. H. (2000) Making a Reality of Lifelong Learning, Inaugural Lecture, University of Southampton.

Fullan, M. (1994) *Prisoner of Time*, Washington, DC: National Commission on Time and Learning.

Fullan, M. (1995) The school as a learning organisation: distant dreams, *Theory into Practice*, vol. 34, no. 4, pp. 230–5.

Fullan, M. (1996) Leadership for change, in Leithwood, K., Chapman, J., Corson, D., Hallinger, P. and Hart, A. *International Handbook of Educational Leadership and Administration*, vol. 2, London: Kluwer Academic.

Fullan, M. (1999) *Change Forces: The Sequel*, London: Falmer Press.

Fullan, M. (2000) The return of large scale reform, *Journal of Educational Change*, vol. 1, no. 1, pp. 5–28.

Fuwa, K. (2001) Lifelong learning in Japan, a highly school-centred society: educational opportunities and practical educational activities for adults, *International Journal of Lifelong Education*, vol. 20, no. 1, pp. 127–36.

Gershunsky, B. and Pullin, R. (1990) Dilemmas for Soviet secondary education, *Comparative Education*, vol. 26, no. 3, pp. 307–18.

Gewirtz, S., Ball, S. and Bowe, R. (1995) *Markets, Choice and Equity in Education*, Buckingham: Open University Press.

Giere, U. and Piet, M. (1997) *Adult Learning in a World at Risk: Emerging Policies and Strategies*, Hamburg: UNESCO.

Gilham, B. (1995) Moving into the open, in Thomas, D. (ed.) *Flexible Learning Strategies in Higher and Further Education*, London: Cassell.

Gill, R. and Wong, A. (1998) The cross-cultural transfer of management practices: the case of Japanese human resource management practices in Singapore, *International Journal of Human Resource Management*, vol. 9, no. 1, pp. 116–35.

Gipps, C. and MacGilchrist, B. (1999) Primary school learners, in Mortimore, P. (ed.) *Understanding Pedagogy*, London: Paul Chapman Publishing.

Gipson, S. (2000) Tridhos school village: lessons from importing a western model of school design into Thailand, in Dimmock, C. and Walker, A. (eds) *Future School Administration*, Hong Kong: Chinese University Press.

Glatter, R. (ed.) (1989) *Educational Institutions and Their Environments: Managing the Boundaries*, Buckingham: Open University Press.

Goldring, E. (1992) System-wide diversity in Israel: principals as transformational and environmental leaders, *Journal of Educational Administration*, vol. 30, no. 3, pp. 49–62.

Goldring, E. B. (1991) Parents' motives for choosing a privatised public school system: an Israeli example, *Educational Policy*, vol. 5, no. 3, pp. 412–26.

Goldring, E. and Pasternak, R. (1994) Principals' coordinating strategies and school effectiveness, *School Effectiveness and School Improvement*, vol. 5, no. 3, pp. 239–53.

Goldring, E. B. (1997) Parental involvement and school choice: Israel and the United States, in Glatter, R., Woods, P. and Bagley, C. (eds) *Choice and Diversity in Schooling: Perspectives and Prospects*, London: Routledge.

Goldstein, H. (2001) Using pupil performance data for judging schools and teachers: scope and limitations, *British Educational Research Journal*, vol. 27, no. 4, pp. 433–42.

Gonahasa, F. (1991) The role of the Church of Uganda in national development, in Abidi, S. (ed.) *The Role of Religious Organisations in the Development of Uganda*, Kampala: Foundation for African Development.

Goodson, I. (1988) Beyond the subject monolith: subject traditions and sub-cultures, in Westoby, A. (ed.) *Culture and Power in Educational Organisations*, Buckingham: Open University Press.

Gorard, S. (1997) *School Choice in an Established Market*, Aldershot: Ashgate.

Gorard, S. and Fitz, J. (2000) Investigating the determinants of segregation between schools, *Research Papers in Education*, vol. 15, no. 2. pp. 115–32.

Gottelmann-Duret, G. and Hogan, J. (1996) The utilization, deployment and management of primary teachers in South Africa, *Prospects*, vol. 26, no. 3, pp. 559–73.

Gounden, P. K. and Mkize, M. G. (1991) Upgrading underqualified black teachers: perceptions of school principals, *South African Journal of Higher Education*, vol. 5, no. 2, pp. 18–25.

Greenwood, M. (1980) Incremental budgeting and the assumption of growth – the experience of local government, in Wright, M. (ed.) *Public Spending Decisions: Growth and Restraints in the 1970s*, London: Allen and Unwin.

Gronn, P. (2000) Distributed properties: a new architecture for leadership, paper presented at BEMAS Research 2000, Leading educational management in learning societies: research, policy and practice, the 6th International Educational Management and Administration Research Conference, 29–31 March, Robinson College, University of Cambridge.

Gronroos, C. (1997) From marketing mix to relationship marketing – towards a paradigm shift in marketing, *Management Decision*, vol. 35, no. 4, pp. 322–9.

Gunter, H. (1996) Appraisal and the school as a learning organisation, *School Organisation*, vol. 16, no. 1, pp. 89–100.

Hackett, P. (1992) *Success in Management: Personnel*, 3rd edition, London: John Murray.

Haenisch, H. and Schuldt, W. (1994) *The Effectiveness of Schooling and Educational Resource Management: The NordRhein-Westfalen Project*, Landesinstitut für Schule und Weiterbildung.

Hallinger, P. and Heck, R. (1996) The principal's role in school effectiveness: an assessment of methodological progress, 1980–1995, in Leithwood, K., Chapman, J., Corson, D., Hallinger, P. and Hart, A. (eds) *International Handbook of Educational Leadership and Administration*, vol. 2, London: Kluwer Academic.

Hallinger, P. and Kantamara, P. (2000) Educational change in Thailand: opening a window on to leadership as a cultural process, *School Leadership and Management*, vol. 20, no. 2, pp. 189–205.

Hallinger, P., Taraseina, P. and Miller, J. (1994) Assessing the instructional leadership of secondary school principals in Thailand, *School Effectiveness and School Improvement*, vol. 5, no. 4, pp. 321–48.

Handy, C. (1993) *Understanding Organizations*, 4th edition, London: Penguin.

Hanushek, E. (1995) Interpreting recent research on schooling in developing countries, *World Bank Research Observer*, vol. 10, no. 2. (n.p.).

Hanushek, E. (1997) Assessing the effects of school resources on student performance: an update, *Educational Evaluation and Policy Analysis*, vol. 19, no. 2, pp. 141–64.

Harber, C. and Davies, L. (1997) *School Management and Effectiveness in Developing Countries: The Post-Bureaucratic School*, London: Cassell.

Hargreaves, A. (1994) *Changing Teachers, Changing Times: Teachers' Work and Culture in the Post-Modern Age*, London: Cassell.

Hargreaves, A., Lieberman, A., Fullan, M. and Hopkins, D. (eds) (1998) *The International Handbook of Educational Change*, Dordrecht: Kluwer.

Hargreaves, D. (1997) A road to the learning society, *School Leadership and Management*, vol. 17, no. 1, pp. 9–21.

Hargreaves, D. and Hopkins, D. (1991) *The Empowered School*, London: Cassell.

Harley, K. and Wedekind, V. (1999) Vision and constraint in curriculum change: a case study of South African secondary school principals, in Moon, B. and Murphy, P. (eds) *Curriculum in Context*, London: Paul Chapman Publishing.

Harris, A. and Young, J. (2000) Comparing school improvement programmes in England and Canada, *School Leadership and Management*, vol. 20, no. 1, pp. 31–42.

Harrison, G. (1995) Satisfaction, tension and interpersonal relations: a cross-cultural comparison of managers in Singapore and Australia, *Journal of Managerial Psychology*, vol. 10, no. 8, pp. 13–19.

Harrison, G. (1997) The management of teaching and learning at Queen Elizabeth's Grammar School, in Bowring-Carr, C. and West-Burnham, J. (eds) *Managing Learning for Achievement*, London: Pitman.

Havelock, R. and Huberman, A. (1977) *Solving Educational Problems*, Paris: UNESCO.

Heck, R. (1993) School context, principal leadership, and achievement: the case of secondary schools in Singapore, *Urban Review*, vol. 25, no. 2, pp. 151–66.

Heck, R. (1996) Leadership and culture: conceptual and methodological issues in comparing models across cultural settings, *Journal of Educational Administration*, vol. 34, no. 5, pp. 74–97.

Henveld, W. (1994) Planning and monitoring the quality of primary education in Sub-Saharan Africa, *AFTHR Technical Note No. 14*, Human Resources and Poverty Division, Washington, DC: World Bank.

Herzberg, F. (1966) *Work and the Nature of Man*, Cleveland, OH: World Publishing.

Hess, G. A. (1999) Understanding achievement (and other) changes under Chicago school reform, *Educational Evaluation and Policy Analysis*, vol. 21 no. 1, pp. 67–83.

Hesselbein, F. (1999) Managing in a world that is round, in Hesselbein, F. and Cohen, P. (eds) *Leader to Leader*, San Francisco: Jossey-Bass.

Ho, E. and Willms, D. (1996) Effects of parental involvement on eighth grade achievement, *Sociology of Education*, vol. 60, no. 1, pp. 126–40.

Hodkinson, P. and Issitt, M. (1995) Competence, professionalism, and vocational education and training, in Hodkinson, P. and Issitt, M. (eds) *The Challenge of Competence*, London: Cassell.

Hofstede, G. (1980) *Culture's Consequences: International Differences in Work-Related Values*, Beverly Hills, CA: Sage.

Hofstede, G. (1991) *Cultures and Organisations: Software of the Mind*, London: McGraw-Hill.

Hofstede, G. (1993) Intercultural conflict and synergy in Europe, in Hickson, D. (ed.) *Management in Western Europe: Society, Culture and Organisation in Twelve Nations*, Berlin: De Gruyter.

Hofstede, G. (1997) Motivation, leadership and organization: do American theories apply abroad? in Pugh, D. (ed.) *Organization Theory*, 4th edition, London: Penguin.

Holman, L. (1998) *National Teacher Motivation Survey*, Kensington: Edu-Must.

Honey, P. (1991) The learning organisation simplified, *Training and Development*, July, pp. 30–3.

Hopkins, D. and Reynolds, D. (2001) The past, present and future of school improvement; towards the Third Age, *British Educational Research Journal*, vol. 27, no. 4, pp. 459–75.

Hossain, M. H. (1994) *Traditional Culture and Modern Systems: Administering Primary Education in Bangladesh*, New York: University Press of America.

Huberman, M. (1992) Teacher development and instructional mastery, in Hargreaves, A. and Fullan, M. (eds) *Understanding Teacher*

Development, London: Cassell/Teachers College Press.

Indonesian Directorate of Primary and Secondary Education (1999) *Primary and Secondary Education in Brief*, Djakarta: Ministry of Education and Culture.

Indonesian Ministry of National Education (2001) *Unit Cost Arrangements for the School Fiscal Year 2001*, Djakarta: Government Finance Division.

Ingulsrud, J. (1996) In-service teacher education: engaging the dialogic communities of teachers, *Language, Culture and Curriculum*, vol. 9, no. 2, pp. 176–85.

Ishumi, A. G. M. (1994) *30 Years of Learning: Education Development in Eastern and Southern Africa from Independence to 1990*, Ottawa: International Development Research Centre.

James, M. (1998) Para-teachers and the school at the end of the dirt road: an under-considered solution for rural schools in low income countries, in Johnson, D., Smith, B. and Crossley, M. (eds) *Learning and Teaching in an International Context: Research Theory and Practice*, Bristol: University of Bristol.

Jansen, J. (1995) Effective schools, *Comparative Education*, vol. 31, no. 2, pp. 181–200.

Jansen, J. (1998) The status of teaching and learning in South African schools, in Johnson, D., Smith, B. and Crossley, M. (eds) *Learning and Teaching in an International Context: Research Theory and Practice*, Bristol: University of Bristol.

Jennings, Z. (1994) Innovations in Caribbean school systems: why some have become institutionalised and others have not, *Journal of Curriculum Studies*, vol. 2, no. 3, pp. 309–31.

Jessop, T. and Penny, A. (1998) A study of teacher voice and vision in the narratives of rural South African and Gambian Primary School teachers, *International Journal of Educational Development*, vol. 18, no. 5, pp. 393–403.

Jin, L. and Cortazzi, M. (1998) Dimensions of dialogue – large classes in China, *International Journal of Educational Research*, vol. 29, no. 4, pp. 739–61.

Johnson, G. and Scholes, K. (1989) *Exploring Corporate Strategy*, 2nd edition, Hemel Hempstead: Prentice Hall.

Jones, P. (1998), Globalisation and internationalism: democratic prospects for world education, *Comparative Education*, vol. 34, no. 2, pp. 143–55.

Joyce, B. (1991) The doors to school improvement, *School Leadership*, May, pp. 59–62.

Kaabwe, E. (forthcoming) The industrial relations and professionalism tension, in Lumby, J., Middlewood, D. and Kaabwe, E. (eds) *Managing People in South African Schools*, London: Commonwealth Secretariat.

Kay, R. and Bawden, R. (1996) Learning to be systemic: some reflections from a learning organisation, *The Learning Organisation*, vol. 3, no. 5, pp. 18–25.

Keitseng, A. (1999) Self-appraisal: a step towards meeting individual development needs for Botswana secondary school teachers, *Journal of In-Service Education*, vol. 25, no. 1, pp. 23–37.

Kenny, T. (1994) From vision to reality through values, *Management Development Review*, vol. 7, no. 3, pp. 17–20.

Khan, M. B. (2000) Teachers' professional development: a way of improving education in Pakistan, *International Studies in Educational Administration*, vol. 28, no. 1, pp. 57–67.

Kirton, M. J. (1976). Adaptors and innovators: a description and a measure, *Journal of Applied Psychology*, vol. 61, pp. 622–9.

Klein, G. (1994) A tale of two conferences and much besides, *Multicultural Teaching*, vol. 12, no. 3, summer, pp. 5–16.

Kotler, P. and Fox, K. (1995) *Strategic Marketing for Educational Institutions*, 2nd edition, New York: Prentice Hall.

Kotter, J. (1999) Making change happen, in Hesslebein, F. and Cohen, P. (eds) *Leader to Leader*, San Francisco: Jossey-Bass.

Kouzes, J. (1999) Finding your leadership voice, in Hesselbein, F. and Cohen, P. (eds) *Leader to Leader*, San Francisco: Jossey-Bass.

Kraak, A. and Hall, G. (1999) *Transforming Further Education and Training in South Africa*, vol. 1, Pretoria: HSRC.

Kremer-Hayon, L. and Goldstein, Z. (1990) The inner world of Israeli secondary school teachers: work centrality, job satisfaction and stress, *Comparative Education*, vol. 26, pp. 285–9.

Kudomi, Y. (1994) The competitive education in Japan, *Hitotsubashi Journal of Social Studies*, vol. 26, no. 2, pp. 31–40.

Laine, R., Greenwald, R. and Hedges, L. (1997) Money does matter: a research synthesis of a new universe of education production function studies, in Picus, L. O. and Wattenbarger, J. L. (eds) *Where Does the Money Go? Resource Allocation in Elementary and Secondary Schools*, Thousand Oaks, CA: Corwin Press.

Lamie, J. (1998) Teacher education and training in Japan, *Journal of In-Service Education*, vol. 24, no. 3, pp. 515–34.

Lauder, H. and Hughes, D. (1999) *Trading in Futures: Why Markets in Education Don't Work*, Buckingham: Open University Press.

Lauder, H., Jamieson, I. and Wikeley, F. (1998) Models of effective schools: limits and capabilities, in Slee, R., Tomlinson, S. and Weiner, G. (eds) *School Effectiveness for Whom?* London: Falmer Press.

Lave, J. and Wenger, E. (1991) *Situated Learning: Legitimate Peripheral Participation*, Cambridge: Cambridge University Press.

Le Metais, J. and Tabberer, R. (1997) Why different countries do better: evidence from examining curriculum and assessment frameworks in 16 countries, *International Electronic Journal for Leadership in Learning*, vol. 1, no. 3, accessed online 4 March 2002 http://www.acs.ucalgary.ca/~iejll/.

Lee, J. (2000) Teacher receptivity to curriculum change in the implementation stage: the case of environmental education in Hong Kong, *Journal of Curriculum Studies*, vol. 32, no. 1, pp. 95–115.

Leithwood, K., Lawrence, L. and Sharratt, L. (1998) Conditions fostering organizational learning in schools, *Education Administration Quarterly*, vol. 34, no. 2, April, pp. 243–76.

Leithwood, K., Steinbach, R. and Begley, P. (1992) Socialization experiences: becoming a principal in Canada, in Parkray, F. and Hall, G. *Becoming a Principal: The Challenges of Beginning Leadership*, Boston, MA: Allyn and Bacon.

Levačić, R. (1995) *Local Management of Schools: Analysis and Practice*, Buckingham: Open University Press.

Levačić, R. (2000) Linking resources to learning outcomes, in Coleman, M. and Anderson, L. (eds) *Managing Finance and Resources in Education*, London: Paul Chapman Publishing.

Li, Y. and Kaye, M. (1999) Measuring service quality in the context of teaching: a study on the longitudinal nature of students expectations and perceptions, *Innovations in Education and Training International*, vol. 36, no. 2 pp. 145–54.

Lingard, B., Ladwig, J. and Luke, A. (1998) School effectiveness in postmodern conditions, in Slee, R., Tomlinson, S. and Weiner, G. (eds) *School Effectiveness for Whom?* London: Falmer Press.

Lloyd, B. (1996) The paradox of power and learning, *Management Development Review*, vol. 9, no. 3, pp. 5–7.

Lo, L. (1999) Raising funds and raising quality for schools in China, *School Effectiveness and School Improvement*, vol. 10, no. 1, pp. 31–54.

Lumby, J. (1997) Developing managers in further education. Part 1: the extent of the task, *Journal of Further and Higher Education*, vol. 21, no. 3, pp. 357–66.

Lumby, J. (1998) Understanding strategic change, in Middlewood, D. and Lumby, J. (eds) *Strategic Management in Schools and Colleges*, London: Paul Chapman Publishing.

Lumby, J. (1999) Strategic planning in further education: the business of values, *Educational Management and Administration*, vol. 27, no. 1, pp. 71–83.

Lumby, J. (2000) Technical colleges in South Africa: planning for the future, *Journal of Vocational Education and Training*, vol. 52, no. 1, pp. 101–18.

Lumby, J. (2000a) Restructuring vocational education in Hong Kong, *International Journal of Educational Management*, vol. 14, no. 1, pp. 16–22.

Lumby, J. (2001) *Managing Further Education Colleges: Learning Enterprise*, London: Paul Chapman Publishing.

Lumby, J. (2001a) Framing learning and teaching for the 21st century, in Middlewood, D. and Burton, N. (eds) *Managing the Curriculum*, London: Paul Chapman Publishing.

Lumby, J. (forthcoming) Identifying and meeting development needs, in

Lumby, J., Middlewood, D. and Kaabwe, E. (eds) *Managing People in South African Schools*, London: Commonwealth Secretariat.

Lumby, J. (forthcoming a) Managing change in South African schools, in Bush, T., Thurlow, M. and Coleman, M. (eds) *Leadership and Strategic Management in South African Schools*, London: Commonwealth Secretariat.

Lumby, J. and Foskett, N. H. (1999) *Managing External Relations in Schools and Colleges*, London: Paul Chapman Publishing.

Lumby, J. and Li, Y. (1998) Managing vocational education in China, *Compare*, vol. 28, no. 2, pp. 197–206.

Lundy, O. and Cowling, A. (1996) *Strategic Human Resource Management*, London: Routledge.

MacGilchrist, B., Myers, K. and Reed, J. (1997) *The Intelligent School*, London: Paul Chapman Publishing.

Maguire, M., Ball, S. and MacRae, S. (2001) 'In All Our Interests': internal marketing at Northwark Park School, *British Journal of Sociology of Education*, vol. 22, no. 1, pp. 35–50.

Maha, A. (1997) Community participation in school administration in Papua New Guinea, *International Studies in Educational Administration*, vol. 25, no. 1, pp. 35–43.

Makau, B. and Coombe, C. (1994) *Teacher Morale and Motivation in Sub-Saharan Africa: Making Practical Improvements*, London: Commonwealth Secretariat.

Malen, B., Ogawa, R. T. and Kranz, J. (1990) What do we know about school-based management? A case study of the literature – a call for research, in Clune, W. H. and Witte, J. E. (eds) *Choice and Control in American Education – the Practice of Choice, Decentralization and School Restructuring*, New York: Falmer Press.

Marquardt, M. (1995) Building a global learning organization: lessons from the world's top organisations, *Industry and Higher Education*, August, pp. 217–26.

Martinez, P. and Munday, F. (1998) 9,000 voices: student persistence and dropout in further education, *FEDA Report*, vol. 2, no. 1, London: FEDA.

Maslow, A. (1943) A theory of human motivation, *Psychological Review*, vol. 50, pp. 370–96.

Maynard, C. (1995) Competence in practice – Cheshire Certificate in Education: further education, in Hodkinson, P. and Issitt, M. (eds) *Challenge of Competence*, London: Cassell.

McGregor, D. (1970) *The Human Side of Enterprise*, Maidenhead: McGraw-Hill.

Memon, M., Ali, R. N., Simkins, T. and Garrett, V. (2000) Understanding the Headteacher's role in Pakistan: emerging role demands, constraints and choices, *International Studies in Educational Administration*, vol. 28, no. 1, pp. 48–56.

Menlo, A. and Poppleton, P. (1990) A five-country study of the work perception of secondary school teachers in England, the United States, Japan, Singapore and West Germany (1986–88), *Comparative Education*, vol. 26, nos 2/3, pp. 173–82.

Middlewood, D. (1997) Managing recruitment and selection, in Bush, T. and Middlewood, D. (eds) *Managing People in Education*, London: Paul Chapman Publishing.

Middlewood, D. (1999) Managing relationships between schools and parents, in Lumby, J. and Foskett, N. (eds) *Managing External Relations in Schools and Colleges*, London: Paul Chapman Publishing.

Middlewood, D. and Cardno, C. (eds) (2001) *Managing Teacher Appraisal and Performance: A Comparative Approach*, London: Routledge.

Middlewood, D. and Lumby, J. (1998) *Human Resource Management in Schools and Colleges*, London: Paul Chapman Publishing.

Moller, J. (2000) School principals in transition. conflicting expectations, demands and desires, in Day, C., Fernandez, A., Trond, E. and Moller, J. (eds) *The Life and Work of Teachers*, London: Falmer Press.

Morgan, G. (1986) *Images of Organization*, London: Sage.

Morley, L. and Rasool, N. (2000) School effectiveness: new mangerialism, quality and the Japanization of education, *Journal of Education Policy*, vol. 15, no. 2, pp. 169–83.

Morris, P. and Adamson, B. (1998) Primary schooling in Hong Kong, in Moyles, J. and Hargreaves, L. (eds) *The Primary Curriculum: Learning from International Perspectives*, London: Routledge.

Morris, P., Chan, K. and Lo, M. L. (2000) Changing primary schools in Hong Kong: perspectives on policy and its impact, in Day, C., Fernandez, A., Trond, E. and Moller, J. (eds) *The Life and Work of Teachers*, London: Falmer Press.

Morris, P. and Lo, M. L. (2000) Shaping the curriculum: contexts and cultures, *School Leadership and Management*, vol. 20, no. 2, pp. 175–88.

Mortimore, P., Sammons, P., Ecob, R. and Stoll, L. (1988) *School Matters: The Junior Years*, Salisbury: Open Books.

Munton, A., Mooney, A. and Korintus, M. (1999) Quality in group day care provision: UK self-assessment models in Hungarian day care centres, *International Journal of Early Years Education*, vol. 7, no. 2, pp. 173–84.

Mutshekwane, M. (1995) In-service education and training of teachers in Venda, *South African Journal of Higher Education*, vol. 9, no. 2, pp. 155–9.

Mwamwenda, T. (1995) Job satisfaction among secondary school teachers in Transkei, *South African Journal of Education*, vol. 15, no. 2, pp. 84–7.

Naisbett, J. and Aburdene, P. (1988) *Mega Trends 2000*, London: Sidgwick and Jackson.

Namibian Ministry of Education and Culture (1993) *Towards Education for All: A Development Brief for Education, Culture and Training*, Windhoek: Ministry of Education and Culture.

Neider, L. (1980) An experimental field investigation utilising an expectancy theory view of participation, *Organisational Behaviour and Human Performance*, vol. 26, no. 3, pp. 425–42.

Ng, H. M. (2001) 'Creation of Income' by Schools in China, *Educational Management and Administration*, vol. 29, no. 4, pp. 379–95.

Nimomaya, A. and Okato, T. (1990) A critical analysis of job-satisfied teachers in Japan, *Comparative Education*, vol. 26, nos 2–3, pp. 249–57.

Nkata, J. and Thody, A. (1996) Who is allowed to speak? Ugandan and English school governance, *International Studies in Educational Administration*, vol. 24, no. 1, pp. 67–76.

Nsaliwa, C. and Ratsoy, E. (1998) Educational decisions in Malawi, *International Studies in Educational Administration*, vol. 26, no. 2, pp. 63–71.

O'Hear, A. (1991) *Education and Democracy against the Educational Establishment*, London: Claridge.

Oduaran, A. (2000) Globalization and lifelong education: Reflection on some challenges for Africa, *International Journal of Lifelong Education*, vol. 19, no. 3, pp. 266–80.

O'Neill, J. (1994) Organisational structure and culture, in Bush, T. and West-Burnham, J. (eds) *The Principles of Educational Management*, Harlow: Longman.

O'Sullivan, C. and O'Sullivan, T. (1995) There's beauty in candlelight: relationship marketing in the non-profit sector, *Proceedings of the Annual Conference of the Marketing Education Group*, Bradford: MEG.

O'Sullivan, F., Jones, K. and Reid, K (1997) The development of staff, in Kydd, L., Crawford, M. and Riches, C. (eds) *Professional Development for Educational Management*, Buckingham: Open University Press.

Ogawa, R. and Bossert, S. (1997) Leadership as an organizational quality, in Crawford, M. (ed.) *Leadership and Teams in Educational Management*, Buckingham: Open University Press.

Olson, J., James, E. and Lang, M. (1999) Changing the subject: the challenge of innovation to teachers' professionalism in OECD countries, *Journal of Curriculum Studies*, vol. 31, no. 1, pp. 69–82.

Oman Ministry of Information (2000) *Oman*, Oman: MoI.

Oplatka, I. (2002) The emergence of educational marketing: lessons from the experiences of Israeli principals, *Comparative Education Review*, vol. 2, pp. 56–71.

Organisation for Economic Cooperation and Development (OECD) (1996) *Lifelong Learning for All*, Paris: OECD.

Organisation for Economic Cooperation and Development (OECD) (1997) *Parents as Partners in Schooling*, Paris: OECD.

Osbourne, D. and Gaebler, T. (1993) *Reinventing Government: How the Entrepreneurial Spirit is Transforming the Public Sector*, New York: Penguin.

Ouston, J. (1998) Educational reform in Japan: some reflections from

England, *Management in Education*, vol. 12, no. 5, pp. 15–19.

Paine, L. and Ma, L. (1993) Teachers working together: a dialogue on organisational and cultural perspectives of Chinese teachers, *International Journal of Educational Research*, vol. 19, pp. 675–97.

Parkray, F. and Hall, G. (1992) Overview, in Parkray, F. and Hall, G. (eds) *Becoming a Principal: The Challenges of Beginning Leadership*, Boston, MA: Allyn and Bacon.

Parry, G. (1995) Concerns and issues related to teacher appraisal in the USA, *Education and the Law*, vol. 7, no. 1, pp. 17–29.

Parsons, T. (1966) *Societies*, Englewood Cliffs, NJ: Prentice-Hall.

Parsons, W. (1995) *Public Policy*, Cheltenham: Edward Elgar.

Peacock, A. (1993) The in-service training of primary teachers in science in Namibia, *British Journal of In-service Education*, vol. 19, no. 2, pp. 21–6.

Pell, A. (1998) Primary schooling in rural South Africa, in Moyles, J. and Hargreaves, L. (eds) *The Primary Curriculum: Learning from International Perspectives*, London: Routledge.

Pepin, B. (2000) Culture of didactics: teachers' perceptions of their work and their role as teachers in England, France and Germany, paper presented at the European Conference on Educational Research, Edinburgh, 2–23 September.

Peshardis, P. (2000) Multi-cultural societies and educational leadership: Cyprus and the Balkans, *Management in Education*, vol. 14, no. 4, pp. 8–10.

Plomp, T. (1998) The potential of international comparative studies to monitor the quality of education, *Prospects*, vol. 28, no. 1, pp. 45–59.

Poppleton, P. (1992) The significance of being alike: the implications of similarities and differences in the work-perceptions of teachers in an international five-country study, *Comparative Education*, vol. 28, no. 2, pp 215–23.

Prawat, R. S. (1996) Learning community, commitment and school reform, *Journal of Curriculum Studies*, vol. 28, no. 1, pp. 91–110.

Prosser, J. (ed.) (1998) *School Culture*, London: Paul Chapman Publishing.

Pugh, D. (1993) Understanding and managing organizational change, in Mabey, C. and Mayon-White, B. (eds) *Managing Change*, London: Paul Chapman Publishing.

Qui, Y. (1988) The vocational education of young people in the People's Republic of China, *International Review of Education*, vol. 34, no. 2, pp. 270–80.

Quinn, J. (1980) *Strategies for Change: Logical Incrementalism*, Homewood, IL: Irwin.

Quong, T., Walker, A. and Stott, K. (1998) *Values-Based Strategic Planning*, Singapore: Simon and Schuster.

Rajpu, J. and Walia, K. (1998) Assessing teacher effectiveness in India: overview and critical appraisal, *Prospects*, vol. 28, no. 1, pp. 137–50.

Ramos, E. and Fletcher, T. (1998) Special education and education reform in New Mexico: providing quality education to a diverse student population, *European Journal of Special Needs Education*, vol. 13, no. 1, pp. 29–42.

Razali, S. (1998) Women in educational management in Sarawak: a study of traditional and professional challenges, EdD thesis, University of Bristol.

Reynolds, D. (1992) School effectiveness and school improvement: an updated review of the British literature, in Reynolds, D. and Cuttance, P. (eds) *School Effectiveness: Research, Policy and Practice*, London: Cassell.

Reynolds, D. and Teddlie, C. (2000) The processes of school effectiveness, in Teddlie, C. and Reynolds, D. (eds) *The International Handbook of School Effectiveness Research*, London: Falmer Press.

Rhoten, D. (2000) Education decentralization in Argentina: a 'global-local conditions of possibility' approach to state, market and society change, *Journal of Education Policy*, vol. 15, no. 6, pp. 593–620.

Ribbins, P. (1999) Producing portraits of leaders in education, *Leading and Managing*, vol. 5, no. 2, pp. 78–99.

Roberts, V. (2001) Global trends in tertiary education quality assurance: implications for the anglophone Caribbean, *Educational Management and Administration*, vol. 29, no. 4, pp. 425–40.

Robertson, I. and Smith, M. (1989) Personnel selection methods, in Smith, M. and Robertson, I. (eds) *Advances in Selection and Assessment*, Chichester: John Wiley.

Robinson, C. (2001) The learning and skills future: lessons from the Australia experience, *College Research*, vol. 4, no. 2, pp. 14–15.

Rodriguez, C. (1994) Chile: system of education, in Husen, T. and Postlethwaite, T. N. (eds) *The International Encyclopaedia of Education*, 2nd edition, pp. 738–46.

Roelofs, E. and Terwel. J. (1999) Constructivism and authentic pedagogy: state of the art and recent developments in the Dutch national curriculum in secondary education, *Journal of Curriculum Studies*, vol. 31, no. 2, pp. 201–27.

Rogers, E. M. (1983) *Diffusion of Innovations*, New York: Free Press.

Roth, G. and Niemi, J. (1996) Information technology systems and the learning organization, *International Journal of Lifelong Education*, vol. 15, no. 3, May–June, pp. 202–15.

Rowley, C. (1998) Introduction: comparisons and perspectives on HRM in the Asia Pacific, in Rowley, C. (ed.) *Human Resource Management in the Asia Pacific Region: Convergence Questioned*, London: Frank Cass.

Rutter, M., Maughan, B., Mortimore, P. and Ouston, J. (1979) *Fifteen Thousand Hours: Secondary Schools and Their Effects on Children*, Wells: Open Books.

Ryan, P., Chen, X. and Merry, R. (1998) In search of understanding: a qualitative comparison of primary school management in the Shaanxi region of China and England, *Compare*, vol. 28, no. 2, pp. 171–82.

Sammons, P., Hillman, J. and Mortimore, P. (1995) *Key Characteristics of Effective Schools: A Review of School Effectiveness Research*, London: OFSTED.

Sara, N. (1981) A comparative study of leader behaviour of school principals in four developing countries, *Journal of Educational Administration*, vol. 19, no. 1, pp. 21–32.

Satow, T. and Zhong-Ming, W. (1994) Cultural and organizational factors in human resource management in China and Japan, *Journal of Managerial Psychology*, vol. 9, no. 4, pp. 3–11.

Sayer, J. (1989) The public context of change, in Sayer, J. and Williams, V. (eds) *Schools and External Relations: Managing the New Partnerships*, London: Cassell Education.

Scheerens, J. and Bosker, R. (1997) *The Foundations of Educational Effectiveness*, Oxford: Pergamon.

Schein, E. H. (1997) *Organizational Culture and Leadership*, 2nd edition, San Francisco: Jossey-Bass.

Scott, D. (1999) Accountability in education systems, in Lumby, J. and Foskett, N. H. (eds) *Managing External Relations in Schools and Colleges*, London: Paul Chapman Publishing

Sebakwane-Mahlase, S. (1994) Women teachers and community control in Lebowa secondary schools, *Multicultural Teaching*, vol. 12, no. 3, pp. 31–41.

Senge, P. (1993) *The Fifth Discipline: The Art and Practice of the Learning Organization*, London: Century Business.

Sernak, K. (1998) *School Leadership – Balancing Power with Caring*, New York: Teachers College.

Shaw, K., Badri, A. and Hukul, A. (1995) Management concerns in the United Arab Emirates state schools, *International Journal of Educational Management*, vol. 9, no. 4, pp. 8–13.

Shimihara, N. (1998) The Japanese model of professional development: teaching as craft, *Teaching and Teacher Education*, vol. 14, no. 5, pp. 451–62.

Silins, H. and Mulford, B. (in press [2002]) Leadership and school results, in Leithwood, K., Hallinger, P., Louis, K., Furman-Brown, G., Gronn, P., Mulford, B. and Riley, K. (eds) *Second International Handbook of Educational Leadership and Administration*, Dordrecht: Kluwer.

Sim, W. (1990) Factors associated with job satisfaction and work centrality among Singapore teachers, *Comparative Education*, vol. 26, nos 2–3, pp. 299–306.

Simkins, T. (1998) Autonomy, constraint and the strategic management of resources, in Middlewood, D. and Lumby, J. (eds) *Strategic Management in Schools and Colleges*, London: Paul Chapman Publishing

Simkins, T., Garrett, V., Memon, M. and Ali, R. N. (1998) The role perceptions of government and non-government headteachers in Pakistan, *Educational Management and Administration*, vol. 26, no. 2, pp. 131–46.

Singapore Department of Education (1987) *Towards Effective Schools*, Singapore: Department of Education.

Siraj-Blatchford, I. and Wong, Y. (1999) Defining and evaluating 'quality' early childhood education in an international context: dilemmas and possibilities, *Early Years*, vol. 20, no. 1, pp. 7–18.

Smyth, J. (1996) The socially just alternative to the 'self-managing school', in Leithwood, K., Chapman, J., Corson, D., Hallinger, P. and Hart, A. (1996) *International Handbook of Educational Leadership and Administration*, vol. 1, London: Kluwer Academic.

South African Department of Education (1995) *Education and Training White Paper Government Gazette 16312*, Pretoria: Department of Education.

Southworth, G. (1996) *Leading Improving Primary Schools: The Work of Headteachers and Deputy Heads*, London: Falmer Press.

Sparrow, P. and Hiltrop, J. (1998) Redefining the field of European human resource management: a battle between national mindsets and forces of business transition? in Mabey, C., Salaman, G. and Story, J. (eds) *Strategic Human Resource Management*, London: Sage.

Spratt, M. (1999) How good are we at knowing what learners like? *System 27*, pp. 141–55.

Staessens, K. and Vandenberghe, R. (1994) Vision as a core component in school culture, *Journal of Curriculum Studies*, vol. 26, no. 2, pp. 187–200.

Steffy, B. and English, F. (1996) The conceptual limitations of systemic education reform in the United States, *International Studies in Educational Administration*, vol. 24, no. 2, pp. 67–82.

Stigler, J. W. and Heibert, J. (1999) *The Teaching Gap*, Glencoe, IL: Free Press.

Stokes, D. (1999) Small enterprise management in the public sector: the marketing of primary schools, unpublished PhD thesis, Kingston University.

Stoll, L. and Fink, D. (1996) *Changing our Schools*, Buckingham: Open University Press.

Stott, K. and Walker, A. (1992) The nature and use of mission statements in Singaporean schools, *Educational Management and Administration*, vol. 20, no. 1, pp. 49–57.

Stromqvist, N. P. (1986) Decentralizing educational decision-making in Peru: intentions and realities, *International Journal of Educational Development*, vol. 6, no. 1, pp. 47–60.

Sugimine, H. (1998) Primary schooling in Japan, in Moyles, J. and Hargreaves, L. (eds) *The Primary Curriculum: Learning from International Perspectives*, London: Routledge.

Summers, A. A. and Johnson, A. W. (1996) The effects of school-based management plans, in Hanushek, E. A. and Jorgenson, D. W. (eds) *Improving America's Schools: The Role of Incentives*, Washington, DC: National Academy Press.

Tam, W. M. and Cheng, Y. C. (1996) Staff development for school education quality, *Training for Quality*, vol. 4, no. 4, pp. 16–24.

Tan, A. (2001) Elementary school teachers' perceptions' of desirable learning activities: A Singaporean perspective, *Educational Research*, vol. 43, no. 1, Spring, pp. 47–61.

Tang, F. J. and Morrison, K. (1998) When marketisation does not improve schooling: the case of Macau, *British Journal of International and Comparative Education*, vol. 28, no. 3, pp. 245–62.

Teddlie, C. and Reynolds, D. (eds) (2000) *The International Handbook of School Effectiveness Research*, London: Falmer Press.

Thaman, K. (1993) Curriculum development in Pacific island countries, in Bacchus, K. and Brock, C. (eds) *The Challenge of Scale: Educational Development in the Small States of the Commonwealth*, London: Commonwealth Secretariat.

Thomas, D. (1995) Learning to be flexible, in Thomas, D. (ed.) *Flexible Learning in Higher and Further Education*, London: Cassell.

Thomas, H. (1998) Developing a strategic plan: a case study from the National University of Lesotho, *Higher Education Policy*, vol. 11, pp. 235–43.

Thrupp, M. (1999) *Schools Making a Difference: Let's Be Realisitic*, Buckingham: Open University Press.

Thurlow, M. with Ramnarain, S. (2001) Transforming educator appraisal in South Africa, in Middlewood, D. and Cardno, C. (eds) *Managing Teacher Appraisal and Performance: A Comparative Approach*, London: Routledge.

Tight, M. (1998) Bridging the learning divide: the nature and politics of participation, *Studies in the Education of Adults*, vol. 30, no. 2, pp. 110–19.

Timperley, H. and Robinson, V. (1997) The problem of policy implementation: the case of performance appraisal, *School Leadership and Management*, vol. 17, no. 3, pp. 333–45.

Trompenaars, F. and Hampden-Turner, C. (1997) *Riding the Waves of Culture: Understanding Cultural Diversity in Business*, 2nd edition, London: Nicholas Brealey Publishing.

Trow, M. (1998) American perspectives on British higher education under Thatcher and Major, *Oxford Review of Education*, vol. 24, no. 1, pp. 111–30.

Tuckett, A.(1997) *Lifelong Learning in England and Wales: An Overview and Guide to Issues Arising from the European Year of Lifelong Learning*, Leicester: NIACE.

Tuohy, D. (1994) Teacher self-evaluation – discipline or dyslexia in a learning organisation? *Irish Educational Studies*, vol. 14, pp. 64–82.

Turner, C. (1990) *Organisational Culture*, Blagdon: Staff College, Mendip Paper 007.

Turner, C. (1992) *Motivating Staff*, Blagdon: Staff College, Mendip Paper 033.

United Nations Educational, Scientific, and Cultural Organisation (UNESCO) (1998) *World Education Report: Teachers and Teaching in a Changing World*, Paris: UNESCO.

Vaill, P. (1984) The purposing of high performance systems, in Sergiovanni, T. and Corbally, J. (eds) *Leadership and Organisational Culture*, Urbana, IL: University of Illinois Press.

Van der Westhuizen, P. and Legotlo, M. (1996) Perceptions of skills for beginning school principals, *South African Journal of Education*, vol. 16, no. 2, pp. 69–74.

Van der Westhuizen, P. and Theron, A. (1994) Human resources management in education: an integrated and holistic approach, *South African Journal of Education*, vol. 14, no. 2, pp. 69–73.

Van Zanten, A. (1995) Market forces in French Education, paper presented to the European Conference on Educational Research, Bath, UK.

Vandevelde, B. R. (1988) *Implications of Motivation Theories and Work Motivation Studies for the Redeployment of Teachers*, Sheffield: Sheffield City Polytechnic Centre for Education Management and Administration.

Verhoeven, J. and Van Heddegem, I. (1999) Parents' representatives in the New Participatory School Council in Belgium (Flanders), *Educational Management and Administration*, vol. 27, no. 4, pp. 415–29.

Verwimp, P. (1999) Measuring the quality of education at two levels: a case study of primary schools in Ethiopia, *International Review of Education*, vol. 45, no. 2, pp. 167–96.

Von Hayek, L. (1976) *Law, Legislation and Liberty – Vol. 2: Rules and Order*, London: Routledge and Kegan Paul.

Vroeijenstijn, A. (1999) The international dimension in quality assessment and quality assurance, *Assessment and Evaluation in Higher Education*, vol. 24, no. 2, pp. 237–47.

Walker, A. and Cheong, Y. C. (1996) Professional development in Hong Kong primary schools: beliefs, practices and change, *Journal of Education for Teaching*, vol. 22, no. 2, pp. 197–216.

Wallace, M. (1992) Flexible planning: a key to the management of multiple innovations, in Bennet, N., Crawford, M. and Riches, C. (eds) *Managing Change in Education*, London: Paul Chapman Publishing.

Wanous, J. and Lawler, E. (1972) Measurement and meaning of job satisfaction, *Journal of Applied Psychology*, vol. 56, pp. 95–105.

Warnet, M. (1994) Towards clarification in determining school strategy, *School Organisation*, vol. 14, no. 2, pp. 219–33.

Washington, K. (1991) School administration in China: a look at the principal's role, *International Journal of Educational Management*, vol. 5, no.

3, pp. 4–5.

Waslander, S. and Thrupp, M. (1997) Choice, competition and segregation: an empirical analysis of a New Zealand secondary school market ꞏ 1990–93, *Journal of Education Policy*, vol. 10, no. 1, pp. 1–26.

Waters, M. (1995) *Globalization*, London: Routledge.

Watkins, D. (2000) Learning and teaching: a cross cultural perspective. *School Leadership and Management*, vol. 20, no. 2, pp. 161–71.

West, A. (1992) Factors affecting choice of school for middle class parents, *Educational Management and Administration*, vol. 20, no. 3, pp. 212–22.

White, L. (1997) Reflection and the infant – quality experience, in Bowring-Carr, C. and West-Burnham, J. (eds) *Managing Learning for Achievement*, London: Pitman.

Wilkinson, D. and Pedler, M. (1994) Strategic thinking in public service, in Garratt, B. (ed.) *Developing Strategic Thought*, Maidenhead: McGraw-Hill.

Willis, D. and Bartell, C. (1990) Japanese and American principals: a comparison of excellence in educational leadership, *Comparative Education*, vol. 26, no. 1, pp. 107–23.

Wisniewski, W. (1990) The job satisfaction of teachers in Poland, *Comparative Education*, vol. 26, nos 2–3, pp. 299–306.

Wolfendale, S. (1996) The contribution of parents to children's achievements in school, in Bastiani, J. and Wolfendale, S. (eds) *Home–School Work in Britain*, London: David Fulton.

Wong, K., Sharpe, F. and McCormick, J. (1998) Factors affecting the perceived effectiveness of planning in Hong Kong self-managing schools, *Educational Management and Administration*, vol. 26, no. 1, pp. 67–81.

Woodhead, M. (1998) 'Quality' in early childhood programmes – a contextually appropriate approach, *International Journal of Early Years Education*, vol. 6, no. 1, pp. 5–17.

Woods, P., Bagley, C. and Glatter, R. (1998) *Schools, Choice and Competition: Markets in the Public Interest?* London: Routledge.

World Bank (1995) *Priorities and Strategies for Education – A World Bank Review*, Washington, DC: World Bank.

Wu, X., Li, W. and Anderson, R. (1999) Reading instruction in China, *Journal of Curriculum Studies*, vol. 31, no. 5, pp. 571–86.

Yin C. C. (1999) The pursuit of school effectiveness and educational quality in Hong Kong: *School Effectiveness and School Improvement*, vol. 10, no. 1, pp. 10–30.

INDEX